D1369301

Microsoft

ACCESS® 2 For Windows™

Step by Step

Catapult **Microsoft**Press®

PUBLISHED BY
Microsoft Press
A Division of Microsoft Corporation
One Microsoft Way
Redmond, Washington 98052-6399

Library of Congress Cataloging-in-Publication Data
Microsoft Access 2 for Windows step by step / Catapult, Inc.
     p.   cm.
  Includes index.
  ISBN 1-55615-593-X
  1. Data base management.   2. Microsoft Access.   I. Catapult, Inc.
II. Title: Microsoft Access two for Windows step by step.
QA76.9.D3M555   1994
005.75'65--dc20   94-2359
                                        CIP

Printed and bound in the United States of America.

       8 9   MLML   9 8 7 6

Distributed to the book trade in Canada by Macmillan of Canada, a division of Canada Publishing Corporation.

A CIP catalogue record for this book is available from the British Library.

Microsoft Press books are available through booksellers and distributors worldwide. For further information about international editions, contact your local Microsoft Corporation office. Or contact Microsoft Press International directly at fax (206) 936-7329.

Macintosh is a registered trademark of Apple Computer, Inc. Avery is a registered trademark of Avery Dennison Corporation. Paradox is a registered trademark of Ansa Software, a Borland Company. dBASE, dBASE III, and dBASE IV are registered trademarks of Borland International, Inc. 1-2-3 and Lotus are registered trademarks of Lotus Development Corporation. FoxPro, Microsoft, Microsoft Access, Microsoft Press, and MS-DOS are registered trademarks and Windows is a trademark of Microsoft Corporation. Btrieve and Xtrieve are registered trademarks of Novell, Inc. Paintbrush is a trademark of Zsoft Corporation.

Companies, names, and/or data used in screens and sample output are fictitious unless otherwise noted.

For Catapult, Inc.
Managing Editor: Donald Elman
Project Editor: Ann T. Rosenthal
Production/Layout Editor: Jeanne K. Hunt
Writer: Emily M. Rainey

For Microsoft Press
Acquisitions Editor: Casey D. Doyle
Project Editor: Laura Sackerman

Catapult, Inc. & Microsoft Press

Microsoft Access 2 Step by Step has been created by the professional trainers and writers at Catapult, Inc., to the exacting standards you've come to expect from Microsoft Press. Together, we are pleased to present this self-paced training guide, which you can use individually or as part of a class.

Catapult, Inc. is a software training company with years of experience in PC and Macintosh instruction. Catapult's exclusive Performance-Based training system is available in Catapult training centers across North America and at customer sites. Based on the principles of adult learning, Performance-Based training ensures that students leave the classroom with confidence and the ability to apply skills to real-world scenarios. *Microsoft Access 2 Step by Step* incorporates Catapult's training expertise to ensure that you'll receive the maximum return on your training time. You'll focus on the skills that increase productivity the most while working at your own pace and convenience.

Microsoft Press is the independent—and independent-minded—book publishing division of Microsoft Corporation. The leading publisher of information on Microsoft software, Microsoft Press is dedicated to providing the highest quality end-user training, reference, and technical books that make using Microsoft software easier, more enjoyable, and more productive.

After you've used this *Step by Step* book, please let us know what you think! Incorporating feedback from readers is a key component in continually improving the books in the *Step by Step* series, and your help ensures that our materials remain as useful to you as possible.

Send your comments to:

Microsoft Press
Associate Publisher—Acquisitions
One Microsoft Way
Redmond, WA 98052-6399
Fax (206) 936-7329

WE'VE CHOSEN THIS SPECIAL LAY-FLAT BINDING

to make it easier for you to work through the step-by-step lessons while you're at your computer.

With little effort, you can make this book lie flat when you open it to any page. Simply press down on the inside (where the paper meets the binding) of any left-hand page, and the book will stay open to that page. You can open the book this way every time. The lay-flat binding will not weaken or crack over time.

It's tough, flexible, sturdy—and designed to last.

Contents

Part 1   Data Basics

About This Book

Microsoft Access for Windows, version 2, is a powerful data management tool that you can use for sorting, organizing, and reporting the important information you need every day. Its ease of use makes it an excellent tool for those who are new to databases, as well as for those who are experienced with databases. *Microsoft Access 2 for Windows Step by Step* shows you how to take advantage of the power of Microsoft Access to find and manage all kinds of data.

You can use *Microsoft Access 2 for Windows Step by Step* as a tutorial to learn Microsoft Access at your own pace and your own convenience, or you can use it in a classroom setting. As you go through the lessons, you'll get hands-on experience using the practice files on the accompanying disk. Instructions for copying the practice files to your computer hard disk are given in "Getting Ready," the next section in this book.

Each lesson is designed to take an average of 20 to 45 minutes, and ends with a brief exercise called "One Step Further." This part of the lesson builds on the skills you have learned so far, and extends your understanding by introducing you to a new feature, a helpful option, or a shortcut technique to improve your productivity with Microsoft Access.

This book is divided into five major parts, each containing lessons covering related skills and activities. At the end of each part, there is a Review & Practice scenario that gives you the opportunity to practice many of the skills you learned in that part. Each Review & Practice allows you to test your knowledge and prepare for your own work.

Finding the Best Starting Point for You

This book is designed both for people who are learning Microsoft Access for the first time and for experienced users who want to learn about the new features in Microsoft Access 2. In either case, *Microsoft Access 2 for Windows Step by Step* will help you get the most out of Microsoft Access.

Each lesson builds on concepts presented in previous lessons. Since all the lessons use one database, database elements created or modified in earlier lessons might be expanded upon in subsequent lessons. It is therefore recommended that you work through the lessons in order.

The following table recommends starting points depending on your Microsoft Access experience.

If you are	Follow these steps
New to a computer or graphical environment, such as Microsoft Windows	Read "Getting Ready," the next section in this book, and follow the instructions to install the practice files. Carefully read the sections on "If You Are New to Microsoft Windows" and "If You Are New to Using a Mouse." Next work through the lessons in order.
New to Microsoft Access	Read "Getting Ready," the next section in this book, to install the practice files, and then read those sections that contain information new to you. Next work through the lessons in order.
Experienced with some parts of Microsoft Access	Read "Getting Ready," the next section in this book, to install the practice files. Read "New Features in Microsoft Access 2." Next work through the lessons in order.

Using This Book As a Classroom Aid

If you're an instructor, you can use *Microsoft Access 2 Step by Step* for teaching Microsoft Access to computer users who are new to the product and for teaching specific features of Microsoft Access to experienced users. You can choose from the lessons to tailor classes to your students' needs.

If you plan to teach the entire book, you should probably set aside two to three full days of classroom time to allow for discussion, questions, and any customized practice exercises you might create.

Conventions Used in This Book

Notational Conventions

- Words or characters you are to type appear in **bold** lowercase type.
- Important terms (where first defined) and titles of books appear in *italic* type.
- Names of files, paths, or directories appear in ALL CAPITALS, except where they are to be directly typed in.

Procedural Conventions

- Procedures you are to follow are given in numbered lists (1, 2, and so on). A triangular bullet (▶) indicates a procedure with only one step.
- The word *choose* is used for carrying out a command from a menu or a dialog box.
- The word *select* is used for highlighting fields or text in a list, for selecting menu bars and options, and for selecting options in a dialog box.

Mouse Conventions

- If you have a multiple-button mouse, it is assumed that you have configured the left mouse button as the primary button. Any procedure that requires you to click the secondary button will refer to it as the right mouse button. Clicking the right mouse button opens a shortcut menu that provides easy access to commands associated with the current action.

- *Click* means to point to an object, and then quickly press and release the mouse button. For example, "Click the Zoom button on the toolbar."

- *Drag* means to press and hold down the mouse button while you move the mouse. For example, "Drag the Cost field name to the filter grid."

- *Double-click* means to rapidly press and release the mouse button twice. For example, "Double-click the Control-menu box on the Customer Review form."

- You can adjust the mouse tracking speed and double-click speed in the Windows Control Panel. For more information, see your Windows documentation.

Keyboard Conventions

- Names of keys are in small capital letters, for example, TAB and SHIFT.

- A plus sign (+) between two key names means that you must press those keys at the same time. For example, "Press SHIFT+SPACEBAR" means that you hold down the SHIFT key while you press the SPACEBAR.

- A comma between two key names means that you must press them consecutively, not together. For example, "Press ALT, T, X" means that you press and release each key in sequence. "Press "Press ALT+W, L" means that you first press ALT and W together, and then release them and press L.

- You can choose menu commands with the keyboard. Press the ALT key to activate the menu bar, and then sequentially press the keys that correspond to the highlighted or underlined letter of the menu name and of the comand name. For some commands, you can also press a key combination listed in the menu.

Other Features of This Book

- You can carry out many commands by clicking a button on the toolbar. If a procedure instructs you to click a button, a picture of the button appears in the left margin of the book.

- Text in the left margin provides tips, additional useful information, or tells you where to get more information in this book.

- The optional "One Step Further" exercise at the end of each lesson introduces new options or techniques that build on the skills you used in the lesson.

- Each lesson has a summary list of the skills you have learned in each lesson and gives a brief review of how to accomplish particular tasks.

- The optional "Review & Practice" activity at the end of each part provides an opportunity to use the major skills presented in the lessons completed so far. These activities present problems that reinforce what you have learned and encourage you to recognize new ways that you can use Microsoft Access.

Cross-References to the Microsoft Access Documentation

References to *Microsoft Access Getting Started, Microsoft Access User's Guide,* and online Help at the end of each lesson direct you to specific chapters for additional information. Use these materials to take full advantage of the features in Microsoft Access.

- *Microsoft Access Getting Started* explains how to set up and start Microsoft Access. It also uses a series of brief, hands-on sessions with real-life examples to show you how to organize and work with data using Microsoft Access.

- *Microsoft Access User's Guide* is a comprehensive guide to creating and working with a Microsoft Access database. It provides in-depth information and examples to help you build and use a database.

- Online Help provides reference and how-to information for all Microsoft Access tasks. You'll learn more about using Help in "Getting Ready," the next section in this book.

Getting Ready

This section of the book prepares you for your first steps in using Microsoft Access. You will review some useful Microsoft Windows techniques as well as some terms and concepts important in your understanding of how to use Microsoft Access.

You will learn how to:

- Install and use the Step by Step practice files.
- Start and quit Microsoft Access.
- Identify the elements of a database.
- Open a database.
- Use important features of the windows, menus, and dialog boxes in the Microsoft Windows graphical operating system
- Use the online Help system and Cue Cards in Microsoft Access.

Installing the Step by Step Practice Files

At the back of this book, you will find a disk labeled "Practice Files for Microsoft Access 2 for Windows Step by Step." These practice files include the database file SWEET.MDB, called the Sweet database, which contains the tables, forms, reports, and other database objects used in this book.

The Sweet database is a collection of data used to manage a fictitious company named Sweet Lil's Chocolates. Sweet Lil's Chocolates sells boxes of gourmet chocolates by phone and mail order. For these lessons, imagine that you are in charge of the database that handles all the operations information for Sweet Lil's. As the company's business increases, more and more requests for specific information come to you. You use Microsoft Access to manage the data, and to provide answers to the various departments at Sweet Lil's.

The practice files also include the following files:

- ALMOND.BMP, CASHEW.BMP, and PECAN.BMP. These are pictures of bonbons that you'll add to the database in Lesson 2, "Getting the Best View of Your Data."
- LOGO.BMP. This is a picture of Sweet Lil's corporate logo. You'll add this logo to forms in Lesson 12, "Using Pictures and Other Objects."
- SHIPPING.DB and SHIPPING.PX. These are Paradox files that you'll use in Lesson 7, "Attaching and Importing Data."

A special program on the Practice Files disk copies the practice files to your computer hard disk into a directory named PRACTICE.

Copy the practice files to the hard disk

1 Turn on your computer.

2 Insert the Practice Files disk into drive A or B of your computer.

3 If Windows is already running, open Program Manager and choose <u>R</u>un from the <u>F</u>ile menu. If you have not started Windows yet, skip to step 5.

4 In the Command Line box, type **a:\install** (or **b:\install**), choose OK, and then skip to step 6.

Do not type a space between the drive letter and the slash.

5 At the MS-DOS command prompt (usually C:\>), type **a:\install** (or **b:\install**) and press ENTER.

Do not type a space between the drive letter and the slash.

6 Follow the instructions on the screen to complete the installation process.

The Step by Step setup program copies the practice files from the floppy disk to the hard disk in a subdirectory called PRACTICE of the Microsoft Access for Windows home directory (called ACCESS, or whatever it happens to be named on your system). You'll need to remember the name of the drive and directory where the practice files are stored to open the Sweet database.

Starting Microsoft Windows and Microsoft Access

This book assumes that you have Microsoft Windows and Microsoft Access installed on your system. Use the following procedures to start Microsoft Windows and Microsoft Access. Your screen might be different from the following illustrations, depending on your particular setup and the applications installed on your computer. For more information about Microsoft Windows, see *Microsoft Windows User's Guide*.

Start Microsoft Windows from the MS-DOS command prompt

1 At the command prompt, type **win**

2 Press ENTER.

After the initial startup, the Program Manager window looks like the following illustration. You can start all of your applications, Microsoft Access, from Program Manager.

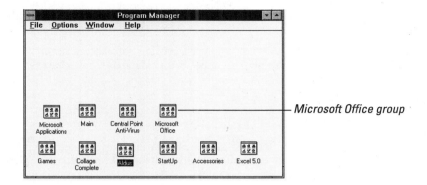

— *Microsoft Office group*

When Microsoft Windows is active, everything on your screen (called the *desktop*) is displayed in *windows*. You can adjust each window to the size you want, and you can move windows anywhere on the desktop. You can have multiple windows open at the same time to compare and share information easily.

Within the Program Manager window are symbols called *icons* that represent applications and documents. The icons are organized in program groups, usually related to applications. The normal installation of Microsoft Access creates a new group called Microsoft Office, and then creates an icon within that group for the Microsoft Access program. Double-clicking the group icon for Microsoft Office opens the program group window that holds the icon for Microsoft Access.

As you become more familiar with Windows, you will find that you can customize the startup screen to your personal working style.

Start Microsoft Access

Microsoft Office

1 In Windows Program Manager, double-click the Microsoft Office group icon.

Microsoft Access

2 Double-click the Microsoft Access program icon.

The first time you start Microsoft Access after installing it, Microsoft Access displays the Welcome To Microsoft Access box. This box offers you choices on how to get started with Microsoft Access using Cue Cards, an online learning tool. You'll learn more about Cue Cards later in "Getting Ready."

3 If the Welcome To Microsoft Access box appears, choose the Close button to close it.

Microsoft Access displays the Microsoft Access startup window. From here, you can create a new database, open a database, or do basic database administration tasks.

What Is a Database?

A *database* is a collection of information that's related to a particular topic or purpose. The key to efficient storage and retrieval of your data is the planning process. By first identifying what you want the database to do for you, you will be able to create a practical design that will result in a faster, more accurate data management tool.

Planning for a New Database

When you design your own database, you first go through a planning process that identifies what the database is for and what information you need to track. Before building your own database in Microsoft Access, consider the following questions:

- What information do I want to get from my database?
- What separate subject areas do I need to store facts about?
- How are these subjects related to each other?
- What facts do I need to store about each subject?

Microsoft Access helps you to manage your database by providing an efficient structure to store and retrieve information. The place you assemble the information about each subject you decide to track is called a *table*, and each category of facts collected in your table is called a *field*. Microsoft Access can automatically produce a *form* for you to fill in all your data. After you have entered some data, you can ask Microsoft Access to display a selected part of the information by using procedures called *find*, *sort,* or *query*. Finally, Microsoft Access helps you print just the part of the information you want to see in a *report*. At any time, you can customize the look or edit the contents of any part of your database.

Because Microsoft Access is a *relational database management system (RDBMS)*, you can organize data about different subject areas into tables, and then you can create relationships between the tables. This approach makes it easy to bring related data together when needed. By establishing relationships between individual tables instead of storing all of your information in one large table, you avoid a lot of duplication of data, you save storage space in your computer, and you maximize the speed and accuracy of working with your data. For more explanation about RDBMSs, see Chapter 1, "Concepts and Terms," in *Microsoft Access Getting Started*.

Microsoft Access has many automated processes and online Help features to assist you in creating and enhancing each element of your database. These processes, which include wizards and toolbar buttons, are covered throughout the lessons in this book. More information about the Help features is contained in "Using Help" and "Using Cue Cards" later in this section.

For more information about creating a new database, see Part 2, "Building a Database," in *Microsoft Access Getting Started*, and Chapter 2, "Designing a Database," in *Microsoft Access User's Guide*.

Using an Existing Database

The primary elements of a database—tables, fields, forms, queries, and reports—are all included in the sample database used with this *Step by Step* book. To facilitate your learning about how to work with information in a database, you use the Sweet database throughout these lessons, and then create new elements as needed.

The following illustration lists each table of the Sweet database with all of its fields, and shows how the tables are related to each other.

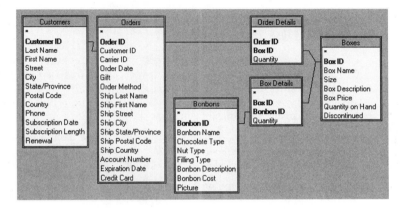

Tables in the Sweet database

In the Sweet database, data about customers is stored in the Customers table and information about orders is stored in the Orders table. The two tables are related to each other, so that Microsoft Access can easily show customer information with related order information (such as a customer's name and phone number with the customer's orders). Later in this book, you'll learn more about the advantages of organizing your data in this way.

When you look at the data contained in a table, each field is displayed as a column in the table. For example, if you want to see only Sweet Lil's 12-ounce boxes, you tell Microsoft Access to show you the boxes with 12 in the Size field. Microsoft Access shows you only those boxes. You'll have many opportunities to use this concept throughout this book.

You often use the values in fields to pinpoint the data you want to see.

Each field in the Boxes table contains data that
describes a box of chocolates that Sweet Lil's sells.

Box ID	Box Name	Size	Box Description	Box Price	Quantity on Hand	Discontinued
ALLS	All Seasons	8	Blueberries, raspberries, and strawberries to enjoy all season, both bitter and sweet.	$14.00	700	No
ALPI	Alpine Collection	12	Straight from the high Cascades, alpine blueberries and strawberries in our best chocolate.	$20.75	400	No
AUTU	Autumn Collection	16	Family-size box of Autumn favorites--Marzipan Maple, Oakleaf, Finch, and Swallow.	$43.00	200	No

Creating and Opening a Database

Using Microsoft Access, you might want to create an entirely new database or to work
with a database that has already been developed. In this *Step by Step* book, you will be
using an existing database so that you can learn how to work with all the objects that
are necessary for any database. You will also create new objects just as you would if
you were starting a database from scratch.

When you need to do so, you can easily create a new database using Microsoft Access.
The first step in creating a successful database is to plan it out before you begin to use
your software, as discussed earlier in this chapter.

In the following steps, you will learn how to start a new database. Then you will close
it, and begin to use the Step by Step sample database.

Create a new database

When you start Microsoft Access, no database is open. Microsoft Access displays the
Database window, a container for the objects you store in the database.

1   From the File menu, choose New Database. Or, click the New Database button on
the toolbar.

New Database

2   In the File Name box, type **New** as the filename for the new database, and then
choose the OK button.

At this point, you would create all of the objects you need, such as tables, forms,
reports, queries and macros. A quick way to get started is to use wizards to help
you create each new object for your database.

3   From the File menu, choose New.

4   Select Table.

Each time you select an item from this list, you can use a Wizard to step you
through the creation process. You will learn about Wizards throughout this *Step by
Step* book. For now, choose Cancel.

5 From the File menu, choose Close Database to close your new database.

For more information about creating a brand new database, see Part 2, "Building a Database," in *Microsoft Access Getting Started*, Chapter 2, "Designing a Database," in *Microsoft Access User''s Guide,* and Chapter 3, "Setting Up and Managing Database Objects" in *Microsoft Access User's Guide.*

Open the Sweet database

You installed the SWEET.MDB file in the PRACTICE subdirectory with the other practice files. This file contains the only database file you'll use in the course of this book, and you'll use it in every lesson. This book refers to the SWEET.MDB database file as "the Sweet database."

1 If Microsoft Access isn't started yet, start it.

2 From the File menu, choose Open Database.

The Open Database dialog box appears.

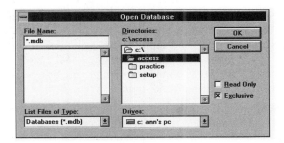

3 In the Directories list, double-click the PRACTICE subdirectory to open it.

If you have no PRACTICE subdirectory, see "Installing the Step by Step Practice Files" earlier in this section.

4 In the File Name list, double-click SWEET.MDB.

The Database window for the Sweet database appears in the Microsoft Access window.

The Database window shows the tables that store data about Sweet Lil's business. From the Database window, you can open and work with any object in the database. To work with a table, you double-click the name of the table you want. To work with another type of object, you click the *object button* for the type of object you want. For example, to work with a form, you click the Form object button. Microsoft Access displays a list of forms in the database. Then you can double-click the name of the form you want to use.

Note   Microsoft Access databases are different from Paradox or dBASE database files. In Paradox and dBASE, each table is a separate DB or DBF file, and other objects, such as forms and reports, are also stored in separate files. In Microsoft Access, your data and all the tools you need to work with your data are stored in a single database file.

If You Are New to Microsoft Windows

For new Microsoft Windows users, this section provides a general overview of what you can accomplish within this graphical environment. Windows is designed to be easy to use while still providing sophisticated functions. It helps you handle all of the daily work that you carry out with your computer. Microsoft Windows provides an interface that has elements in common among many different application programs—both in the way they share data and in the way you control their operation.

After you become familiar with the basic elements of Microsoft Windows, you can apply these skills to learn and use Microsoft Access, as well as many other types of applications including word processing and graphics.

Using Microsoft Windows

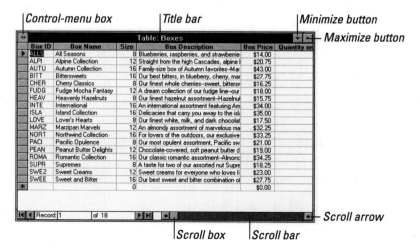

You can scroll, move, size, and close a window by using the mouse.

To	Do this
Scroll through a window	Click the scroll bars or drag the scroll box.
Change the size of a window	Drag any of the window edges or corners.
Enlarge a window to fill the screen	Double-click the title bar or click the Maximize button.
Shrink a window to an icon	Click the Minimize button.
Restore a window to its previous size	Click the Restore button. (See the following illustration.)
Move a window	Drag the title bar.
Close a window	Double-click the Control-menu box.

Using Windows in Microsoft Access

Like any Windows-based application, Microsoft Access has a main program window
that displays the application name, "Microsoft Access," in the title bar. This window
can be maximized to fill the entire screen, restored to fill part of the screen, or
minimized to an icon at the bottom of the screen.

Minimize button
— Restore button

Using Menus

In Microsoft Access, menus and commands work according to Microsoft Windows
conventions. Menu names appear in the *menu bar* across the top of the screen. To
choose a command, you click the menu name to open the menu, and then click the
command you want.

The following illustration shows the Edit menu opened from the Microsoft Access
menu bar.

Some options have a *shortcut key* combination listed to the right of the command name. After you are familiar with the menus and commands, these shortcut keys can save you time.

All commands have keyboard equivalents. To select a command from a menu, you press ALT and type the underlined character when the menu appears.

When a command name appears dimmed, it doesn't apply to your current situation and is unavailable. For example, the Paste command on the Edit menu appears dimmed if you have not first used either the Copy command or the Cut command.

When a command name is preceded by a check mark, the command is already in effect.

Command in effect

When a command name is followed by an arrow, another level of choices appears when you choose the command. For example, when you choose the Quick Sort command from the Records menu, a list of further choices appears. You can choose Ascending or Descending to sort your records.

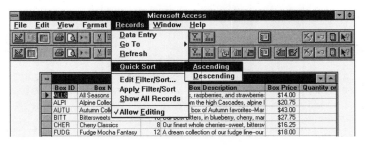

To close a menu without choosing a command, click the menu name again, or press ESC.

Using Dialog Boxes

When you choose a command that is followed by an ellipsis (...), Windows-based applications display a *dialog box* so that you can provide more information. Depending on the dialog box, you type the information or select from a group of options.

After you enter information or make selections in the dialog box, you can click the OK button with the mouse or press ENTER to carry out the command. You can also choose the Cancel button or press ESC to close a dialog box without carrying out an action.

For example, the Find dialog box appears when you choose the Find command from the Edit menu. In the dialog box, you specify the options you want.

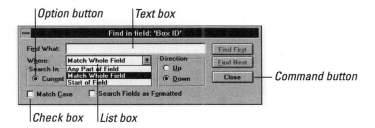

Every dialog box has one or more of the following types of *controls* to help you supply the information necessary to carry out the command.

Text box   You type information in a text box. For example, in the Find dialog box, you can type the text you want to find in the text box.

List box   Available choices appear in a list. If the list is longer than the box, you can use the scroll bar or the down arrow to see the rest of the list. In the Find dialog box, you click the down arrow next to the Where box to display the list.

Option buttons   You can select only one option at a time from a group of option buttons. A selected option button has a black dot in its center.

Check boxes   You can select multiple check boxes at a time from a group of check boxes. A selected check box has an X in its center.

Command buttons   You choose a command button to carry out an operation or to display more options. If a command button is dimmed, it is unavailable. An ellipsis following the name of a command button means that more options are available. In the Find dialog box, you can choose the Close button to close the dialog box and apply the options, or you can press ESC to cancel.

Selecting Dialog Box Options

To move around in a dialog box, you can simply click the item you want. You can also hold down ALT and press the key for the underlined letter at the same time. Or, you can press TAB to move between items.

Use the procedures in this table to select options in a dialog box with the mouse.

To	Do this
Select an option button	Click the option button.
Clear an option button	Select another option button.
Select or clear a check box	Click the check box.
Select an item in a list	Click the item.
Move to a text box	Click the text box.
Select text in a text box	Double-click a word or drag through the characters.
Scroll through a list	Use the scroll bars.
Select a tab	Click the tab.

Using Toolbars

Located below the menu bar are the *toolbars*. When you first install and start Microsoft Access, the Database toolbar is displayed. This bar contains buttons that are shortcuts for choosing commands and for working with Microsoft Access. For example, clicking the Open Database button on the toolbar is the same as choosing the Open Database command from the File menu.

You can select different toolbars, depending on the tools you need. To change to a different toolbar, use the Toolbars command on the View menu, and then select the toolbar you want from the list.

Although initially you might feel more comfortable using the keyboard for making menu selections, it is generally much faster to use the mouse to click a button on the toolbars. The instructions in this book emphasize using the toolbars as the most efficient method for most of the basic Microsoft Access operations.

If You Are New to Using a Mouse

Menu bars, toolbars, and many other features of Microsoft Access and other Windows-based applications are designed for working with a mouse. Although you can use the keyboard for most actions in Microsoft Access, many of these actions are easier to do with the mouse.

Using the Mouse

The mouse controls a symbol on the screen called the *pointer*. You move the pointer by sliding the mouse over a flat surface in the direction you want the pointer to move. If you run out of room to move the mouse, you can lift it up and put it down again. The pointer moves only when the mouse is touching a flat surface.

Moving the mouse pointer across the screen does not affect the document; the pointer simply indicates a location on the screen. When you press the mouse button, an action occurs at the location of the pointer.

When the mouse pointer passes over different parts of the Microsoft Access window, it changes shape, indicating what you can do with it at that point. Most of your work in this book will use the following mouse pointers.

This pointer	Appears when you point to
⌖	The menu bar and toolbars to choose a command or a button, the title bar to move a window, or the scroll bars to scroll through a document.
I	Text in a text box or text in a cell in Datasheet view. When you click the mouse in text, a blinking vertical bar called the *insertion point* appears.
↔ ↕	A column heading boundary or row heading boundary to change column width or row height.

The following describes the four basic mouse actions that you use throughout the lessons in this book.

Pointing   Moving the mouse to place the pointer on an item is called *pointing*.

Clicking   Pointing to an item on your screen, and then quickly pressing and releasing the mouse button once is called *clicking*. You select items on the screen and move around in a document by clicking.

When you click with the right mouse button, you get a shortcut menu of commands that apply to the current operation. Microsoft Access 2 for Windows has several shortcut menus that you'll use throughout this book to access commands quickly.

Double-clicking   Pointing to an item, and then quickly pressing and releasing the mouse button twice is called *double-clicking*. This is a convenient shortcut for many tasks.

Dragging   Holding down the mouse button as you move the pointer is called *dragging*.

Using Help

Microsoft Access includes Help, a complete online reference. You can access Help information in several ways.

To get Help information	Do this
By topic or activity	From the Help menu, choose Contents.
While working in a window or dialog box	Press F1 or choose the Help button in the dialog box.
About a specific command, tool, or other element on the screen	Click the Help button on the toolbar, and then click the command, tool, or other screen element.
By keyword	Double-click the Help tool. In the Search dialog box, type a keyword, and then select a Help topic.

Display the list of Help topics

▶ From the Help menu, choose Contents.

The Microsoft Access Help Contents window looks similar to the following illustration.

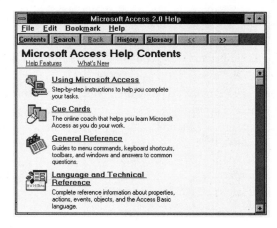

You can size, move, and scroll through a Help window. You can switch between the Help window and Microsoft Access, or you can choose the Always On Top command to keep the Help window on top of other windows so that you can refer to Help while you work.

Getting Help on Help

To learn how you can make best use of all the information in Help, you can read through instructions for using Help.

Learn to use Help

1   Press F1.

The Contents For How To Use Help list appears.

2   In the first paragraph, locate the phrase, "scroll bar," which has a dotted underline, and click it.

A definition of the term appears in a pop-up box. Clicking an underlined term "jumps" you to a related topic. Clicking a term with a dotted underline displays a pop-up definition in a topic window.

3   Click the phrase again.

The definition popup box closes.

4   Locate the phrase "Help Basics," which has a solid underline, and click it.

A new screen appears with information about Help.

5   Click the term "jumps," which has a dotted underline.

Another pop-up definition appears.

6   Click the term again to close the definition.

The definition closes.

Use the Contents list

1   In the Help window, click the Contents button.

The Contents list appears.

2   Scroll downward in the list, and click any topic that is underlined in green.

A new screen appears with information about the topic.

3   From the File menu, choose Exit.

Getting Help on a Topic

The Help system allows you to find information on a topic in several ways. First, the Contents list allows you to choose from a list of functionally organized topics and subtopics. Second, the Search option allows you to quickly locate Help topics by using a key word. If you know the command or term you want help on, you can go directly to the topic. You can also use the Index or the Help button on the Standard toolbar to find Help.

In the next exercises, you look for information using the the Search option.

Search Help for a topic

This book and the Microsoft Access documentation contain references to Help for additional information about the task at hand. Sometimes the reference tells you to search Help for a keyword. For example, it might tell you to search Help for "opening tables." To follow the reference, you use the Search command on the Help menu.

1   From the Help menu, choose Search. (If the Help window is already open, you can choose the Search button.)

The Search dialog box appears.

2   Type the keyword in the dialog box. For example, type **opening tables**

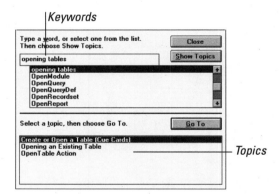

3   Choose the Show Topics button.

4   In the lower portion of the Search dialog box, double-click the topic you want to read. For example, double-click "Opening an Existing Table."

Microsoft Access displays the Help topic.

5   When you're finished looking at Help, double-click the Control-menu box on the Help window to close it.

Using Cue Cards

Microsoft Access includes Cue Cards, online learning tools that provide instructions to help you learn Microsoft Access while you build and use your own database. Cue Cards walk you through a task from start to finish. They provide graphical examples, guidance, and shortcuts to online reference material. The following steps show you how to start and quit Cue Cards.

Open Cue Cards

Cue Cards

1 From the Help menu, choose Cue Cards. Or, click the Cue Cards button on the toolbar.

The main Cue Cards menu appears.

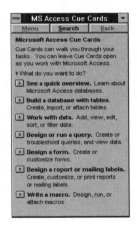

Here you can select what you want to do first. For an introduction to the parts of a database and how you can use them, select the first option, See A Quick Overview.

2 Explore different topics using the Cue Cards.

Close Cue Cards

▶ When you finish using Cue Cards, double-click the Control-menu box on the Cue Cards window to close it.

Control-menu box

Quitting Microsoft Access

If you are ready to start working with a database in Microsoft Access, go to Lesson 1 now. If you are ready to take a break, you can quit Microsoft Access.

Quit Microsoft Access

▶ Double-click the Control-menu box in the Microsoft Access window. Or, from the File menu, choose Close.

Before shutting down, Microsoft Access closes any other database objects you might have open. If you made changes to the data in a table before exiting, your changes are saved.

Quitting Microsoft Windows

If you would like to quit Windows, here is a simple way to exit the program.

Quit Microsoft Windows

1   From the File menu, choose Exit Windows.

2   When you see a box with the message "This will end your Windows session," press ENTER.

New Features in Microsoft Access 2

The following table lists the major new features in Microsoft Access 2 for Windows that are covered in this book. The table shows the lesson in which you can learn about each feature. For more information about new features, see *Microsoft Access User's Guide*.

To learn how to	See
Size a column to its best fit by double-clicking.	Lesson 2
Cut text easily using a Shortcut menu.	Lesson 3
Sort records quickly using the Sort Ascending and Sort Descending buttons.	Lesson 4
Automatically create a new table with the Table Wizard.	Lesson 6
Filter a table to see only the records you want to see.	Lesson 6
Export only part of a table to an Excel worksheet.	Lesson 7
Sketch the design of your database or see all the relationships at once by using the Relationships window.	Lesson 8
See how Microsoft Access automatically relates tables in a query with matching fields.	Lesson 9
Automatically format a convenient layout for your data by using a Query Wizard to create a crosstab query.	Lesson 10
Set a field property easily by using a Build button to help you select choices.	Lesson 11
Fine-tune the placement of controls on a form by moving them just one grid point at a time.	Lesson 11
Open a form from within a form by creating a Command Button.	Lesson 13
Set a field property to require data in a field.	Lesson 14
Create a quick detail report by using the Tabular Report Wizard.	Lesson 15
Customize the default style of a report created with a Report Wizard.	Lesson 15
Improve the printed look of a report by keeping groups together on a page with the Keep Together property.	Lesson 16
Add an expression to a report that prints page numbers with customized text.	Lesson 16

Part

1 Data Basics

Adding Data to a Database

The most convenient place to keep the information you need is right at your desk. You might keep stacking paper forms in a file folder next to the phone, as long as the stack doesn't get too big. But you have a problem if you try to keep *all* the information you need at your desk—pretty soon you can't find the desk!

You can use Microsoft Access to organize and store all kinds and quantities of information and have it available, with only a few clicks of your mouse. In this lesson, you'll find out how to open a Microsoft Access database, use a form to add new data, and move from record to record.

You will learn how to:

- Open a database.
- Open a form.
- Enter data.
- Select an option or a check box.
- Move from record to record.
- Open a table.
- Quit Microsoft Access.

Estimated lesson time: 20 minutes

What Is Data?

Data is anything you want to store and refer to again. In Microsoft Access, data can be text, numbers, dates, and pictures. For example, if you sell boxes of bonbons, you can store the names, pictures, and recipes of your bonbons, the prices and quantities of boxes, and the dates of sales.

In most cases, the easiest way to enter data is by using a *form*. Database forms resemble the paper forms we see in offices, find in junk mail, and lose from magazines. You type the data in the form, and Microsoft Access stores it in a table.

A *record* is a set of information that belongs together, such as all the information on one job application or magazine subscription card. A database can hold many records.

Setting the Scene

Sweet Lil's Chocolates, Inc., a fast-growing gourmet chocolate company, has switched to Microsoft Access to store data on its product lines and sales. To attract new customers, Sweet Lil's started a monthly newsletter called *Chocolate Gourmet*. After seeing how much time the database saved and how many errors it prevented, the Newsletter department wants to keep subscription information in the database as well.

They've recruited you to be the first person to enter data using a new form called "Subscriptions." The Sweet database contains the form you need. You'll open the database, open the Subscription form, and enter subscription data. The records you enter will be stored in the Customers table.

Note   If you have just completed the steps in "Getting Ready" earlier in this book for starting Microsoft Access and opening a database, skip "Opening a Database," and go to the following section, "Opening a Form."

Opening a Database

If you quit Microsoft Access at the end of "Getting Ready," or if you are just starting to use *Microsoft Access 2 for Windows Step by Step* with this lesson, perform these steps for starting Microsoft Access and opening a database.

Start Microsoft Access from Microsoft Windows

Microsoft Office

1   Double-click the Microsoft Office group icon shown at the left to display the group window. (Or open whichever group contains Access 2.0.)

2   To start Microsoft Access, double-click the Microsoft Access icon shown at the left.

Microsoft Access

3   If the Welcome To Microsoft Access box appears, double-click the Control-menu box to close it.

The Microsoft Access startup window appears. From here, you can create a new database, open a database, or do basic database administration tasks.

Open a database

Open Database

1   From the File menu, choose Open Database, or click the Open Database button on the toolbar.

To create a new database from scratch, see "Getting Ready," or refer to your Microsoft Access documentation.

The Open Database dialog box appears.

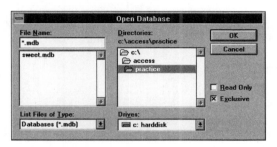

2   In the Directories list, double-click the PRACTICE subdirectory to open it.

The PRACTICE subdirectory is probably in your ACCESS directory. If you need help finding the PRACTICE subdirectory, see "Getting Ready" earlier in this book.

3   In the File Name list, double-click SWEET.MDB.

The Database window for the Sweet database appears.

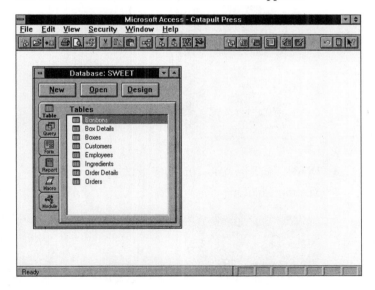

The Database window shows the tables that store data about Sweet Lil's business. From the Database window, you can open and work with any object in the database.

Opening a Form

Now that you're in the Sweet database, you can open the Subscription form to enter the subscription information for a new customer.

Open a form

1   If the Microsoft Access window doesn't fill your screen, click the Maximize button to maximize the window.

Maximize button

2   In the Database window, click the Form object button.

A list of the forms in the Sweet database appears.

3   Double-click the Subscription form.

The form appears.

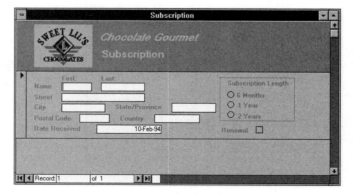

The Subscription form contains blank boxes—or fields—where you type the information from the paper form. A *field* is an area on a form where you enter data, such as a last name or an address.

The *insertion point* indicates where the information appears when you type. You can move the insertion point by clicking a different field or by pressing the TAB key. In general, forms are set up so that when you press TAB, the insertion point moves from left to right and from top to bottom.

Notice that Microsoft Access fills in the current date in the Date Received field automatically so you don't have to type it.

Entering Data

You'll use the blank Subscription form on your screen to enter the subscription for a *Chocolate Gourmet* fan from Ohio. Here's what his paper subscription form looks like.

Add a name

1   Type **Earl** in the First Name field.

As soon as you start typing, a new blank form appears below the one you're working in.

If you make a mistake, just press the BACKSPACE key, and then retype.

2   Press TAB to move the insertion point to the Last Name field (or click anywhere in the Last Name field).

You'll find that pressing TAB is convenient for moving to the next field when your hands are already on the keyboard, or use SHIFT + TAB to move to the previous field.

3   Type **Lee** in the Last Name field.

Add an address

▶ Type the following address information, pressing TAB to move from field to field.

Street:	**28 Dorothy**
City:	**Fairborn**
State/Province:	**OH**
Postal Code:	**45324**
Country:	**USA**

Note   From now on, you'll see instructions on how to move to the next field only if you need to do something other than press TAB. For a list of all the keys you can use while editing data in a form, press F1 to open Help, and then click the word "Keyboard" near the top of the Help window.

Selecting an Option Button or a Check Box

When you press TAB after typing "USA" in the Country field, Microsoft Access draws a dotted line around "6 Months" in the Subscription Length field instead of displaying the insertion point.

Subscription Length is an *option group*. Because an option group presents a set of options to select from, you don't have to type the data yourself—you just select an option. In this case, Earl Lee wants a 2-year subscription.

Select an option button

▶ Click the circle next to 2 Years. Or, press the DOWN ARROW key twice.

A dot appears in the button next to 2 Years, indicating that this option is selected.

Next, you'll fill out the Renewal field.

Select a check box

Earl Lee's subscription is a renewal. Renewal is a *check box*. When this kind of field is selected, you see an X in the box.

▶ Click the Renewal check box.

An X appears in the box.

Tip   To clear a selected check box, click it again. If you prefer to use the keyboard, you can press the SPACEBAR to select or clear a check box.

Moving from Record to Record

All the information in Earl Lee's subscription makes up one complete record. Now that you've entered Earl Lee's subscription, you're ready to start the next subscription.

Depending on the way a form is designed, you can see one or more records at a time while you use the form. If you can see the next record, you can move to it by clicking in it. Whether you can see the next record or not, you can move to it by pressing TAB from the last field in the current record (the record you're in now).

Save the record and move to the next record

▶ Click in the First Name field of the next record. Or, in the Renewal field of the current record, press TAB.

Microsoft Access saves Earl Lee's subscription information automatically when you go to a new record. You don't have to do anything else to save the first subscription.

Return to the previous record

Looking over your first entry, you notice that you didn't type "St." in Earl Lee's street address. You'll return to the previous record to make the change.

1   Click after the "y" in "Dorothy" in the Street field of Earl Lee's record to return to the record.

You can also use the PAGE UP key to go to the first field in the first record. Then press TAB to move to the Street field.

If you move to a field by pressing TAB, Microsoft Access selects the entire value in the field. To change from the selection mode and place the insertion point at the end of the field, press F2.

2   Press the SPACEBAR to insert a space after "Dorothy," and then type **St.**

3   Click in the First Name field of the next record.

Microsoft Access saves your change to Earl Lee's record.

While you were editing Earl Lee's record, you might have noticed that a pencil symbol appeared in the area on the left side of the form. The pencil indicates that you've changed data in the current record but your changes aren't saved yet. If you haven't changed data in the current record, a triangle appears instead of a pencil. You can see how this works while you add the next subscription from the stack on your desk.

Add the first name

▶ Type **Becky** in the First Name field.

Notice that Becky's last name doesn't look as if it's going to fit in the Last Name field. If you were filling out a paper form, you'd have to squeeze the name in the space. But Microsoft Access forms can accommodate long names.

Add text to scrollable fields

1 Type **Sawyer-Roundstone** in the Last Name field.

As soon as you type one more letter than fits in the Last Name field, Microsoft Access scrolls the name so you can keep typing. The entire name is saved, even if you can't see it all at once.

2 Type **260 Kent Street Station 1551** in the Street field.

Finish entering the subscription

▶ Type the data below, pressing TAB to move from field to field.

City:	**Ottawa**
State/Province:	**Ontario**
Postal Code:	**K1A 0E6**
Country:	**Canada**
Subscription Length:	**6 Months**
Renewal:	**No**

It's almost break time. Before you stop, proofread your entries. When you're finished, close the Subscription form.

Close the form

▶ Double-click the Control-menu box in the Subscription form window. Or, from the File menu, choose Close.

Be sure that you double-click the Control-menu box for the form, not the Control-menu box for the Microsoft Access window.

Click here.

Opening a Table

The records you just added using the Subscription form were saved in the Customers table in the Sweet database. Take a look at your new records in the Customers table.

Display table names in the Database window

▶ In the Database window, click the Table object button.

The list of tables in the Sweet database appears.

Open the Customers table

▶ Double-click the Customers table.

The Customers table opens and its records appear.

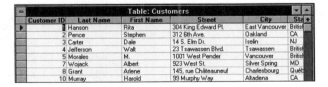

The two records you added are at the end of the list of customers. You can use the navigation buttons at the bottom of the form window to move directly to the first, previous, next, or last record.

Move to the last record

▶ In the lower-left corner of the window, click the navigation button for the last record.

Previous record   *Next record*

First record   *Click here for the last record.*

The last records in the table appear. The last two records are the ones you just added for Earl Lee and Becky Sawyer-Roundstone. Notice that Microsoft Access automatically assigned Earl and Becky customer ID numbers. You'll learn how to set up a table that automatically assigns ID numbers in Part 2, "Expanding a Database."

Tip   You can use the keyboard or the vertical scroll bar to move between records, but the fastest way to move in a large database is with the navigation buttons.

Quitting Microsoft Access

Since you're going on a break, it's best to quit Microsoft Access. That way, no one can damage your data while you're away. You can close the Customers table and quit Microsoft Access all in one step.

Quit Microsoft Access

▶ Double-click the Control-menu box in the Microsoft Access window.

Click here.

Before shutting down, Microsoft Access closes the Customers table (and any other database objects you might have open). If you made changes to the data in the Customers table before exiting, your changes are saved.

One Step Further

You're ready to fill out more subscriptions. To make corrections faster, you can move between the forms quickly by using such keys as PAGE DOWN and HOME.

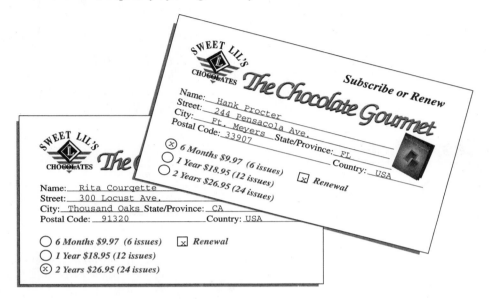

Enter two more subscriptions

Add information for two subscriptions to the Subscription form in the Sweet database.

1   Start Microsoft Access and open the Sweet database.

2   In the Database window, click the Form button to see the list of forms, and then double-click the Subscription form in the list to open it.

3   Add the subscription information for Hank Proctor as shown in the previous illustration.

4   Press PAGE DOWN to move to the next record.

You can immediately see a new blank form.

5   Add the subscription information for Rita Courqette.

In reviewing the paper form, you realize that Rita's last name is misspelled.

6   To move quickly to the first field of the record, press HOME. Then press TAB to move to the Last Name field.

7   To replace her name, be sure the whole word is selected, and then type **Corquette**

If You Want to Continue to the Next Lesson

▶ Double-click the Control-menu box on the Subscription form. Or, from the File menu, choose Close.

This closes the form, but it does not exit the Microsoft Access program.

If You Want to Quit Microsoft Access for Now

▶ In the Microsoft Access window, double-click the Control-menu box. Or, from the File menu, choose Exit.

This closes the form and exits the Microsoft Access program. The changes you made to the data in the Subscription form are saved.

Lesson Summary

To	Do this	Button
Open a database	From the File menu, choose Open Database, or click the Open Database button on the toolbar.	
Open a form	In the Database window, click the Form object button, and then double-click the form you want to open.	
Select an option in an option group	Click the option button. *or* Press the DOWN ARROW key until the option is selected.	
Select or clear a check box	Click the check box. *or* Press TAB to move to the check box, and then press the SPACEBAR.	
Move to the next record on a form	Click the Next Record button at the bottom of the form. *or* From the last field, press TAB.	
Move from field to field	Click the field you want to move to. *or* Press TAB to move to the next field; press SHIFT+TAB to move to the previous field.	

To	Do this
Move to the previous record on a form	Press PAGE UP. *or* Click the Previous Record button at the bottom of the form.
Save data	Microsoft Access automatically saves your data. This usually happens when you move to another record or window, close the form, or exit Microsoft Access.
Open a table	In the Database window, click the Table object button, and then double-click the table you want to open.

For more information on	See
Adding and saving data with a form	Chapter 4, "Creating a Form" in *Microsoft Access Getting Started*
	Chapter 4, "Adding and Editing Data" in *Microsoft Access User's Guide*
Looking at information in a table	Chapter 2, "Microsoft Access Basics" in *Microsoft Access Getting Started*
	Chapter 7, "Table Basics" in *Microsoft Access User's Guide*

For online information about	From the **Help** menu, choose **Search** and then type
Opening databases	opening databases
Moving between records	moving between records
Saving data	saving data
Opening tables	opening tables

Preview of the Next Lesson

In the next lesson, you'll use a form to look at records in two ways: one at a time arranged like a form, and several records at once, arranged like a table in row-and-column format. You'll copy data from one record to another and add a picture to a record.

Getting the Best View of Your Data

The best view of data isn't just one view—it depends on what you're doing at the time. When you add a new product, you might want to see all the details about that product at once. When you review a group of related products, you might prefer seeing all the products in a list. However the data is arranged, you need easy, convenient ways to add and edit data.

Microsoft Access forms have the flexibility to show you both kinds of views. In this lesson, you'll find out how to see different views of data using the same form, and you'll learn more techniques for adding and editing data on a form.

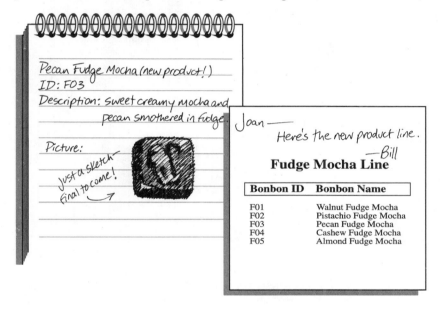

You will learn how to:

- Switch between Form view and Datasheet view of a form.
- Change the way a datasheet looks.
- Copy and move data.
- Select values from a list.
- Insert a picture in a record.

Estimated lesson time: 40 minutes

Understanding Views

A paper form shows one arrangement of your data. To see another arrangement, you have to use another form. A Microsoft Access form provides the flexibility of two views—Form view and Datasheet view. In Form view, the fields are arranged to show individual records to their best advantage. Datasheet view shows the same fields arranged in rows and columns, like a spreadsheet, so you can see multiple records at the same time.

One form...

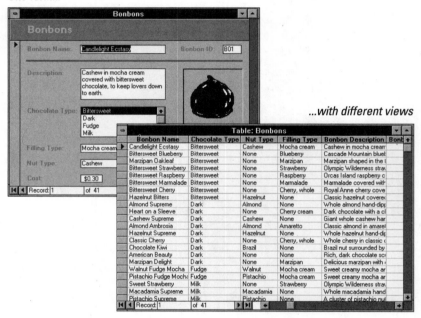

...with different views

In Datasheet view, you can rearrange columns and resize columns and rows. In either view, Microsoft Access provides powerful editing features you can use to keep your data current.

Start the lesson

▶ If Microsoft Access isn't already started, start it and open the Sweet database as described in Lesson 1. If the Microsoft Access window doesn't fill your screen, maximize the window.

Switching Between Views of a Form

You've just been put in charge of Sweet Lil's new Fudge Mocha line. You'll use the Bonbons form to update existing records for Fudge Mocha bonbons and to add records for several new bonbons.

Open a form

1   In the Database window, click the Form object button.

A list of the forms in the Sweet database appears.

2   Double-click the Bonbons form.

The Bonbons form opens, and the record for Candlelight Ecstasy appears.

In Form view, the fields on the Bonbons form are arranged so you can see all the information about an individual bonbon at a glance. Except for your current task, a row-and-column format would make it easier to compare fields from different Fudge Mochas.

Switch to Datasheet view

Datasheet View

▶   On the toolbar, click the Datasheet View button.

The records in the Bonbons form appear in a row-and-column layout. The triangle next to the Candlelight Ecstasy record marks it as the current record.

You can see that two of the bonbons in the new Fudge Mocha line—Walnut Fudge Mocha and Pistachio Fudge Mocha—are already in the database. These are the records you want to work with.

Move to a different record

▶   Click anywhere in the row for Walnut Fudge Mocha.

Now the record for Walnut Fudge Mocha is the current record. The triangle at the left edge of the datasheet is now pointing to the Walnut Fudge Mocha record. If you switch back to Form view, that's the record you'll see on the form.

Switch views

Form View

1   On the toolbar, click the Form View button to switch to Form view.

The record for Walnut Fudge Mocha appears in the form.

2   Click the Datasheet View button to return to Datasheet view.

The form appears in Datasheet view. Walnut Fudge Mocha is still the current record.

Changing the Way a Datasheet Looks

The Bonbon Description field describes each bonbon in a sentence or two. You'll include these descriptions in Sweet Lil's catalog, so you want to make sure that the text is just right. With the datasheet laid out as it is now, you can see only part of each bonbon's description. To read an entire description, you'd have to use the arrow keys and the HOME and END keys to scroll through the text.

You'll change the datasheet layout so you can read the entire description at once.

To change the height of rows in a datasheet, you use the *record selectors* on the left side of the records. You use the *field selector* at the top of a column to change the column width.

Field selectors

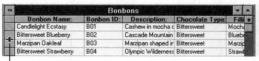

Record selectors

You'll start by changing the row height, so you can see all of a bonbon's description at once.

Change the height of rows in a datasheet

1   Position the pointer on the lower border of any record selector (on the left side of the record).

The pointer changes shape to show that you can resize the rows.

2   Drag the border downward to make the rows higher.

Microsoft Access resizes all the rows. (You can't resize just one row.)

3   If necessary, adjust the height of the rows until you can read the entire description for Bittersweet Blueberry.

Now that you've resized the rows, you'll adjust the width of some of the columns.

Change the width of a column in a datasheet

The column for the Bonbon ID field is wider than necessary. If you make the column narrower, you'll be able to see more of the other fields in the datasheet.

1   Position the pointer on the right border of the field selector for the Bonbon ID field.

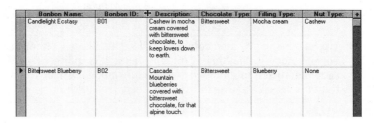

2   Double-click the right edge of the column.

You can also resize to a measurement you choose by dragging the border to the left to make the column narrower.

Microsoft Access sizes the column to fit its widest value, but it also retains the complete field name at the top of the column.

Next you'll make the Cost field narrower.

3   At the bottom of the form window, click in the scroll bar to see the rest of the fields.

Click here.

Microsoft Access scrolls the columns horizontally.

4   Click the arrows at either end of the scroll bar to scroll one field (one column) at a time.

5   Make the column for the Cost field narrower by double-clicking the right border of the field selector.

Hide a column

The Format menu also contains a Hide Columns command. When you choose the command, it hides the column that contains the insertion point.

The column for the Picture field doesn't show pictures for the bonbons in this view. (You can see pictures on forms in Form view, but not in Datasheet view.) Since the pictures aren't visible anyway, you can hide the Picture column.

▶   Drag the right border of the Picture column all the way to its left border.

Microsoft Access hides the column.

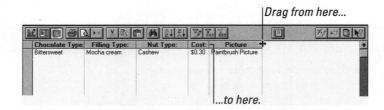

Drag from here...

...to here.

Tip   To display hidden columns, choose the Show Columns command from the Format menu. If the Show Columns dialog box indicates the column is already showing, then it might not be completely hidden. Check to be sure you dragged its right border *all the way* to its left border.

Freeze a column

Notice that when you scroll to the fields on the right side of the datasheet, you can't see the Bonbon Name field, so you can't tell which bonbon records you're viewing. It would be more convenient to be able to scroll horizontally through the fields with the Bonbon Name field anchored, or frozen, on the left. You can do that by freezing the column.

1   Scroll backward to the left side of the form.

Click here.

2   Click in any row in the Bonbon Name column.

3   From the Format menu, choose Freeze Columns.

Microsoft Access displays a bold line on the right border of the Bonbon Name column. Now the column is frozen.

4   Scroll horizontally to see the fields on the right side of the record, and then scroll backward to the left side of the form.

This column doesn't scroll.

All other columns scroll.

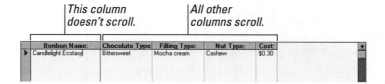

Save the layout of a form's datasheet

You can save this convenient layout so the datasheet appears this way every time you use it.

▶   From the File menu, choose Save Form.

Scroll through a set of records

You're ready to work with the records in the Fudge Mocha line. But now that you've widened the rows in your datasheet, the records you want aren't visible. You can use either the vertical scroll bar or the PAGE DOWN key to scroll through the records.

1   Click below the scroll box in the vertical scroll bar. Or, press PAGE DOWN.

— *Scroll box*
— *Click here.*

Microsoft Access scrolls downward one page (window).

To scroll upward or downward one record at a time, click the arrows at the top or bottom of the scroll bar.

2   Continue to click below the scroll box until you see the Fudge Mochas in the list.

Notice that each time you click below the scroll box, the box moves down the scroll bar to show your relative position in the records.

Tip   If you know the relative position of the records you're looking for, you can move to them very quickly by dragging the scroll box. For example, if you're looking for a record in the middle of the list, drag the scroll box to the middle of the vertical scroll bar. When you release the mouse button, Microsoft Access displays the records in the middle of the list.

Copying and Moving Data

You keep a database current and accurate by updating data in fields. Microsoft Access has convenient editing features that help you edit, move, copy, and delete data in fields. You'll find most editing features on the Edit menu and on the toolbar.

When you edit in Microsoft Access, keep in mind a principle called *select then do*. If you want to copy, delete, or change something, you first *select* it, and then you *do* it by choosing the action you want from the menu or by using buttons on the toolbar. There are also convenient keyboard shortcuts that you can use, which are listed to the right of many menu commands. For example, if you want to delete text, first you drag to select it, and then you choose Cut from the Edit menu (or press the shortcut keys CTRL+X).

When you cut or copy text or an object, Microsoft Access stores it in the Windows storage area called the *Clipboard*. When you paste, Microsoft Access pastes whatever is on the Clipboard at the current location of the insertion point. You can copy text from one field and then paste it into another field or into as many other fields as you need. That's because Windows keeps the Clipboard contents until you copy or cut something else.

Add text to a field

Market research tells you that chocolate fudge is a key ingredient for the success of your new line. You'll add the phrase "smothered in fudge" to the end of each bonbon description.

1 In the Description field for the Walnut Fudge Mocha bonbon, click between the "t" in "walnut" and the period.

The insertion point appears where you click.

2 Press the SPACEBAR to insert a space, and then type **smothered in fudge**

Copy text from one field to another

Rather than type the phrase again, you can copy it to the Description field for the Pistachio Fudge Mocha bonbon.

1 Select the phrase "smothered in fudge," including the space in front of "smothered" but not the period at the end.

Hint: Click in the space after the "t" in "walnut." Drag to select the text you want.

Copy

2 From the Edit menu, choose Copy. Or, click the Copy button on the toolbar.

Microsoft Access places a copy of the selected text on the Clipboard.

3 In the Description field for the Pistachio Fudge Mocha bonbon, position the insertion point between the "o" in "pistachio" and the period.

Paste

4 From the Edit menu, choose Paste. Or, click the Paste button on the toolbar.

Microsoft Access pastes the text from the Clipboard.

Cut

Note   You use the same steps to move text, except you choose Cut instead of Copy from the Edit menu (or click the Cut button to the left of the Copy button on the toolbar). Microsoft Access removes the text and places a copy of it on the Clipboard. Then you can paste the text where you want it.

Switch to Form view

Next, you'll enter records for Sweet Lil's three new Fudge Mochas—Pecan, Cashew, and Almond. You can add new records in either Datasheet view or Form view, but it's easier in Form view because you can see all the fields in a record at once.

Form View

▶ Click the Form View button on the toolbar.

The Bonbons form appears in Form view.

Begin a record

There's a new, blank record after the last record. You can use the navigation buttons to go to it quickly.

1 Click the navigation button for the last record, and then click the navigation button for the next record.

Click here...

...and then click here.

The new record appears at the end of the last record.

2 Type this data in the first two fields:

Bonbon Name: **Pecan Fudge Mocha**
Bonbon ID: **F03**

3 In the Description field, type **Creamy sweet mocha and nutty pecan**

The next part of the description, "smothered in fudge," is still on the Clipboard. Instead of typing it, you can paste it again.

Paste

4 Click the Paste button on the toolbar.

5 Type a period at the end of the description.

Delete text

"Nutty" is redundant as an adjective for "pecan," so you'll delete it.

▶ Select the word "nutty" and the space after it, and then press DELETE.

Replace text

To match the other Fudge Mocha descriptions, you want this description to start with "Sweet creamy" rather than "Creamy sweet." You can replace the old text at the same time that you type the new text, without deleting it first.

1 Select "Creamy sweet" in the Description field.

2 Type **Sweet creamy**

Microsoft Access replaces the selected text with the text you type. Now your description is correct.

Selecting Values from Lists

A *value* is an individual piece of data, such as a last name, an address, or an ID number. Selecting a value from a list is often quicker than typing the value yourself. But lists have another advantage besides speed—they help keep your data accurate. When you select a value from a list, you know that it's spelled consistently and that it's a valid entry.

The Chocolate Type field on the Bonbons form is a special kind of field called a *list box*. List boxes display a list of values to select from. You can use either the mouse or the keyboard to select a value from the list.

The Nut Type and Filling Type fields are both *combo boxes*. With a combo box, you can either type the value yourself or select it from the list.

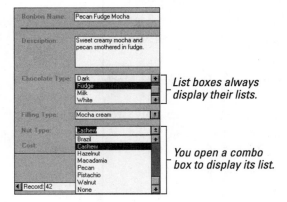

List boxes always display their lists.

You open a combo box to display its list.

Select a value in a list box

▶ In the Chocolate Type field, click "Fudge" to select it, or press TAB to move to the Chocolate Type field, and then type **f**

"Fudge" is the only value in the Chocolate Type list box that starts with "f," so you can select "Fudge" by typing the first letter of the word. If the list box had more than one "f" value, you could type "f" to go to the first one, and then use the DOWN ARROW key to move down the list.

Select a value in a combo box

You can either type the value you want in the Filling Type combo box, or you can select a value from the list. Often, it's easier and more accurate to do the latter.

1 Click the arrow in the Filling Type field to display the list. Or, press TAB to move to the Filling Type field, and then press F4.

This list shows you the fillings that Sweet Lil's uses.

2   Select Mocha cream from the list.

To select the value without using the mouse, type **mo**, the first two letters in Mocha. Because Mocha cream is the only value that starts with those two letters, Microsoft Access selects it. If you wanted to select Marmalade instead of Marzipan, you'd type **marm**.

3   Type **Pecan** in the Nut Type field, or select it from the list.

Enter the bonbon cost

▶   Type **.25** in the Bonbon Cost field, and then press TAB to move to the last field on the form.

Notice that when you leave the Bonbon Cost field, Microsoft Access automatically formats the value to show that it's a currency value.

You're ready to add the last value to this record—the bonbon's picture.

Adding a Picture to a Record

You can store most any kind of information in your database, including pictures, graphs, sounds, and other objects from other applications. An *OLE object* is any piece of information created with an application for Windows that supports *object linking and embedding* (OLE). Microsoft Access stores OLE objects in a field in a table. You can store a different OLE object in each record, just as you can store a different name or address in a text field for each record. You can display the objects in any form or report.

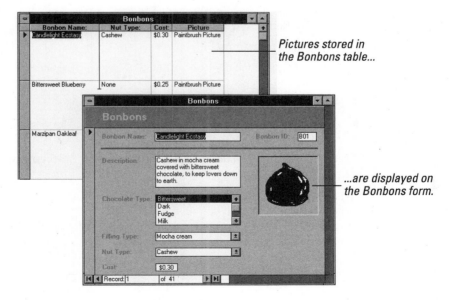

Pictures stored in the Bonbons table...

...are displayed on the Bonbons form.

The Picture field on the Bonbons form is a special type of field called an *object frame*. You use this type of field to add, edit, or view OLE objects in your tables.

Insert a picture into a record

The picture for Pecan Fudge Mocha is in a file called PECAN.BMP. The PECAN.BMP file was copied to your PRACTICE directory when you copied the practice files to your hard disk. You'll *insert* the picture in the record for Pecan Fudge Mocha.

1 Be sure the Picture field is selected, and then from the <u>E</u>dit menu, choose Insert Object.

The Insert Object dialog box appears.

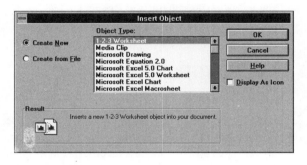

To draw a picture from scratch, you double-click Paintbrush Picture. Paintbrush starts with an empty drawing area for you to draw in.

2 Scroll down the list of object types and select Paintbrush Picture.

Because the picture already exists in a file, you need to tell Microsoft Access where to find it.

3 Select the Create From File option.

You can either type the name of the file you want to place, or choose the Browse button.

4 Choose the Browse button.

You'll learn more about using OLE in Microsoft Access in Lesson 12, "Using Pictures and Other Objects."

5 If you're not in the PRACTICE directory, use the Directories list to switch to the PRACTICE directory, and then double-click PECAN.BMP.

The name of the picture file appears in the Insert Object dialog box.

6 Choose the OK button.

The picture appears in the Picture field.

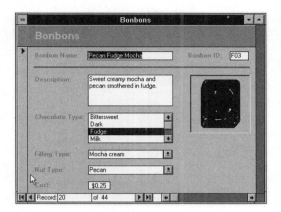

One Step Further

You're ready to add the other two Fudge Mocha bonbons to the database.

The fields for the Fudge Mocha line are all very similar. You could copy and paste the information and then edit it, but to speed up entry of data that is similar, you can use the Ditto key, CTRL+' (single quotation mark). You can also modify the pictures, if you want.

Add two more records

Use the Bonbons form to add the records for Cashew Fudge Mocha and Almond Fudge Mocha to the database. The following tables show the data for the two records.

Remember that to display a new, empty record, you click the navigation button for the last record, and then click the button for the next record. The navigation buttons are in the lower-left corner of the window.

1   Enter the data for Cashew Fudge Mocha.

Field	Data
Bonbon Name	**Cashew Fudge Mocha**
Bonbon ID	**F04**
Description	**Sweet creamy mocha and cashew smothered in fudge.**
Chocolate Type	**Fudge**
Filling Type	**Mocha cream**
Nut Type	**Cashew**
Cost	**.24**
Picture	**CASHEW.BMP**

2   Click the Next Record button to move to a new record. Then enter the data for Almond Fudge Mocha. Click each field and use the Ditto key, CTRL+' (single quotation mark), to repeat any similar data from the Cashew Fudge Mocha record. Edit the information as necessary.

Field	Data
Bonbon Name	**Almond Fudge Mocha**
Bonbon ID	**F05**
Description	**Sweet creamy mocha and almond smothered in fudge.**
Chocolate Type	**Fudge**
Filling Type	**Mocha cream**
Nut Type	**Almond**
Cost	**.19**
Picture	**ALMOND.BMP**

Edit a picture

You can edit a bonbon's picture directly from the Bonbons form. The background of the picture for Almond Fudge Mocha doesn't match the other bonbon pictures, which all have light gray backgrounds. You'll fix the Almond Fudge Mocha picture to be like the others.

1   In the record for Almond Fudge Mocha, double-click the Picture field.

Paintbrush starts and the picture appears in the Paintbrush window.

For help using Paintbrush, press F1 or see your Windows documentation.

2   To change the background to light gray, click the light gray color in the palette at the bottom of the window, and then click the paint roller tool.

3   With the paint roller tool selected, click the white background of the picture. If you make a mistake, choose the Undo command from the Edit menu.

4   When you're finished editing the picture, choose the Exit & Return To Bonbons command from the File menu.

5   When Paintbrush asks if you want to update the object, choose Yes.

If You Want to Continue to the Next Lesson

1   Double-click the Control-menu box on the Bonbons form. Or, from the File menu, choose Close.

2   If Microsoft Access asks if you want to save your changes, choose Yes.

This closes the form, but it does not exit the Microsoft Access program.

If You Want to Quit Microsoft Access for Now

▶   Double-click the Control-menu box in the Microsoft Access window. Or, from the File menu, choose Exit.

This closes the form and exits the Microsoft Access program. The changes you made to the data in the Bonbons form are saved.

Lesson Summary

To	Do this	Button
Switch between Form view and Datasheet view	Click the Datasheet View button or the Form View button on the toolbar.	▦ ▦
Change the height of rows or the width of a column in a datasheet	Drag the lower border of any record selector to resize rows. To resize a column, drag the right border of the column's field selector.	
Hide a column in a datasheet	Drag the right border of the column's field selector all the way to its left border, or click in the column and from the Format menu choose Hide Columns.	
Show hidden columns in a datasheet	From the Format menu, choose Show Columns.	
Freeze the leftmost column or columns in a datasheet	Select the column or columns, and then, from the Layout menu, choose Freeze Columns.	
Copy text from one field to another	Select the text. Click the Copy button on the toolbar. Place the insertion point where you want the text to appear. Click the Paste button on the toolbar.	▦ ▦
Move text from one field to another	Follow the copy text procedure above, but use the Cut button instead of the Copy button.	✂
Insert a picture in a record	Select the field that will contain the picture, and then choose Insert Object from the Edit menu. In the Insert Object dialog box, select the object type. Select the Create From File option, and then double-click the picture you want. Choose OK.	
Edit a Paintbrush picture in a field	Double-click the picture.	

For more information on	See
Viewing data and changing the display of a form in Datasheet view	Chapter 4, "Adding and Editing Data," in *Microsoft Access User's Guide*
Adding and editing OLE objects in your database	Chapter 19, "Using Pictures, Graphs, and Other Objects," in *Microsoft Access User's Guide*

For online information about	From the <u>H</u>elp menu, choose <u>S</u>earch and then type
Keyboard shortcuts for data entry	keyboard: data entry keys
Changing column widths	column width
Hiding a column	hide columns
Freezing columns	freeze columns
Copying or moving text from one field to another	copy data; move data
Inserting a picture in a record	insert object

Preview of the Next Lesson

In the next lesson, you'll use the Sweet Boxes form to add a new box of bonbons to the database. This form contains a subform that shows which bonbons are in each box.

Saving Time with Forms

When you fill out a paper form, it's easy to make a small mistake that wastes a lot of time later, when you're ready to use the information. A simple subtraction error can result in a frustrating hour checking figures; a forgotten bit of information can eat up time while you look for the missing information and record it correctly. What you need is a form that does calculations for you, looks up missing information, and warns you if the data you enter isn't correct.

Microsoft Access forms can do all this for you. In this lesson, you'll find out how to use forms that help you start and stay with the right data.

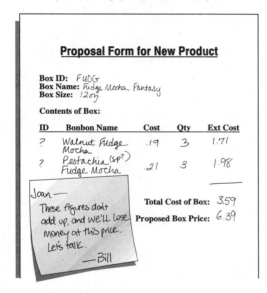

You will learn how to:

- Use a form with a subform to add and change data.
- Use a validation message to help you enter the right data.
- Undo your edits.
- Use a command button to perform a complicated task.
- Delete a record.

Estimated lesson time: 20 minutes

Understanding Forms That Have Subforms

The form you'll use in this lesson—Boxes—is more complex than either the Subscription form or the Bonbons form that you used in the first two lessons. But with Microsoft Access forms, "more complex" doesn't necessarily mean "harder."

The Boxes form contains a *subform* that displays the contents of each box of bonbons. That means you can look at information about the whole box on the main form at the same time you look at information about the bonbons in the box on the subform. You can scroll through the records in the subform, adding and deleting bonbons, until the box has the contents you want.

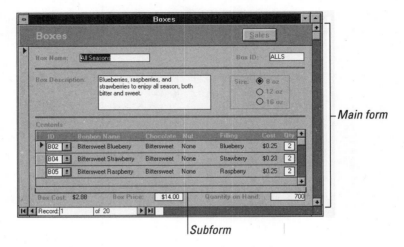

Main form

Subform

The advantage of using a form with a subform is that you can work with data from two different tables at the same time. In the Boxes form, data you enter on the main form is stored in the Boxes table. Data you enter on the subform is stored in the Box Details table. You'll learn how to create a form with a subform in Lesson 13, "Showing Related Records and Calculations on Forms."

Start the lesson

▶ If Microsoft Access isn't started yet, start it and open the Sweet database as described in Lesson 1. If the Microsoft Access window doesn't fill your screen, maximize the window.

Adding a Record to a Form That Has a Subform

You'll use the Boxes form to add a new box of bonbons called Winter Collection to Sweet Lil's line of products.

Open a form and go to the new record

1   Open the Boxes form. If tables are currently listed in the Database window, be sure to click the Form object button first. Otherwise, you'll open the Boxes table instead of the Boxes form.

Microsoft Access displays the record for All Seasons — the first box in the Boxes table.

2   Click the navigation button for the last record, and then click the navigation button for the next record.

The new blank record appears at the end of the existing records.

Enter data in the main form

1   Type the following data in the fields on the main form:

Box Name: **Winter Collection**
Box ID: **WINT**
Box Description: **Nuts and berries coated with chocolate and fudge for those long winter evenings by the fire.**

2   Select 12 oz in the Size option group.

3   Press TAB to move to the subform.

The insertion point moves to the first field in the subform. You'll add six different bonbons to the Winter Collection, each one containing either berries or nuts.

Enter a record in the subform

The first field in the subform will contain the Bonbon ID for the first bonbon in the Winter Collection box. The bonbon you want is Bittersweet Blueberry, but you're not sure of its ID number. The ID combo box can help you find the ID you want.

You'll learn how to create a combo box like this in Lesson 14, "Making Your Forms Easy to Use."

1   Open the list for the ID combo box.

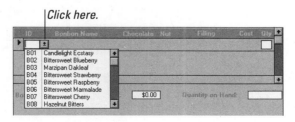

Click here.

The list shows two columns: IDs in the first column and the corresponding bonbon names in the second column. When you select a row, only the ID is stored in the field. The names are there to help you make the right selection.

2   Select the row for Bittersweet Blueberry.

The Bonbon ID, B02, appears in the ID field, and the Bonbon Name, Chocolate, Nut, Filling, and Cost fields are filled in automatically. Notice that the fields you fill in are displayed in white and all others have a gray background.

3   Press TAB to move to the next field.

The insertion point skips fields that are already filled in and moves to the Qty field.

4   Type **3** in the Qty field, and then press TAB.

Microsoft Access saves the first record in the subform and moves the insertion point to the first field in the second record.

Enter more subform records

While you add the remaining bonbons to the subform in this exercise, notice that the Box Cost field in the lower-left corner of the main form changes for each new record in the subform. How much a box costs Sweet Lil's depends on which bonbons are in the box. The Boxes form figures the box cost automatically while you're adding bonbons to the box.

1   Add the following two bonbons to the Winter Collection:

ID		Qty
B05	Bittersweet Raspberry	3
D03	Cashew Supreme	3

The record for the Cashew Supreme bonbon fills up the subform, but you have two more bonbons to add to the box. Notice the vertical scroll bar on the right side of the subform. The presence of the scroll bar means the subform can contain more records, and you can scroll upward and downward through the records to see them.

2   After filling in the quantity of the Cashew Supreme record, press TAB to move to the next record in the subform.

The subform scrolls to show another new, blank record.

3   Add the following three bonbons to the Winter Collection:

ID		Qty
D07	Classic Cherry	3
F01	Walnut Fudge Mocha	3
F02	Pistachio Fudge Mocha	3

4   When you're finished adding the records, scroll upward and downward in the subform to check your work. Make sure each record is correct before going on.

Moving out of a subform

Now that you've added all the bonbons to the new box, you're ready to fill in the fields in the lower portion of the main form—Box Price and Quantity On Hand.

▶ Press CTRL+TAB to move to the next field on the main form.

The insertion point moves out of the subform to the Box Price field on the main form. You can also move to the Box Price field by clicking it, but when you're entering new records, it's often easier to keep your hands on the keyboard rather than move back and forth between the mouse and the keyboard.

Tip When you're using a form with a subform, you can think of the CTRL key as the "subform" key. Just as pressing TAB moves you to the next field within a subform or main form, pressing CTRL+TAB moves you from the subform to the next field in the main form. And just as pressing SHIFT+TAB moves you to the previous field within a subform or main form, pressing CTRL+SHIFT+TAB moves you from the subform to the previous field in the main form.

Entering the Right Data

You've already seen a number of ways that a Microsoft Access form can help you enter the right data. For example, the ID combo box in the subform helps you pick the right ID by showing you bonbon names as well as IDs. After you pick a bonbon, Microsoft Access automatically fills in fields, such as the Bonbon Name and Chocolate fields, saving you time and the possibility of data entry errors in those fields. While you're adding bonbons to the box, Microsoft Access automatically figures the cost of the box and displays it in the Box Cost field, saving you the effort of making the calculation yourself.

A form can also help you enter the right data by displaying a message when you enter incorrect information.

Get help correcting wrong data

The note you have from Sweet Lil's Marketing department says to start the new box at the special introductory price of $7.50.

1 Type **7.50** in the Box Price field, and then press TAB.

Microsoft Access displays a validation message that tells you the value you entered is incorrect and gives you information on how to correct the problem.

> **Note**   If the message doesn't appear, the problem might be in the Box Cost field. The Box Price field checks the value in the Box Cost field and displays its message if the price is less than twice the cost. The Box Cost field is calculated automatically from the records entered in the subform. If you don't see the message, be sure you entered the subform records correctly.

2   Choose the OK button.

After calling the Marketing department, you find out that they made a mistake on their note and meant to start the box at $17.50.

3   Type a **1** before the 7 in the Box Price field, and then press TAB.

Microsoft Access accepts this price, adds a dollar sign, and moves the insertion point to the Quantity On Hand field.

4   Type **0** (zero) in the Quantity On Hand field.

This is a new box, so you don't have any in stock yet.

Microsoft Access rejected the price of $7.50 because the Box Price field has a *validation rule* attached to it. The value you enter in the field is checked against the rule, and if the value breaks the rule, a message appears. You can't leave the field until you correct the invalid data.

Suppose you need to look up a value on a different form before you can correct the error. You have to leave the current form to correct the error, but you can't leave the form as long as the invalid data you entered is still there. In this case, you can choose the OK button when the message appears, and then press the ESC key. Microsoft Access replaces your value with the original value (in this example, the field was empty), and then treats the field as if you had never changed it, so you can leave the field or form.

Undoing Your Edits

With Microsoft Access, you can use the Undo button on the toolbar to undo your most recent action, or the Undo Current Field/Record button to undo changes you have made to the current field or record. You can also use the Undo commands on the Edit menu to undo recent actions.

Make changes and then undo your most recent action

1   Select "Nuts and berries" at the beginning of the description for the Winter Collection, and then type **Berries and nuts**

2   Place the insertion point in front of "fire," type **roaring**, and then press the SPACEBAR.

After looking over the changes, you decide that "roaring" doesn't sound quite right.

Undo

3   On the toolbar, click the Undo button.

Microsoft Access deletes "roaring," your most recent change.

Undo all edits in the current field

After making numerous changes to the text in a field, you might decide that you prefer the original text.

*Undo Current
Field/Record*

▶   On the toolbar, click the Undo Current Field/Record button.

All the edits you made to the field since moving the insertion point into the field are undone. If you click this button again, all changes you have made to the current form would be removed.

Using a Command Button

Sometimes one task turns into many related tasks. For example, you might be looking at information about the contents of a product on one form and realize that you want to see sales information for the product, too. So you open a sales form and find the appropriate sales information. This related task can require a number of steps to complete.

A *command button* on a form condenses related tasks into a single step. A command button can perform one action or a series of actions, depending on how the button is defined.

Now that you've added the Winter Collection box to the database, you'll use a command button to check on the sales of one of Sweet Lil's best sellers — the Autumn Collection.

Go to a specific record

The Autumn Collection is the third box in the Boxes form.

1   To the right of the word "Record," in the lower-left corner of the window, select the current record number, and then type **3**

|Replace the current record number with 3.

2   Press ENTER.

The record for the Autumn Collection—the third record in the table—appears.

Use a command button to perform a task

The Boxes form shows the contents of the Autumn Collection box. You can use the Sales command button to see the sales for this box.

1   Click the Sales button at the top of the Boxes form.

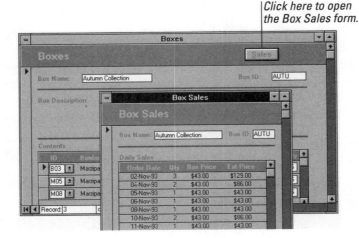

Click here to open the Box Sales form.

The Box Sales form appears. Like the Boxes form, the Box Sales form has a subform. The main form shows the name of the box at the top and the total sales for the box at the bottom of the form. The subform shows daily sales for the box.

2 Scroll through the records in the Daily Sales subform to see all the sales.

3 When you're finished looking at the sales of the Autumn Collection, double-click the Control-menu box in the Box Sales form to close it (or choose Close from the File menu).

4 Close the Boxes form.

Deleting Records

In most databases, the only real constant is that data is constantly changing. You add records when you have to keep track of new people or things. You change records when the data changes. And you delete records when you no longer need to track the people or things that the records are about.

Sweet Lil's receives this note in the morning's mail:

Dear Sweet Lil's:

My son buys your chocolates frequently and loves them. In fact, he told me that he recently gave you my name to add to your customer list. I'm trying to lose some weight, so please don't add me to your list. No need to waste the catalog.

Thank you,
Francois Marcus

Go to the record you want to delete

Francois Marcus was just added to the Customers table last night. Using the View Customers form, you'll delete his record now.

1 Open the View Customers form.

2 Click the navigation button for the last record.

If you followed the steps in Lesson 1, the four new customers you added to the database are at the end of the records, and Francois Marcus's record is right before theirs. If you didn't do Lesson 1, Francois Marcus's record is the last record.

3 If necessary, click the Previous Record button until you see Francois Marcus's record.

Delete a record

To delete a record, you must first select it.

1 Click the record selector at the left edge of the form. Or, click in any field in the record, and then choose Select Record from the Edit menu.

Click here.

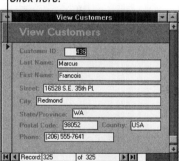

The record selector darkens to show that the record is selected.

2 Press DELETE. When Microsoft Access asks you to confirm the deletion, choose the OK button.

The record is deleted.

3 Close the View Customers form.

One Step Further

You are ready to add one more season to the bonbon collections. If you change your mind about which items to include in the new collection, you can delete the information from the subform the same way you did in the main form, or you can use a shortcut menu command.

Add a new box

Using the Boxes form, add a new box called Spring Collection.

1 Open the Boxes form.

2 Enter the following data for the new box:

Box Name: **Spring Collection**
Box ID: **SPRI**
Box Description: **Hearts and flowers make the perfect gift for springtime lovers.**
Size: **12 oz**

3 In the Contents subform, enter the following data:

ID		Qty
D02	Heart on a Sleeve	3
D09	American Beauty	3
M06	Lover's Heart	3
M07	Apple Amore	3
M10	Forget-Me-Not	3
W02	Calla Lily	3
W03	Broken Heart	3

4 Finish the Spring Collection by entering this information on the bottom of the main form. Use CTRL+TAB to move to the main form.

Box Price: **$23.50**
Quantity on Hand: **0**

Delete a record in a subform

As you study the new collection, you decide to make some changes in what bonbons are included. Use the following steps to delete information in two different ways.

You decide to take the Lover's Heart and the Apple Amore bonbons out of this collection.

1 Delete the Lover's Heart bonbon from the Spring Collection. Use the same approach to delete a record in a subform as you did in the main form. First select the record by clicking its record selector (but this time on the left side of the subform, not the main form), or by clicking in the record and choosing Select Record from the Edit menu. Then press DELETE.

2   For a quicker method, delete the Apple Amore bonbon from the Spring Collection by using a Shortcut menu choice. Select the record by clicking its record selector with the *right* mouse button, and choose Cut.

3   Add 1 to the quantity of the American Beauty, Forget-Me-Not, and Calla Lily bonbons, so the box contains four of each flower bonbon.

If You Want to Continue to the Next Lesson

1   Double-click the Control-menu box on the Boxes form. Or, from the File menu, choose Close.

2   If Microsoft Access asks if you want to save your changes, choose Yes.

This closes the form, but it does not exit the Microsoft Access program.

If You Want to Quit Microsoft Access for Now

▶   Double-click the Control-menu box in the Microsoft Access window. Or, from the File menu, choose Exit.

This closes the form and exits the Microsoft Access program. The changes you made to the data in the Boxes and View Customers forms are saved.

Lesson Summary

To	Do this	Button
Move from a main form to a field on a subform	Click the field in the subform. *or* From the last field on the main form before the subform, press TAB.	
Move from a subform to a field on a main form	Click the field in the main form. *or* Press CTRL+TAB to move to the next field on the main form; press CTRL+SHIFT+TAB to move to the previous field on the main form.	
Respond to a validation message (a message that says you entered the wrong data in a field)	Choose the OK button, and then correct the data in the field. To leave the form without correcting the data, press ESC.	
Undo your most recent changes	Click the Undo buttons on the toolbar *or* Use the Undo commands from the Edit menu.	

To	Do this
Go directly to a specific record	Type the record number in the Record Number box between the navigation buttons at the bottom of the form.
Delete a record	Select the record by clicking its record selector or by clicking in the record and choosing Select Record from the Edit menu. Then press DELETE.

For more information on	See
Adding and editing data on a form	Chapter 4, "Adding and Editing Data," in *Microsoft Access User's Guide*
	Choose Cue Cards from the Help menu, and then choose "Work with Data."
Understanding subforms	Chapter 17, "Creating Forms Based on More Than One Table," in *Microsoft Access User's Guide*

For online information about	From the Help menu, choose Search and then type
Adding records to a form	records: adding
Undoing changes	undoing changes
Deleting records	delete

Preview of the Next Lesson

In the next lesson, you'll learn how to focus on the data that answers your questions. You'll find out how to filter records to get a set of related records, to sort records, and to find a record that contains a particular value in it.

Finding Information

You ask the questions; Microsoft Access provides the answers. When you're interested in milk chocolates, you don't want to look at data about bittersweets. When you're interested in your Toronto customers, you don't want to see all your other customers.

While you're viewing data in forms, you can focus on the information you're interested in without wading through irrelevant data. In this lesson, you'll learn how to ask questions so that Microsoft Access displays only the data you want to see.

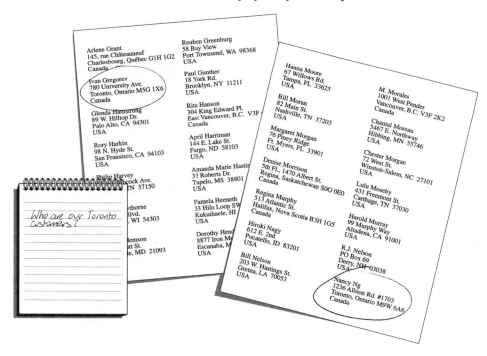

You will learn how to:

- Find a record with a particular value in it.
- Filter records to get a set of related records.
- Sort records.

Estimated lesson time: 35 minutes

Finding One Record or a Group of Records

Microsoft Access is more helpful than a filing cabinet or a pile of paper because you can find just the records you need, sorted the way you want them. Whether your database contains hundreds, thousands, or even millions of records, Microsoft Access finds just what you ask for and sorts the data just the way you want.

For quick searches, when you're looking for only one record, use the Find button on the toolbar. For example, you can find the record for the bonbon named Brazilian Supreme.

When you want to see a particular group of records, such as all the customers in Toronto, you create a *filter* to tell Microsoft Access which records you're interested in. When you create a filter, you give Microsoft Access a set of *criteria* that describes the records you want to see. Microsoft Access then displays the records in a form or in a form datasheet.

Using a filter, you can also *sort* records in alphabetic or numeric order. For example, you could sort your customers alphabetically by last name.

Start the lesson

▶ If Microsoft Access isn't started yet, start it and open the Sweet database as described in Lesson 1. If the Microsoft Access window doesn't fill your screen, maximize the window.

Finding a Record

This morning you found a slip of paper on your desk saying "Call N. Valerio—she's going to cancel her order if you don't get back to her immediately!" But the note doesn't have a phone number on it. You need to look up the number in the Sweet database.

A fast way to get this customer's record is to use the Find button on the toolbar.

Open a form

▶ In the Database window, click the Form button, and then double-click the Customer Review form.

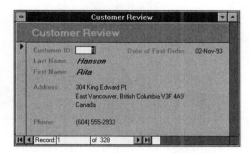

The form opens and the first record appears.

Find a record

1 Click in the Last Name field.

You don't need to select the entire last name—just click anywhere in the field.

Find

2 On the toolbar, click the Find button.

The Find In Field dialog box appears. The title bar of the Find In Field dialog box shows the name of the field you're searching in—Last Name.

If the Find In Field dialog box blocks your view of the form, you can move it out of the way by dragging its title bar.

3 In the Find What box, type **Valerio**

Notice that you have the option of searching in all the fields for Valerio. Since you know the value is in the Last Name field (the current field), you can make the search go faster by searching only in the current field.

4 Choose the Find First button.

The record for Nina Valerio appears.

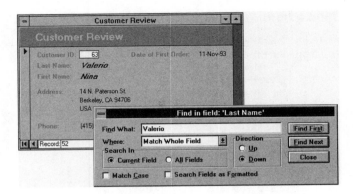

This looks like the customer you need to call, but you'd better check just to make sure there's not another customer with the same last name.

5 Choose the Find Next button.

Microsoft Access doesn't find another Valerio. It asks if you want to continue the search from the beginning of the set of records.

6 Choose the No button, and then click OK to continue.

7 Choose the Close button to close the dialog box.

Now you know that you have only one customer named Valerio, and you can call her.

Find a record even if you don't know much about it

As soon as you hang up the phone with Nina Valerio, you get a call from a clerk in Sweet Lil's Shipping department. He's having trouble reading the address on a shipping label. All he can make out is part of the street name, which starts with "Stew." He asks if you could find the name and address of the customer with this small amount of information.

1 In the Customer Review form, click in the field that contains the street address (the first line in the address).

You don't have to go back to the first record in the table—you can use the Find button from any customer's record.

2 On the toolbar, click the Find button.

Find

The Find In Field dialog box appears. The Find What box still contains your last entry, Valerio.

3 Type **Stew** in the Find What box.

4 In the Where box, select Any Part Of Field.

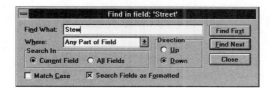

Because "Stew" is only part of the street name, you want to search for it no matter where it occurs in the field.

5 Choose the Find First button.

Microsoft Access finds an address with "Stewart" in the street address.

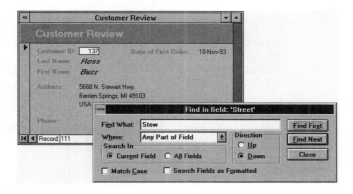

You can make a search case-sensitive (find only text with the same uppercase and lowercase letters) by selecting the Match Case check box.

6 Choose the Find Next button.

Microsoft Access finds a second record with "stew" in the address. Notice that this "stew" doesn't have a capital S, since it appears in the middle of a word.

7 Choose the Find Next button again.

Microsoft Access asks if you want to continue the search from the beginning of the set of records. Because you started this search from the middle of the records, Microsoft Access hasn't searched the first records in the set yet.

8 Choose Yes to search the first records.

Microsoft Access doesn't find another "Stew," so you have two possible customers for the Shipping department.

9 Choose the Close button to close the dialog box, and then close the Customer Review form.

Filtering to Find a Group of Related Records

Suppose you're creating a promotional box of chocolates, and you want to include a bonbon that contains white chocolate. You'd like to review all the bonbons that contain white chocolate before making your choice.

Note   If you followed the steps in Lesson 2, "Getting the Best View of Your Data," your datasheet will look a little different from the following illustration. The appearance of the datasheet doesn't matter, though—you can still follow the steps given in this lesson to create a filter.

Display the Filter window

1   Open the Bonbons form.

The form opens and displays the first record in the Bonbons table. The Bonbons form is designed to display a single record of data. In this case, you want to look at all the bonbons that contain white chocolate at the same time, so you'll switch to the form's Datasheet view.

2   Click the Datasheet View button on the toolbar.

Datasheet View

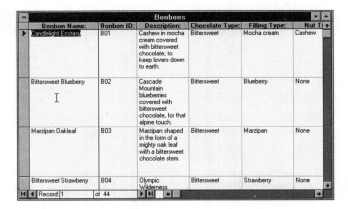

Notice that the form shows the type of chocolate each bonbon contains. For example, Candlelight Ecstasy has bittersweet chocolate.

Edit Filter/Sort

3   Click the Edit Filter/Sort button on the toolbar.

The Filter window opens where you describe the records you want to see.

The upper portion of the Filter window contains a *field list* of all the fields on the Bonbons form. The lower portion is the *filter grid*, where you set criteria for the records you want to see.

Choose fields and specify criteria

You want to see only the white chocolate bonbons, so you'll set criteria that will limit the records to only those bonbons. Start by choosing the field for which you want to set criteria. The type of chocolate is stored in the Chocolate Type field.

1 Drag the Chocolate Type field to the first cell in the Field row of the filter grid.

To drag the field, click it and hold down the mouse button while you move the mouse. Release the mouse button when the field is positioned over the cell.

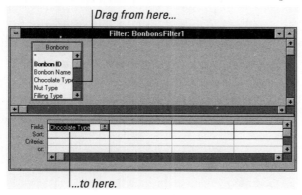

2 Click in the Criteria cell below the Chocolate Type field.

3 Type **white** in the cell, and press ENTER.

Microsoft Access adds quotation marks after you press ENTER. However, if you type a text value that contains commas or periods, you must enclose the value in quotation marks yourself.

Apply the filter and look at the results

Apply Filter/Sort

▶ Click the Apply Filter/Sort button on the toolbar.

Microsoft Access searches for bonbons with white chocolate and displays these records in the datasheet.

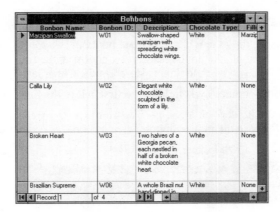

Add more criteria

Since you have to keep the cost of this promotional box down, you'd like to see only the white chocolate bonbons that cost less than $0.30 each. To do this, you will type your request as an *expression*, which specifies exactly what you are searching for, and might require Microsoft Access to perform a calculation.

1   Click the Filter window to make it the active window.

The Filter window still displays the filter you created earlier to find the bonbons with white chocolate.

2   In the field list, scroll downward until you see the Bonbon Cost field.

3   Drag the Bonbon Cost field from the field list to the cell in the Field row next to the Chocolate Type field.

4   In the Criteria cell for the Bonbon Cost field, type **<.30** and then press ENTER.

This expression tells Microsoft Access to select all the white chocolate bonbons that cost less than $0.30.

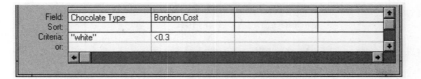

Apply Filter/Sort

5   Click the Apply Filter/Sort button on the toolbar.

6   To see all the records again, click the Show All Records button.

Show All Records

All the records in the datasheet appear, not just the records for bonbons with white chocolate.

Sorting Records

Suppose you want to introduce your new assistant to the different kinds of bonbons that Sweet Lil's makes. She knows the names of the bonbons, but you'd like her to learn more about their ingredients, too. To make the bonbons easier for her to find, you'll sort them in alphabetical order.

You can create your own filter in the Filter window, but Microsoft Access also has a quicker way to set this kind of filter.

Delete the previous criteria

Since you already have been working in the Filter window, it contains some criteria you don't need for the next sort.

1   Click the Filter window to make it the active window.

The criteria for white chocolate bonbons that cost less than $0.30 is still in the Filter window.

2   From the Edit menu, choose Clear Grid.

Microsoft Access deletes all information from the filter grid.

Apply Filter/Sort

3   On the toolbar, click the Apply Filter/Sort button so that all your data is again ready to be sorted.

Sort records alphabetically with a sort button

You can sort alphabetically directly in the form window.

1   In the Bonbon form window, click any record in the Bonbon Name field.

Sort Ascending

2   On the toolbar, click the Sort Ascending button. Or choose Quick Sort from the Records menu, and then choose Ascending.

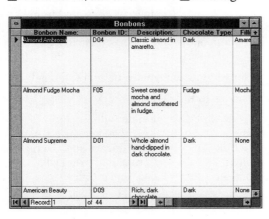

Ascending means records are sorted from A to Z. Descending means Z to A. Using the Sort Ascending or Sort Descending button, or the Quick Sort command, automatically creates and applies a filter.

3   Click the Filter window to view the current filter and sort order.

Sort records numerically with a sort button

Your assistant wants to know which bonbons are the most expensive. Sort the records so that the datasheet displays the most expensive bonbons first.

1   Click the Bonbons window to make it the active window.

2   Click any record in the Cost field.

Sort Descending

3   Click the Sort Descending button on the toolbar. Or, choose Quick Sort from the Records menu, and then choose Descending.

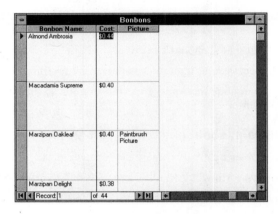

Descending means numerical records are sorted from highest to lowest, so that the most expensive bonbon appears at the top. Using the Sort Ascending or Sort Descending button, or the Quick Sort command, automatically creates and applies a filter.

4   Click the Filter window to view the current filter and sort order.

5   Close the Bonbons form.

Microsoft Access doesn't save the filter with the form. The next time you open the Bonbons form, the records won't be filtered or sorted. In the lessons in Part 3, "Asking Questions and Getting Answers," you'll learn how to create and use a *query*. A query is like a saved filter. You can use it over and over again to display records that meet certain criteria and are sorted in a particular order.

One Step Further

Sweet Lil's recently launched an expensive marketing promotion in Canada. It's time to decide whether to recommend the promotion for the United States by studying how successful the Canadian campaign was. Working with filters allows you to quickly find and look at particular records. This exercise shows you more ways to specify information for your filter.

Find out who are the new customers from Canada

Create a filter that shows the Canadian customers who were added on or after December 15, 1993, the first day of the promotion.

1   Open the Customer Review form.

Edit Filter/Sort

2   On the toolbar, click the Edit Filter/Sort button to begin building your filter.

3   In the first Field cell of the filter grid, click the down arrow to display the list of fields from the Customer Review form, and then select the Country field.

4   Under Country in the Criteria cell, type **Canada** and press ENTER.

5   Move to the second Field cell, and select the Date Of First Order field from the list.

6   Move to the Sort cell under Date Of First Order, and select Descending from the list.

This sorts the records so that you see the newest customers (those with the most recent Date Of First Order) first.

7   To specify the dates you want to filter, move to the Criteria cell under Date Of First Order, then enter the expression **>=15-Dec-93** for "on or after December 15, 1993," and then press ENTER.

After you enter the expression, Microsoft Access puts number signs (#) around the date, indicating that it is a date/time value.

Apply Filter/Sort

8   On the toolbar, click the Apply Filter/Sort button to apply the filter.

9   On the toolbar, click the Datasheet View button to see all of the filtered records at once.

Datasheet View

If You Want to Continue to the Next Lesson

▶ Double-click the Control-menu box on the Customer Review form. Or, from the File menu, choose Close.

This closes the form, but does not exit the Microsoft Access Program.

If You Want to Quit Microsoft Access for Now

▶ Double-click the Control-menu box in the Microsoft Access window. Or, from the File menu, choose Exit.

This closes the form and exits the Microsoft Access program.

Lesson Summary

To	Do this	Button
Find a specific record	On the toolbar, click the Find button and fill in the dialog box.	
Open the Filter window	Open a form. Then click the Edit Filter/Sort button on the toolbar.	
Choose a field for a filter	In the Filter window, drag a field from the field list to a cell in the Field row of the filter grid.	
Set criteria for a filter	In the filter grid of the Filter window, type your criteria in the Criteria cell below the field for which you want to set criteria.	
Apply a filter	Set criteria for the filter in the Filter window, and then click the Apply Filter/Sort button on the toolbar.	

To	Do this	Button
Sort records in a filter	With the form in Datasheet view, click in a field, and then click the Sort Ascending or Sort Descending button. *or* In the filter grid, select Ascending or Descending in the Sort cell below the field you want to sort on.	
Look at all records after you've applied a filter	Click the Show All Records button.	

For more information on	See in *Microsoft Access User's Guide*
Filtering, sorting, and finding records	Chapter 7, "Finding the Data You Want"
	Chapter 5, "Finding and Sorting Data"
Specifying criteria	Chapter 10, "Query Basics"
	Chapter 15, "Finding and Sorting Data"
Using expressions	Chapter 10, "Query Basics"

For online information about	From the **H**elp menu, choose **S**earch and then type
Specifying criteria	criteria: filters
Using expressions	criteria: queries

Preview of the Next Lesson

In the next lesson, you'll learn how to use reports to print information from your database. You'll print a sales report, and you'll create and print mailing labels.

Printing Reports and Mailing Labels

How many different ways do you use a customer's address or a product's name? The address might appear on an invoice and a mailing label. The product name might appear on the same invoice and on a sales report. Using Microsoft Access forms and reports, you can arrange and combine your data however you want. To present your data to its best advantage in print, use a report.

Reports can show all of the information in the database or just the information you want to highlight. Reports can also show other critical information, such as subtotals and totals. In this lesson, you'll open, preview, and print a sales report. Then you'll create a mailing label report and print your mailing labels.

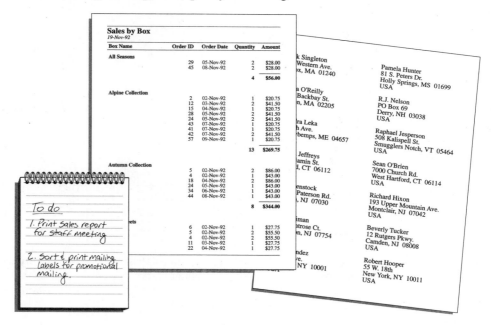

You will learn how to:

- Open and preview a report.
- Print a report.
- Create and print mailing labels.

Estimated lesson time: 25 minutes

What Is a Report?

Up to now, you've used forms to put information in your database and to edit and find that information. Now you'll use reports to print the results of your work.

You can use either a form or a report to print detailed information, such as lists of records. For example, you could use either a form or a report to print a list of all your customers. But a report is especially useful when you want to print summary information, such as subtotals and totals. Microsoft Access calculates these for you and prints them on your report.

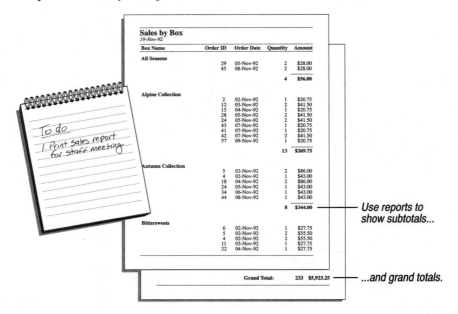

Use reports to show subtotals...

...and grand totals.

A report also gives you greater control than a form over exactly where the data prints on a page. For example, you can use a report to print records in snaking columns, like entries in a phone book. This type of layout is especially useful for printing mailing labels and phone lists.

Start the lesson

▶ If Microsoft Access isn't started yet, start it and open the Sweet database as described in Lesson 1. If the Microsoft Access window doesn't fill your screen, maximize the window.

Previewing a Report

Sweet Lil's marketing staff is planning a mail-order campaign to stimulate sales for assortments of chocolates that aren't selling well. You can print a report on recent box sales that will help you pick which boxes to promote. You'll use the Sales By Box report to see how the assortments have been selling during a one-week period in November.

Preview a report

1   In the Database window, click the Report object button.

2   Double-click the Sales By Box report.

A dialog box appears that asks you to enter the dates for the period you want the report to cover.

3   Type **2-Nov-93** as a starting date, and then press ENTER.

To find out which country your computer is set for, open the Windows Control Panel and double-click the International icon.

Microsoft Access recognizes a number of ways to enter dates. For example, you could have used 11/2/93, another United States format. The Canadian (English) format is 2/11/93.

4   In the next dialog box, type **9-Nov-93** as an ending date, and then press ENTER.

Microsoft Access collects the appropriate data and opens the report in Print Preview.

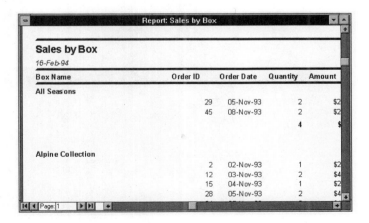

Look at a whole page at once

The report is magnified in Print Preview so that you can clearly read the data. The magnifying glass pointer means you can switch views: Zoom out to see how the data is laid out on the whole page, and zoom in to see the magnified view.

Zoom

▶ Click anywhere on the report with the magnifying glass pointer. Or, click the Zoom button on the toolbar.

The whole page appears.

Zoom in on the data

The layout looks fine. Now you'll check to be sure you have the data you want.

▶ Click anywhere on the report. Or, click the Zoom button on the toolbar.

Now you're looking at the magnified view again.

Move around the page

▶ Use the vertical scroll bar to move up and down the page, and use the horizontal scroll bar to move from left to right.

The data looks right—sales for the week of November 2, 1993.

Move from page to page

Before printing the report, take a quick look at each page. Your report is five pages long. The last page includes the grand total for all the boxes.

▶ Use the navigation buttons at the bottom of the window to page through the report.

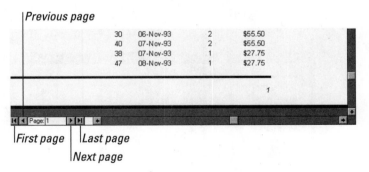

The report looks great—it's ready to print.

Printing a Report

When you print a report, you have the option of specifying a range of pages if you don't want to print the entire report, and you can specify how many copies you want to print. If you print more than one copy, you can have Microsoft Access collate the copies for you. You can also print the report to a file on your disk instead of to the printer so that you can print the file at a later date.

If you're set up to print, you can print the Sales By Box report now.

Print a report from Print Preview

Print

1   On the toolbar, click the Print button.

The Print dialog box appears. In this case, you want to print one copy of the whole report, so you don't need to change any of the settings in the Print dialog box.

2   If you are set up with an active printer, choose the OK button; otherwise, choose Cancel.

3   Close the Sales By Box report.

Tip   As you've seen, when you double-click a report in the Database window, Microsoft Access opens it in Print Preview so you can see how it will look on the page before you print it. To print a report without opening it first in Print Preview, select the report in the Database window, and then choose Print from the File menu.

Creating Mailing Labels

Based on your report, you decide to promote the two slowest-selling boxes by discounting them in a special mailing to all customers. You'll create mailing labels and print the labels sorted by postal code.

To create mailing labels, you use an *Access Wizard*. An Access Wizard is like a database expert who asks you questions about the form or report you want, and then builds it for you according to your answers. You use *Form Wizards* to build forms and *Report Wizards* to build reports. Your mailing labels will be a new report in the database.

Create mailing labels

Because you just printed the Sales By Box report, the Database window is still showing the list of reports.

1   Choose the New button.

The New Report dialog box appears.

2   In the Select A Table/Query box, click the arrow to display the list of tables and queries, and then select the Customers table.

The Customers table contains the names and addresses you want to print in the mailing labels.

3   Choose the Report Wizards button.

Microsoft Access asks which Wizard you want to use.

4   Select Mailing Label, and then click OK.

The Access Wizard displays the first in a series of dialog boxes that you'll use to define your mailing labels. In the first dialog box, you define the label appearance.

Define the label appearance

1   In the Available Fields box, double-click the First Name field.

Microsoft Access adds the field to the first line of your mailing label.

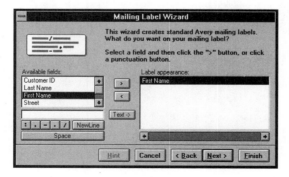

2   Click the Space button to put a space between first names and last names.

3 Double-click the Last Name field.

Microsoft Access adds the Last Name field to the first line of your mailing label.

4 Click the NewLine button to go to the second line of the mailing label.

Left Arrow

5 Define the second, third, and fourth lines of the mailing label as follows. If you make a mistake in a line of text, select the line and use the left arrow between the Available Fields box and the Label Appearance box to remove an item from the mailing label.

- Street field in the second line.

- City, State/Province, and Postal Code fields in the third line, with appropriate punctuation between them.

- Country field in the fourth line.

When you're finished, the box for your mailing label appearance looks like the following illustration.

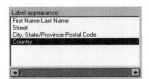

The third line has three fields in it, with a comma and space after the first field and a space between the last two fields.

6 Choose the Next button to move to the next dialog box.

Now that you've defined the mailing label appearance, you'll tell Microsoft Access how to sort the printed labels.

Sort the labels

You want to sort the mailing labels by postal code so that all the labels with the same postal code are printed together.

1 In the Available Fields box, double-click the Postal Code field.

Microsoft Access adds Postal Code to the list of fields that define the sort order.

2 Choose the Next button.

Finally, you can tell Microsoft Access the exact size of your label stock.

Select the mailing label size

You can choose from a wide range of label sizes, listed in either English measurements (inches) or metric measurements. If you have label stock on hand, use the Avery stock number to help you select the label size you want.

1   Under Label Type, select Sheet Feed.

2   Select the label size for Avery number 5095. (Choose EAL O4 if you're using metric measurements.)

3   Choose the Next button.

Choose the font and color for the appearance of your text

You can make selections that will affect the appearance of your text. For now, accept the choices that Microsoft Access already has set.

▶   Choose the Next button.

That's it! You've finished designing your mailing labels.

Preview your mailing labels

▶   Click the Finish button.

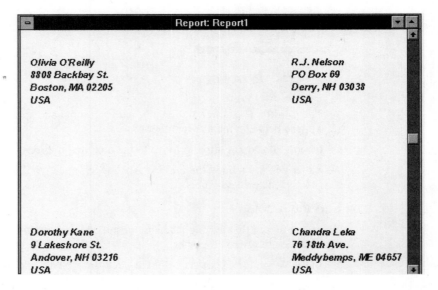

The labels appear as they will print on the page. If you want, you can scroll through the labels.

Note   If the labels don't appear lined up evenly, it might be due to a mismatch between your printer driver and the label size or format. Try different label sizes.

Since you know that you'll be making frequent mailings to your customers, you can save this mailing label report so that it's available anytime you want customer labels.

Save and close the mailing label report

1 From the File menu, choose Save.

The Save As dialog box appears.

2 Type **Customer Mailing Labels** in the Report Name box.

3 Choose the OK button.

4 Close the Customer Mailing Labels report.

Your new report appears in the list of reports in the Database window. Now, whenever you need mailing labels for your customers, you can print this report.

When you saved the Customer Mailing Labels report, you saved the *definition* of the mailing labels but not the actual names and addresses that print on the labels. The data printed on the labels is stored in the Customers table. When Sweet Lil's gets a new customer, you add the customer's information to the Customers table. When a customer moves, you update the address in the Customers table. The next time you print the Customer Mailing Labels report, Microsoft Access automatically draws the most current data from the Customers table and prints a label for each customer.

One Step Further

The Mailing Label Report Wizard makes it easy to create a variety of mailing labels. You can use the Mailing Label Report Wizard to create other types of reports as well.

Create a phone list

Use the Mailing Label Report Wizard to create a handy phone list you can keep beside your phone or in your briefcase.

1 To create a new report, in the Database window choose the Report object button, and then choose the New button.

2 In the Select A Table/Query box, select the Customers table from the list.

3 Choose the Report Wizards button.

4 To answer the question, "Which Wizard do you want?" select Mailing Label, and then click OK.

5   From the Available Fields box, specify the fields in the following illustration by double-clicking each one. Put punctuation between the appropriate fields by clicking the comma and space buttons. Click the New Line button to move to a new line. When you have finished specifying the fields, choose the Next button.

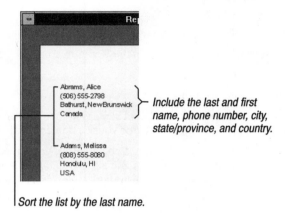

Abrams, Alice
(506) 555-2798
Bathurst, NewBrunswick
Canada

} *Include the last and first name, phone number, city, state/province, and country.*

Adams, Melissa
(808) 555-8080
Honolulu, HI
USA

Sort the list by the last name.

6   To answer the question, "What field(s) do you want to sort by?" double-click Last Name in the Available Fields box, and then choose the Next button.

7   To answer the question, "What label size do you want?" select Avery 5097 (or, select FAB 03 if you're using metric measurements). Choose the Finish button to complete your report.

Zoom

8   To switch the magnification to preview your report, use the Zoom button on the toolbar, or click anywhere on the report with the magnifying glass pointer.

9   When you're finished viewing the report, save the report and name it Customer Phone List.

After you've created a report with an Access Wizard, you can make changes and adjustments in the design to customize the report's appearance. You'll learn how to do this in the lessons in Part 5, "Customizing Your Reports."

If You Want to Continue to the Next Lesson

▶   Double-click the Control-menu box on the Customer Phone List report. Or, from the File menu, choose Close.

This closes the report, but it does not exit the Microsoft Access program.

If You Want to Quit Microsoft Access for Now

▶   After closing the report, double-click the Control-menu box in the Microsoft Access window. Or, from the File menu, choose Exit.

This closes the form and exits the Microsoft Access program.

Lesson Summary

To	Do this	Button
Open and preview a report	In the Database window, click the Report button, and then double-click the report you want.	
Switch between a magnified view of a report in Print Preview and a view of the whole page	Click anywhere on the report. *or* Choose the Zoom button on the toolbar.	
Move from page to page in a report in Print Preview	Use the navigation buttons at the bottom of the window.	
Print a report	In Print Preview, choose the Print button on the toolbar. *or* To print a report directly from the Database window, select the report, and then either choose Print from the File menu or choose the Print button on the toolbar.	
Create mailing labels	In the Database window, click the Report object button, and then choose the New button. Select the table or query that contains the data for the labels, and click the Report Wizards button. Then select the Mailing Label Report Wizard.	
Save and close a mailing label report	From the File menu, choose Save. Enter a filename in the Report Name box, and then choose OK.	

For more information on	See
Setting up a printer	Chapter 8, "Print Manager," in *Microsoft Windows User's Guide*
Reports you can create with Report Wizards	Chapter 20, "Report Basics," in *Microsoft Access User's Guide*
Printing reports	Chapter 9, "Creating Reports and Mailing Labels," in *Microsoft Access Getting Started*
	Chapter 20, "Report Basics," in *Microsoft Access User's Guide*

For online information about	From the <u>H</u>elp menu, choose <u>S</u>earch and then type
Printing reports	printing: reports

Preview of the Next Lessons

Now that you know how to get data into and out of a database, you're ready to start creating tables and forms of your own. In Part 2, you'll learn techniques for expanding a database by adding and relating tables and by attaching and importing data. In the next lesson, you'll learn how to create a new table and use its datasheet to add records to the table.

Review & Practice

In the lessons in Part 1, you learned how to open a database, view and move within your data, use forms and filters, and sort records. If you want an opportunity to refine those skills before going on to Part 2, you can do so in the Review & Practice section that follows.

Part 1   Review & Practice

Before you begin to expand your database by working with tables, you can use the steps in this Review & Practice section to practice the skills and techniques you learned in Part 1, "Data Basics."

Scenario

The Human Resources and Accounting departments have asked you to help them manage their information. You update the personnel records and answer questions posed by these departments.

You will review and practice how to:

- Open a database and a database form.
- View your data and move between records.
- Use a form to enter and edit data.
- Use a filter to find specific records.
- Sort records alphabetically and numerically.
- Create a report.

Estimated practice time: 35 minutes

Step 1: Open a Database and View the Data

To become familiar with the human resources information, you open a form called Employees. Use the Datasheet View and Form View buttons to look at the data in different ways. Use the navigational keys at the bottom of the form window to move between records.

1 Start Microsoft Access and open the Sweet database.

2 In the Database window, open the Employees form.

3 Browse through the data by using the navigational keys.

4 Look at a different view of this form by using the Datasheet View button.

5 Change the width of the columns so that you can see more information in Datasheet view.

6 Switch back to Form view.

For more information on	See
Starting Microsoft Access	Getting Ready, Lesson 1
Opening a database	Lesson 1
Opening a form	Lesson 1
Moving between records	Lesson 1
Switching views of a form	Lesson 2

Step 2: Enter and Edit Data in a Form

The Human Resources department has given you some changes for the personnel files. Enter new data and change existing data.

1 A new employee has been hired. If necessary, switch to Form view, and then move to the next blank form.

2 Add the following information for the new employee.

First Name: **Joseph**
Last Name: **Wood**
Title: **Technician**

3 Add the following department information to the form.

Department: **Operations**
Extension   **778**
Birthdate: **4/5/58**
Date Hired: **3/1/94**

4 Ursula Halliday, employee ID number 6, has gotten married. Move to her record, and change the last name to Martin.

5 Adrienne Snyder, employee ID number 5, has left the company. Switch to Datasheet view. Select her record by using the record selector, and then delete the record using DELETE.

6 Switch back to Form view.

For more information on	See
Entering data in a form	Lesson 1
Moving around a form	Lesson 1
Choosing data from a combo box	Lesson 2
Editing text in a field	Lesson 2
Deleting a record from a form	Lesson 3

Step 3: Find One or More Records

An employee has put in a requisition for vacation, signed with a first initial and a last name, but the signature is hard to read. The Human Resources department can make out "Woo" at the beginning of the last name, and they ask you to determine from whom this memo might have come. Find and display records that match the information you have.

1 While in Form view, select the Last Name field, and then use the Find feature to search for "Woo".

2 Note the first occurrence, and then search for any additional occurrences.

For more information on	See
Finding records	Lesson 4

Step 4: Use a Filter to Find Specific Records

The company adopted its current name, Sweet Lil's, in 1985. The Human Resources department would like to know which employees were with the company before the name change. Use a filter to specify dates to find the answer.

1 While in Form view, use a filter to learn which employees were hired prior to 1985. Click in the Date Hired field, and then use the Edit Filter/Sort feature.

2 Move the Date Hired field name to the filter grid. In the Criteria cell below Date Hired, type an expression that indicates that the date hired was during or before 1984.

3 Initiate an ascending sort. Use the navigation buttons to look at each record.

4 Switch to Datasheet view to see more records at one time.

For more information on	See
Using a filter to find records	Lesson 4
Using an expression	Lesson 4, Appendix A
Sorting records	Lesson 4

Step 5: Sort Records Alphabetically or Numerically with a Button

The company accountant is checking a monthly phone bill and needs to know who has extension 787. Sort the records to make it easy to find out who it is.

1 While in Datasheet view, click in any row of the Extension column.

2 Sort the records by extension in ascending order.

3 Find extension 787 in the Extension column.

4   Close the Employees form.

For more information on	See
Sorting Records	Lesson 4

Step 6: Create a Report

To facilitate the scheduling of department meetings, you are asked to produce a report that will contain the names, departments, and extensions of all the employees, sorted by the department name.

1   In the Database window, create a mailing label report.

2   Select the Employees table.

3   Use a Report Wizard to define a report that contains the following information:

Last Name, First Name
Department Name
Extension

4   Sort by Department Name and then by Last Name.

5   Choose Finish to end the Report Wizard, and then view your report.

6   Save your report as **Department List**

For more information on	See
Using a Report Wizard	Lesson 5
Viewing a report	Lesson 5

If You Want to Continue to the Next Lesson

▶ Double-click the Control-menu box on the Department List report. Or, from the File menu, choose Close.

This closes the window, but it does not exit the Microsoft Access program.

If You Want to Quit Microsoft Access for Now

▶ Double-click the Control-menu box in the Microsoft Access window. Or, from the File menu, choose Exit.

This exits the Microsoft Access program.

Part

2 Expanding a Database

Adding a Table

When information is well organized, it's easy to find and manage. Photographs arranged in family albums, for example, are easier to find than those jumbled together in a box in the attic. In a Microsoft Access database, information is organized in tables. You can display the information in a variety of formats, but it's all stored in tables. You have already examined and changed data displayed in a form, which is one way to look at data from one or more tables.

In this lesson, you'll learn how to create a table, define its fields, and add records in the table's datasheet.

You will learn how to:

- Use a Table Wizard to create a table.
- Add records using a table's datasheet.
- Design a new table.
- Add fields to a table.
- Set a table's primary key.
- Set field properties.

Estimated lesson time: 35 minutes

What Is a Table?

A database *table* is a collection of data with the same subject or topic. One table might contain data about customers, such as each customer's name, address, and phone number. Another table might contain data about bonbons, such as each bonbon's name, picture, and cost.

A Microsoft Access database is a collection of tables—or at least one table—that you use to store related information. The tables in the Sweet database, for example, all contain data relating to different parts of Sweet Lil's business.

You worked with fields when you added records using the Boxes form in Lesson 3. In this lesson, you'll learn how to define the fields in a table, and you'll see how fields and records are displayed in tables.

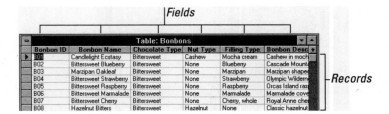

Each field appears as a column in the table and contains a category of information. For example, each field in the Bonbons table contains a different category of information that describes a bonbon, such as the name, chocolate type, or filling in the bonbon.

Each record appears as a row in the table and contains all the information about a particular person, item, or event (depending on the table's subject). Each record in the Bonbons table, for example, contains all the information about a particular bonbon. Each record in the Customers table contains all the information about a particular customer.

When you create a new table, you define how many fields the table has and what kind of data can be stored in each field. After naming and saving the table, you can add data to it.

Planning for New Tables

Sweet Lil's Chocolates is growing fast. More and more customers who order chocolates on Sweet Lil's toll-free telephone line want their gift orders to arrive very quickly, often overnight. To meet the increased demand, Sweet Lil's needs to increase the amount of candy they make, and speed up the process of getting candy to the customer. Therefore, Sweet Lil's has decided to make communication with its candy ingredient suppliers more efficient by having a main contact person at each supplier. To meet its customers' requirements for faster delivery, Sweet Lil's will begin using three shipping carriers instead of one, so that customers can choose air delivery if they want.

First you'll use a Table Wizard to create a table in the Sweet database, called Suppliers. This table lists information about your primary contact person in each vendor company. Then you'll design a table, called Carriers, to hold data on the three carrier companies.

Creating a Table with a Table Wizard

Microsoft Access can guide you through the table creation process with a Table Wizard. It is a quick way to get started in a new database, or to add a new table to an existing database. If you create a table with a Table Wizard, you can go back at a later time and edit or change anything in the table.

Start the lesson

▶ If Microsoft Access isn't started yet, start it and open the Sweet database. If the Microsoft Access window doesn't fill your screen, maximize the window.

Create a table with a Table Wizard

1 In the Database window, be sure that the Table object button is selected so that the list of tables appears, and then choose the New button.

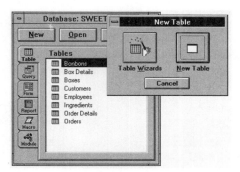

2 In the New Table dialog box, choose the Table Wizards button.

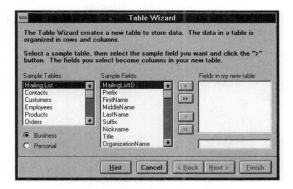

3 In the Sample Tables list, select Suppliers.

4 In the Sample Fields list, double-click each of the following fields to move it to the Fields In My New Table list:

SupplierName
ContactName
PhoneNumber
FaxNumber

5   Choose the Next button.

Below "What do you want to name your table?" the name "Suppliers" appears. This is what you want to call your table, so you don't have to make any change.

6   With the option "Let Microsoft Access set a primary key for me" selected, choose the Next button.

7   The next question you see is, "Is your new table related to any other tables in your database?" You don't have any tables to relate the Suppliers table to now, so choose the Next button.

8   With the option "Enter data directly into the table" selected, choose the Finish button.

Your new table opens in Datasheet view.

Adding Records in a Table's Datasheet

In the Datasheet view of a table, you add or look at your data. Later in this lesson when you design a new table, you'll work in Design view. You switch between these two views by using the View buttons on the left side of the toolbar.

Datasheet View button

Design View button

Switch to Datasheet view

▶   If you are not in Datasheet view, click the Datasheet View button on the toolbar.

Datasheet View

Start a record

Notice that Microsoft Access has added a SuppliersID field for you to use as the primary key. In the SuppliersID field is the word "Counter," which lets you know that you don't have to fill in this field yourself. Microsoft Access will give each new record a number automatically. You will add the new information about suppliers to the other fields.

1   Press TAB to move to the SupplierName field.

As you begin typing, notice that Microsoft Access gives the record an ID of 1.

2   Type **Chocolate World**, and then press TAB to move to the Contact Name field.

3   Type **Becky Rheinhart**, and then press TAB to move to the Phone Number field.

4   Type **(617) 555-5460**, and then press TAB to move to the Fax Number field.

5   Type **(617) 555-5459** to complete the record.

Save a record

The record is saved when you move to a new row. Before you move to another row, notice the *record indicator* in the field selector to the left of the SuppliersID field. The record indicator looks like a pencil and shows that you have added or changed data in the record but haven't saved the data yet.

Record indicator

▶   Press TAB to move to the next record.

When you move to the next record, Microsoft Access automatically saves the data in the previous record. You don't have to do anything else to save the record.

Add more records

▶   Press TAB to move to the SupplierName field, and then add these two records to the Suppliers table:

Supplier Name:	**Allfresh Nuts**	**Flavorly Extracts, Inc.**
Contact Name:	**Barney Cutter**	**Beverly Sims**
Phone Number:	**(313) 555-9987**	**(515) 555-9834**
Fax Number:	**(313) 555-9990**	**(515) 555-9888**

Close the table

▶   From the File menu, choose Close.

The Suppliers table closes. Notice that this table now appears in the list of tables in the Database window.

Creating a New Table that You Design

Now that you have created a table by using a Table Wizard, you can create a table that is completely customized. Using the following steps, add a table to a new or existing database.

Create a New Table

1   In the Database window, be sure that the Table object button is selected so that the list of tables appears, and then choose the New button.

2   In the New Table dialog box, choose the New Table button.

Naming Fields and Selecting Data Types

You add a field to a table by typing the field name in the upper part of the Design view window, and then selecting the field's *data type*. The data type tells Microsoft Access what kind of data to accept in the field. When you created a table with a Table Wizard, Microsoft Access automatically assigned a data type for all of the fields based on the field you selected from the list. In this exercise, you learn how to choose a data type as you design your table.

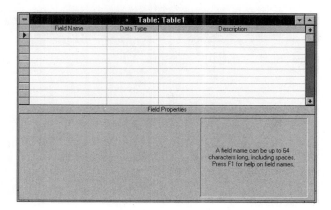

For details on all the data types, click the first box under "Data Type" and press F1.

The following table shows examples of fields with different data types and the data each can hold.

Field	Data type	Data you might enter
Last Name	Text	Houlihan
Box Price	Currency	$18.75
Quantity on Hand	Number	500
Picture	OLE Object	

Data types protect the accuracy of your data by restricting the type of information you can enter in a field. For example, you can't store a picture or a name in a field with the Currency data type.

Now, you're ready to add the first field to your new table. You'll use this field to store an ID number for each carrier.

Name a field

▶ In the first empty cell of the Field Name column, type **Carrier ID**

A field name can contain up to 64 characters, including spaces. It can include any punctuation mark except a period (.), an exclamation point (!), or brackets ([ ]).

Select a data type

You want each carrier to have a unique ID number. As you saw in the Suppliers table, a simple code, such as 1 for the first carrier, 2 for the second carrier, and 3 for the third carrier, will work fine.

1 Press the TAB key to move to the Data Type column.

By default, Microsoft Access gives the field the Text data type. The arrow in the box tells you that you can select the data type you want from a list.

2 Click the down arrow to open the list, and then select Counter.

Notice that Microsoft Access displays properties for the field in the lower portion of the Design view window. Later in this lesson, you'll learn how to set properties to further refine the definition of your fields.

Add a description

A description can help you remember the purpose of a field long after you define it. In addition, when you're adding data to the table, field descriptions can help you enter the right data. You'll see how that works later in this lesson, when you add records to the Carriers table.

1 Press TAB to move to the Description column.

2 Type **Number automatically assigned to new carrier** in the Description box, and then press TAB to move to the next field.

Add more fields

Next you'll add two additional fields: the Carrier Name field and the Delivery Method field. The Carrier Name field will store the names of the three carriers—Wild Fargo Carriers, Grey Goose Express, and Pegasus Overnight. These names are text, so you'll use the Text data type for this field.

1 Type **Carrier Name** in the second Field Name column, underneath where you typed Carrier ID.

2 Press TAB to move to the Data Type column.

Microsoft Access automatically assigns the field the Text data type. This is the data type you want, so you don't need to change it.

3 Press TAB to move to the Description column, type **Company name of carrier**, and then press TAB to move to the next field.

4 Type **Delivery Method** in the third Field Name column.

This field will store data indicating whether the carrier delivers by surface or by air.

5 Press TAB to move to the Data Type column, and then click the down arrow to display the list of data types.

You can see that one of the data types is Yes/No. This is the right data type for the Delivery Method field, since this field can contain one of only two choices (carriers deliver either by surface or by air).

6   Select Yes/No as the data type for the Delivery Method field, and then press TAB.

7   In the Description column, type **Yes for air; no for surface**

Your table should now look like the following.

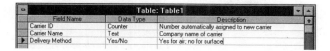

Get Help

Before you finish defining your table, you might want to be sure that the Yes/No data type is really the right choice for the Delivery Method field. To get more information about the data type, you can use the F1 key to get Help.

Microsoft Access Help is *context-sensitive,* which means the context of your screen tells Microsoft Access which Help topic to display when you press F1. For example, if you press F1 with the insertion point in a Field Name box, Help information appears about field names.

1   Click in the Data Type column for the Delivery Method field, and then press the F1 key.

For more information about Help, see "Getting Ready" earlier in this book.

Help appears about the data types. As you can see, the Yes/No data type is appropriate for fields that contain one of two values.

2   Close the Help window by double-clicking the Control-menu box.

Setting the Primary Key

Every table in your database should have a *primary key*—one or more fields whose values uniquely identify each record in the table. The primary key helps Microsoft Access search, find, and combine data as efficiently as possible.

As you saw when you created the Suppliers table with a Table Wizard, a field with a Counter data type makes a perfect primary key. You know the field will contain a unique value for each record because Microsoft Access automatically enters sequential numbers in that field for each new record of data. In the Suppliers table, you let Microsoft Access automatically set the primary key. In this table, you determine that you want to set the Carrier ID field as the primary key.

Set the primary key

1   Click the row selector for the Carrier ID field.

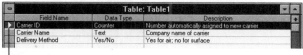

Row selector

Set Primary Key

2   Click the Set Primary Key button on the toolbar.

A key symbol appears in the row selector for the Carrier ID field. This symbol tells you that the Carrier ID field is the table's primary key.

	Field Name	Data Type	Description
🔑▶	Carrier ID	Counter	Number automatically asigned to new carrier
	Carrier Name	Text	Company name of carrier
	Delivery Method	Yes/No	Yes for air; no for surface

Primary key

Your table definition is complete. You're ready to save the table and start adding records to it.

Save the table

1   From the File menu, choose Save.

The Save As dialog box appears.

2   Name the table **Carriers**, and then choose the OK button.

Microsoft Access saves the table. Now you can add the data for the three carriers.

Tip   To remove or edit the primary key, use the Indexes window. For information on indexes, see Chapter 8, "Changing and Customizing Tables," in the *Microsoft Access User's Guide*.

Switching to Datasheet View to Add Records

So far, you've been working with the Carriers table in Design view. As you did with the Suppliers table, you'll use Datasheet view to add data. You use the View buttons on the left side of the toolbar to switch back and forth between these two views.

Switch to Datasheet view

Datasheet View

▶   Click the Datasheet View button on the toolbar.

Add records to the table

Because the Carrier ID is a Counter field, you know that you don't have to fill in the field yourself. Microsoft Access will give each new record a number automatically.

1   Press TAB to move to the Carrier Name field.

2   Type **Wild Fargo Carriers**, and then press TAB to move to the Delivery Method field.

Delivery Method is a field with a Yes/No data type. When you defined the field, you gave it a description that said what Yes and No meant. The field description appears in the status bar, so you can see what value to type.

No is the default for the Delivery Method field. Wild Fargo Carriers uses surface as its delivery method, so you don't have to change the default value.

3   Press TAB to save the record and move to the next row.

4   Add two more records to the Carriers table:

Carrier Name: **Grey Goose Express**
Delivery Method: **Yes**

Carrier Name: **Pegasus Overnight**
Delivery Method: **Yes**

Setting Field Properties

Each field in a table has *properties* that you can use to control how Microsoft Access stores, handles, and displays data in the field. For example, to display numbers in a field as percentages, you would set the field's Format property to Percent.

Each data type has a different set of properties associated with it. Fields with the Text and Number data types, for example, have a property called Field Size that sets the maximum size of data you can store in the field. Fields with the Yes/No data type, on the other hand, don't have a Field Size property because the values stored in a Yes/No field have a fixed size.

All data types have a Caption property. You use the Caption property to display a column heading in Datasheet view that's different from the field name. Since the Delivery Method field will display Yes or No, you'd like its caption in Datasheet view to be Air Delivery instead of Delivery Method. You can give the field a custom caption by setting its Caption property.

Set a field property

Design View

1   Click the Design View button on the toolbar to switch to Design view.

2   Click anywhere in the row for the Delivery Method field.

The field properties appear in the property box in the lower-left portion of the table window.

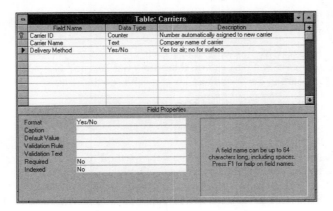

3   Click in the Caption property box, and type **Air Delivery**

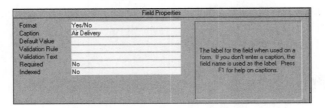

Tip   For fast, detailed information on any property, just click in the property box and press F1.

Datasheet View

4   Switch to Datasheet view to see the new caption for the Delivery Method field. When Microsoft Access asks if you want to save the changes, choose the OK button.

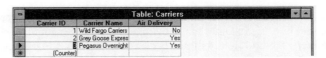

Close the table

▶ From the File menu, choose Close.

The Carriers table closes. Notice that this table now appears in the list of tables in the Database window.

One Step Further

Before you begin another project with the Carriers table, you receive a note from Sylvia in the Shipping department. To accommodate the information she wants in the Carriers table, you will set some new types of field properties, and then add the data on her memo. Later you receive a call asking you to identify a carrier from just part of a contact person's name. You will use a filter to find the information.

INTEROFFICE MEMO

    Could you please add this information about our
carriers to the database so we can look them up any time?
Our contacts and their phones seem to change weekly, and
we need a convenient place to keep them up-to-date.

Carrier	Contact Person	Contact Phone
Wild Fargo Carriers	Clyde Houlihan	(212) 555-7837
Grey Goose Express	Bella Lamont	(503) 555-9874
Pegasus Overnight	Morris Jantz	(206) 555-8988

    Thanks,

    Sylvia G.

Set field properties for new fields in a table

Add new field names and field properties to the Carriers table in Design view.

1 In the Database window, click the Table object button, and then select the Carriers table.

2 Click the Design button to open the Carriers table in Design view.

3 In the Field Name column, add two new fields called Contact Person and Contact Phone, with Text as the data type. Type the appropriate text in the Description property box.

4 Set the FieldSize property of the Contact Phone field to 24.

5 Choose the Datasheet View button to switch to Datasheet view and add the names and numbers from Sylvia's note to the Contact Person and Contact Phone fields.

Datasheet View

6   Save your changes and close the table.

Filter a table to find a record

You receive a call from the Shipping department telling you that someone took a message from a person named Clyde asking which orders are to be sent by air. The Shipping department needs you to identify which carrier called. Use a filter with a table as you did with a form in Lesson 4.

1   In the Database window, open the Carriers table in Datasheet view.

2   Click the Edit Filter/Sort button on the toolbar to display the Filter window.

Edit Filter/Sort

3   Drag the Contact Person field from the field list to the filter grid.

4   Since Clyde could be a first or last name, in the Criteria cell type ***Clyde*** to indicate that the name Clyde is only part of the field.

5   Choose the Apply Filter/Sort button to see the results of your filter.

Apply Filter/Sort

If You Want to Continue to the Next Lesson

▶   Double-click the Control-menu box on the Carriers table. Or, from the File menu, choose Close.

This closes the table, but it does not exit the Microsoft Access program.

If You Want to Quit Microsoft Access for Now

▶   Double-click the Control-menu box in the Microsoft Access window. Or, from the File menu, choose Exit.

This closes the table and exits the Microsoft Access program.

Lesson Summary

To	Do this
Create a table	In the Database window, click the Table object button, and choose the New button. In the New Table dialog box, either choose the Table Wizards button or the New Table button.
Add records to a table	Display the table in Datasheet view. Then type the data in the fields.
Add a field to a table	In the first empty row in Design view, type a field name in the Field Name box. Select a data type from the drop-down list in the Data Type column. Add a description in the Description column.

To	Do this	Button
Get Help on any field property	Click in the property box, and then press F1.	
Set a table's primary key	In Design view, select the table rows that define the fields you want to include in the primary key, and then click the Primary Key button on the toolbar.	
Set properties for a field	Click the row that defines the field in the upper portion of the Design view window, and then set the property in the lower portion of the window.	
Add or modify fields in a table	Select the table in the Database window, and then choose the Design View button. Move to the Field Name column, and then make your changes.	

For more information on	See in *Microsoft Access User's Guide*
Deciding what tables belong in your database	Chapter 2, "Designing a Database"
Adding fields and setting a primary key	Chapter 7, "Table Basics"
Setting field properties	Chapter 8, "Changing and Customizing Tables"

For online information about	From the <u>H</u>elp menu, choose <u>S</u>earch and then type
Creating a table	tables: creating tables: Wizards
Adding or making changes to a field in a table	tables: fields
Adding records to a table	tables: adding records
Setting a table's primary key	primary key
Setting properties for a field	field properties

Preview of the Next Lesson

In the next lesson, you'll learn how to access data that's stored outside your Microsoft Access database in a different file format, and you'll learn how to import the data to make a new Microsoft Access table.

Attaching and Importing Data

Suppose you have sales data in a file that's not part of a Microsoft Access database. Can you use Microsoft Access to work with the data? The answer is probably *yes*. If the data is in Microsoft Excel, in Lotus 1-2-3, or in a text file, you can import it. If the data is in another database file format, such as a Paradox or Microsoft SQL Server file, you can import it, or you can attach it to your Microsoft Access database and use Microsoft Access to work with it.

In this lesson, you'll learn how to attach a table in a different database format to your Microsoft Access database and how to use Microsoft Access to work with data in the external table. You'll also learn how to import data into your Microsoft Access database and export data from Microsoft Access to a different file format.

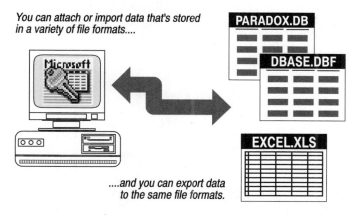

You can attach or import data that's stored in a variety of file formats....

PARADOX.DB

DBASE.DBF

EXCEL.XLS

....and you can export data to the same file formats.

You will learn how to:

- Attach an external table.
- Work with data in an attached table.
- Use a Form Wizard to create a form for an attached table.
- Import a file from a different database.

Estimated lesson time: 30 minutes

Using Data from Different Sources

When you *import* data into your Microsoft Access database, Microsoft Access copies the data from its source into a table in your database. You can import data from these file formats:

- A spreadsheet file, such as a Microsoft Excel or a Lotus 1-2-3 file.

- A text file, such as a file you might create with a word processing program or a text editor.

- A file in another database format, such as a FoxPro file, a Paradox version 3.x or 4.x file, a dBASE III or dBASE IV file, a Btrieve file (with an Xtrieve dictionary file), a Microsoft SQL Server file, or another Microsoft Access database file.

If your file is a Microsoft Access, Paradox, dBASE, Btrieve, or Microsoft SQL Server database file, you also have the choice of *attaching* the external table. An attached table isn't copied into your Microsoft Access database; the table stays in its original file format. You create a link between your Microsoft Access database and the external table. That way, you can use Microsoft Access to work with the data, and someone else can still use the table in its original application.

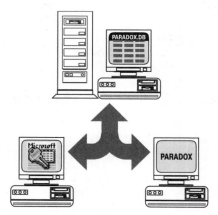

You can use Microsoft Access to work with data at the same time someone else uses another application to work with the same data.

In this lesson, you'll start by attaching a Paradox table to the Sweet database. Later, you'll import the data so that it's a Microsoft Access table.

Start the lesson

▶ If Microsoft Access isn't started yet, start it and open the Sweet database. If the Microsoft Access window doesn't fill your screen, maximize the window.

Attaching an External Table

If you attach an external table to your Microsoft Access database, you can view and update the data even if others are using it in the table's source application. You can create Microsoft Access forms and reports based on the external table. You can even use a *query* to combine external data with the data in your Microsoft Access tables. You'll learn more about using a query to combine data from different tables in Lesson 9, "Joining Tables to See Related Data."

As a small company, Sweet Lil's charged a flat shipping rate. Now that it has expanded nationwide and uses three carriers, you plan to base shipping charges to customers on the destination state or province and the selected carrier. A colleague in the Shipping department has a Paradox version 3.5 table that contains the data.

Your colleague wants to continue using Paradox for the time being to keep track of his shipping data, so instead of importing the table into the Sweet database, you'll attach it. That way, your colleague can continue to use Paradox to work with the table while you work with it using Microsoft Access.

Attach an external table

1   From the File menu, choose Attach Table.

The Attach dialog box appears.

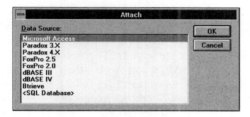

2   Double-click Paradox 3.x to select the external table's file format.

The Select File dialog box displays the files you can attach. The Paradox version 3.5 file, SHIPPING.DB, was copied to your PRACTICE directory when you copied the practice files to your hard disk.

If this file does not appear, use the Directories list to open the PRACTICE directory, and then select the file.

3   In the File Name box, double-click SHIPPING.DB.

Microsoft Access attaches the table to your database, and then displays a message to let you know that the table was successfully attached.

4   Choose the OK button to close the message box, and then choose the Close button to close the Select File dialog box.

Now the SHIPPING table appears in the Database window along with the other tables in the Sweet database.

|
A special icon shows this
is an attached table.

Note   In addition to SHIPPING.DB, a Paradox index file, named SHIPPING.PX, was copied to your PRACTICE directory when you copied the practice files to your hard disk. Paradox stores information about the table's primary key in this file. Microsoft Access needs the .PX file to open the attached table. If you delete or move the .PX file, you won't be able to open the attached table. For more information about attaching Paradox tables, see Chapter 9, "Importing, Exporting, and Attaching" in *Microsoft Access User's Guide.*

Working with Data in the Attached Table

After you attach an external table to your Microsoft Access database, you can use it much as you would a regular Microsoft Access table. You can't change the structure of an attached table (add, delete, or rearrange fields), but you can set field properties in Design view to control the way Microsoft Access displays data from a field. You can also use field properties to give a field a default value or to check new data entered in a field to be sure it meets a rule you specify.

Open an attached table

▶ In the Database window, double-click the SHIPPING table.

The table opens in Datasheet view, and its data appears.

Carrier ID	Ship State/Prov	Shipping Charge
1	AK	3.35
1	AL	3.7
1	AR	3.35
1	AZ	3.35
1	Alberta	3.35
1	British Columbia	3.35
1	CA	3.35
1	CO	3.35
1	CT	4.25
1	DC	4.05

Change a field property

You'd like to see the data in the Shipping Charge field displayed as currency. One of the Microsoft Access data types is Currency; maybe you can use it to display the data the way you want.

Design View

1   Click the Design View button on the toolbar.

Microsoft Access displays a message to let you know that you can't modify some properties of an attached table. It asks if you want to open the table anyway.

2   Choose the OK button.

The SHIPPING table appears in Design view.

3   Click the Data Type box for the Shipping Charge field.

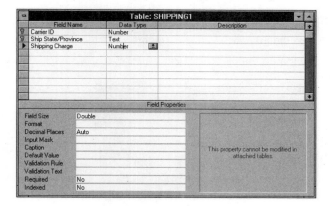

The properties of the Shipping Charge field appear in the lower portion of the window. Notice that the Hint box beside the properties says that this property (Data Type) can't be modified in attached tables. But you can still modify how Microsoft Access displays the data by setting the field's Format property.

4   In the lower portion of the window, click in the Format property box.

Now the Hint box displays a hint about setting the Format property.

5   Click the down arrow in the Format property box, and then select Currency.

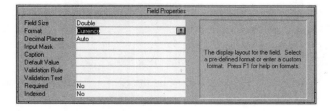

Datasheet View

6 Click the Datasheet View button on the toolbar. In the message box, choose the OK button to save your changes.

Now the data is formatted the way you want.

7 Close the SHIPPING table.

Importing a Table

Your colleague in the Shipping department has decided to use Microsoft Access instead of Paradox to manage his shipping data. This means you don't need to keep the Paradox file of shipping charges anymore; you can import it so that it's part of the Sweet database. Remember that when you attach a table, it retains its original file format. When you import a table, the data is converted to Microsoft Access format.

Import a table

1 From the File menu, choose Import.

The Import dialog box appears.

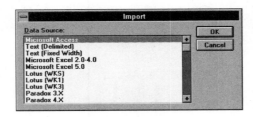

2 In the Data Source list, double-click Paradox 3.x.

The Select File dialog box appears.

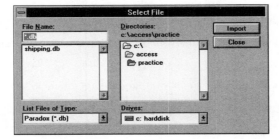

3 In the File Name list, double-click SHIPPING.DB.

4 When you see the message that the file has been successfully imported, choose the OK button.

5 Close the Select File dialog box.

Since your attached table is named SHIPPING, Microsoft Access gives the imported table the name SHIPPING1. (You can't have two tables with the same name in one database)

6 In the Database window, note that the imported table has been added to the list.

Delete a table or an attachment to an external table

Now that the data is stored in a Microsoft Access table, you don't need the attached SHIPPING table in Paradox format, and you can delete it from your list of tables.

1 In the Database window, select the attached SHIPPING table, and then press DELETE.

2 When you see the message asking if you want to remove the attachment, choose the OK button.

Since the SHIPPING table is an external Paradox file, only the attachments to the Paradox files are deleted. The Paradox files are still in your PRACTICE directory.

Note You use exactly the same procedure to delete a Microsoft Access table permanently from your database.

Rename a table

Since you now have only one table with shipping data, you can rename the imported file from SHIPPING1 to Shipping.

1 In the Database window, select the SHIPPING1 table.

2 From the File menu, choose Rename.

The Rename dialog box appears.

3 In the Table Name box, type **Shipping**, and then choose the OK button.

Working with Data in the Imported Table

The data in the imported table is now part of your Microsoft Access database, but you want to change some aspects of the table. You can customize the table's design, as you would with a table you created yourself. In this case, you will change some of the properties so that the values are displayed in a format you choose. And you will set two fields as the primary key so that when you are ready to relate tables together in the next lesson, you have already identified unique information for each record in this table.

You might wonder why you use two fields (Carrier ID and Ship State/Province) to make a primary key for the Shipping table. These two fields make a good primary key because, taken together, their two values are unique for each record in the table. To see how this works, look at the table in Datasheet view. Each carrier ID appears in the table 59 times—once for every state and province. And each state or province appears in the table three times—once for every carrier. But the combination of a specific carrier ID and a specific state or province—1 and AK, for example—appears in the table only once.

Change properties and set two primary keys

1 Open the Shipping table in Design view by clicking the Design button in the Database window.

2 Click in the Field Size property box for the Carrier ID field, click the down arrow, and then select Long Integer.

Long Integer limits values in the field to whole numbers. In addition, it enables you to create a relationship between the Carriers table and the Shipping table. You'll do that in Lesson 8, "Relating Tables."

3 Click in the Data type cell of the Shipping Charge field, click the down arrow, and then select Currency.

Primary Key

4 Set the table's primary key to both the Carrier ID and the Ship State/Province fields. When both rows are selected, click the Set Primary Key button on the toolbar.

To set two fields for the primary key, you need to select the rows for both fields. To do that, drag through the row selector for each field. Or, select the row for the first field, and then hold down the SHIFT key while you select the row for the second field.

5 From the File menu, choose Save. In the message box, choose the OK button.

You won't lose data in this case because the data in the fields is smaller than the new size limits.

6 Double-click the Control-menu box to close the table.

Using a Form Wizard to Base a Form on a Table

A table datasheet is a convenient way to work with all the records in the table at the same time, but for ease of entering data and to cut down on the possibility of making editing errors, you might prefer to use a form. Microsoft Access provides a fast way to create a form based on a table—use a Form Wizard.

Create a form with a Form Wizard

All three of Sweet Lil's carriers are now shipping to both Puerto Rico and Guam. You want to create a form to enter the new shipping information. A Form Wizard guides you through the creation process.

1 In the Database window, click the Form object button.

2 Choose the New button.

The New Form dialog box appears.

3 In the Select A Table/Query box, click the down arrow to display the list of tables and queries, and then select the Shipping table.

4 Choose the Form Wizards button.

The first Form Wizard dialog box appears and asks which wizard you want to use.

5 Double-click Single-Column.

The Single-Column Form Wizard displays the fields for each record lined up vertically, with the field names on the left.

6 Click the first double-arrow button to add all the fields in the Shipping table to the form.

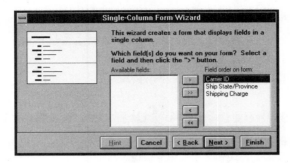

7 Choose the Next button.

8 Click the Standard option button, and then choose the Next button.

9 "Shipping" is the title you want for the form, so you don't have to make a change. Choose the Finish button to display the form.

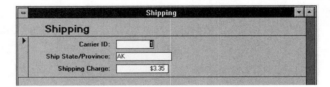

A Single-Column form based on the Shipping table opens.

Add information with the new form

Add the new shipping information using the new form.

1 Use the navigation keys to move to the next new record.

2 Enter the new information, using PR for Puerto Rico and GU for Guam.

Carrier ID	Ship State/Province	Shipping Charge
1	PR	$3.85
1	GU	$10.50
2	PR	$5.36
2	GU	$4.30
3	PR	$8.52
3	GU	$7.51

3 Close the Shipping form when you have finished entering the information.

4 When you see the message "Save changes to Form 'Form1'?" choose Yes and name the form **Shipping**

One Step Further

You might want to use a spreadsheet program to analyze the data in one of your database tables. For example, you can export the whole table, or just part of the table, to a Microsoft Excel file.

Export data from a table to a Microsoft Excel file

You want to examine some price breakdowns of the sizes of the boxes Sweet Lil's sells compared with the box prices. You are interested in all boxes that sell for less than $30.00. You could export the whole Boxes table to Microsoft Excel, but since you don't need the information from all of the fields, you can export only the cells you select. All you need is the information from the Box Name, Size, Box Description, and Box Price fields.

1 In the Database window, click the Table object button, and then double-click the Boxes table to open it.

Sort Descending

2 To see the prices of boxes you need all together, click in the Box Price column, and then choose the Sort Descending button on the toolbar.

3 To select only the data you need, drag through all of the records that have a box price less than $30.00. Include only the information from the Box Name, Size, Box Description, and Box Price fields.

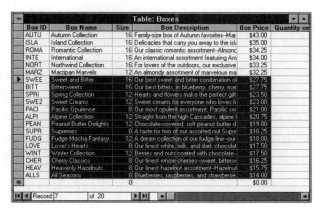

4 From the File menu, choose Output To.

5 From the Select Format list, select Microsoft Excel. Under Output, be sure that the Selection option is selected. Choose the OK button.

6 In the File Name box, be sure **BOXES.XLS** is the name of the exported file. Choose the OK button to complete the export of the file.

7 If you have Microsoft Excel installed on your computer, open the BOXES.XLS file in Microsoft Excel to look at the exported data.

If You Want to Continue to the Next Lesson

▶ Double-click the Control-menu box on the Boxes table. Or, from the File menu, choose Close.

This closes the table, but it does not exit the Microsoft Access program.

If You Want to Quit Microsoft Access for Now

▶ Double-click the Control-menu box in the Microsoft Access window. Or, from the File menu, choose Exit.

This closes the table and exits the Microsoft Access program.

Lesson Summary

To	Do this
Attach an external table to a Microsoft Access database	Open the Database. From the File menu, choose Attach Table.
Change field properties of an attached table	In Design view, click the property you want to change. (The Hint text will let you know if it's a property you can't change.)
Use a Form Wizard to create a form based on a table	In the Database window, click the Form button, and then click the New button. Select a table, and then click the Form Wizards button.
Import a table	In the Database window, choose Import from the File menu. From the Data Source list, select the source file program. In the File Name box, select the file. In the message box, choose the OK button, and then close the dialog box.
Delete an attachment to an external table	In the Database window, select the attached table, and then press DELETE. Microsoft Access deletes only the attachment, not the external table.
Rename a table	Select the table in the Database window, and from the File menu, choose Rename.

For more information on	See in *Microsoft Access User's Guide*
Importing, exporting, and attaching tables	Chapter 9, "Importing, Exporting, and Attaching"
Setting a table's primary key	Chapter 7, "Table Basics"

For online information about	From the <u>H</u>elp menu, choose <u>S</u>earch and then type
Attaching an external table	tables: attaching
Creating a form based on a table	forms: creating forms: Wizards
Importing a table	tables: importing
Renaming a table	renaming objects

Preview of the Next Lesson

In the next lesson, you'll learn how to create relationships between tables so they're automatically joined in queries. You'll also learn more about designing tables for a relational database.

Relating Tables

Some encounters are temporary; others last a lifetime. You might have a few things in common with the person sitting next to you on an airplane, for example, but that doesn't mean you'll ever see the person again. In contrast, you probably have daily contact with a co-worker, a friend, a parent, or a child. It's similar with relationships between tables. If you want to see related information from two tables again and again, you can create a permanent relationship between them. That helps Microsoft Access automatically associate the information in the two tables whenever you use them together in a query, form, or report.

In this lesson, you'll learn how to create a relationship between two tables. You'll also learn how to evaluate relationships and to structure your tables so that they're related correctly.

You will learn how to:

- Create a relationship between two tables.
- Relate tables that contain multiple-field primary keys.
- Detect a many-to-many relationship and use a linking table.

Estimated lesson time: 40 minutes

Understanding Relationships

Microsoft Access is a relational database, and therefore, you can use data from more than one table at a time. After you create tables in your database and set each table's primary key, you can create relationships between the tables. A relationship can help Microsoft Access associate the data in any new query, form, or report that includes the two related tables.

You can create two types of relationships in Microsoft Access: a *one-to-many* relationship or a *one-to-one* relationship. One-to-many relationships are by far the most common. In this type of relationship, *one* record in one table can have *many* related records in the other table. For example, one customer can place one or more orders. So one record in a Customers table (called the *primary* table in the relationship) can have many matching records in an Orders table (called the *related* table).

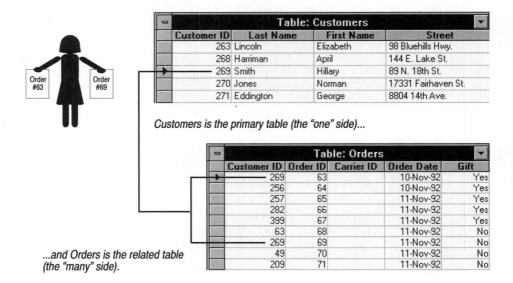

Customers is the primary table (the "one" side)...

...and Orders is the related table (the "many" side).

In a one-to-one relationship, on the other hand, one record in the primary table can have only one matching record in the related table. This type of relationship is less common than the one-to-many relationship. One reason you might use a one-to-one relationship would be when you want to separate information about employees into public and restricted data. For example, you might put public information, such as names and job titles, in one table and restricted information, such as salary information, in another table. These two tables would have a one-to-one relationship because each record in the public table would have only one matching record in the restricted table.

Note   You can also have relationships between your tables that help ensure that the data in the relationship makes sense—for example, that you don't have orders in the Orders table with no matching customer in the Customers table. For details, see "Referential Integrity" in Chapter 7, "Table Basics," in *Microsoft Access User's Guide.*

Start the lesson

In this lesson, you'll create a relationship between the Carriers table created in Lesson 6 and the Shipping table imported in Lesson 7. If you don't have these two tables, see Lessons 6 and 7 for instructions on adding them to the Sweet database. Then you can complete the exercises in this lesson.

▶ If Microsoft Access isn't started yet, start it and open the Sweet database. If the Microsoft Access window doesn't fill your screen, maximize the window.

Creating a Relationship Between Two Tables

Before you can create a relationship between two tables, the tables must contain matching fields. You relate the primary key field in the primary table (on the "one" side of the relationship) to a matching field in the related table. The matching field is sometimes called a *foreign key*.

Before creating a relationship, determine which table is the primary table (the table on the "one" side of the relationship) and which is the related table. If the related table doesn't contain a field with data that matches the data in the primary key field in the primary table, add the field to the related table so that you can create the relationship.

After you create a relationship between two tables, you can't modify or delete the fields on which the relationship is based without deleting the relationship first.

Display the Relationships window

In the relationship between the Carriers and Shipping tables in the Sweet database, the Carrier ID field is the matching field.

Carrier ID is the primary key of the Carriers table...

Table: Carriers				
Carrier ID	**Carrier Name**	**Air Delivery**	**Contact Person**	**Contact Phone**
1	Wild Fargo Carriers	No	Clyde Houlihan	(212) 555-7837
2	Grey Goose Expres	Yes	Bella Lamont	(503) 555-9874
3	Pegasus Overnight	Yes	Morris Jantz	(206) 555-8988
(Counter)				

Record: 1   of 3

Table: Shipping		
Carrier ID	**Ship State/Prov**	**Shipping Charge**
1	AK	$3.35
1	AL	$3.70
1	Alberta	$3.35
1	AR	$3.35
1	AZ	$3.35
1	British Columbia	$3.35
1	CA	$3.35
1	CO	$3.35
1	CT	$4.25
1	DC	$4.05
1	DE	$4.05
1	FL	$3.85

Record: 1   of 192

...and the matching field in the Shipping table.

This is a one-to-many relationship. One carrier can have many different shipping charges, depending on the destination of the package, so the Carriers table is the primary table in the relationship. When you create the relationship between these two tables, you'll relate Carrier ID in the Carriers table to Carrier ID in the Shipping table.

Relationships

▶ From the Edit menu, choose Relationships, or click the Relationships button on the toolbar.

The Relationships window appears. If you've worked with relationships in this database before, the Relationships window appears as you last saved it. If this is the first time you're editing relationships in this database, the window is empty and it might appear behind the Add Table dialog box.

> **Note** For this exercise, the Relationships window should be empty. If yours is not, from the Edit menu, choose Clear Layout, and then choose OK to clear the Relationships window.

Add tables to the Relationships window

Add Table

1 If Microsoft Access didn't display the Add Table dialog box automatically, choose Add Table from the Relationships menu, or click the Add Table button on the toolbar.

2 In the Table/Query list, select the Carriers table, and then choose the Add button.

3 Select the Shipping table, and then choose the Add button.

A picture of each table with its list of fields appears in the Relationships window.

4 Choose the Close button to close the Add Table dialog box.

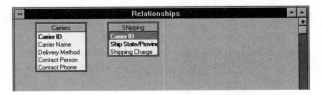

Create a relationship between tables

1 In the Relationships window, drag the Carrier ID field from the Carriers field list to the Carrier ID field in the Shipping field list.

You drag the field from the field list of the primary table (Carriers) to the field list of the related table (Shipping).

When you release the mouse button, the Relationships dialog box appears. Check to be sure that the matching field is listed for both tables. If it is not, you can click the list box down arrow and select the proper field.

2 Choose the Create button.

The Carriers table is now related to the Shipping table. You see a line between the matching fields in the two tables. This relationship remains intact until you delete it.

3   Double-click the Control-menu box on the the Relationships window to close it.

When you close the Relationships window, a message asks if you want to save changes to the Relationships layout. This decision affects only what is graphically displayed in the Relationships window. Any relationships between tables you have created or deleted remain in your database.

4   Choose the Yes button to save the layout of the Relationships window.

Next time you open the Relationships window you will see the display you just saved.

Note   Matching fields don't necessarily have to have the same name as the primary key fields they're related to. But they do have to contain matching data. In addition, they must have the same data type (with one exception), and if they have the Number data type, they must have the same field size.

The exception occurs when the primary key of the primary table has the Counter data type. In that case, the matching field in the related table can have either the Counter or Number data type (with the Field Size property set to Long Integer). For example, the Carrier ID field in the Carriers table has the Counter data type. The Carrier ID field in the Shipping table has the Number data type, with its Field Size property set to Long Integer.

Delete and restore a relationship between tables

Relationships

1   Choose the Relationships button on the toolbar to see the layout of the Relationships window that you saved.

2   Click the line between the Carriers table and the Shipping table.

The line appears heavier.

3   Press DELETE to delete the relationship.

4   In the message box, choose the OK button to delete the relationship.

Microsoft Access erases the line between the two tables. They are no longer related.

5   Re-create the relationship by dragging the Carrier ID field from the Carriers field list to the Carrier ID field in the Shipping field list, and then choosing the Create button in the Relationships dialog box.

6   Close the Relationships window and save the layout.

Relating Tables with Multiple-Field Primary Keys

A table's primary key can consist of one or more fields. If a table with a multiple-field primary key is the primary table in a relationship, you must relate *all* the fields in its primary key to matching fields in the related table. To see why, look at the Shipping and Orders tables in the Sweet database. These two tables have a one-to-many relationship, with Shipping as the primary table.

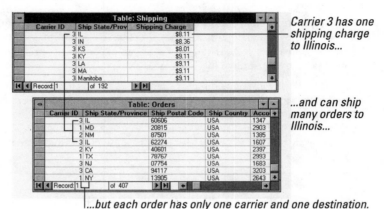

Carrier 3 has one shipping charge to Illinois...

...and can ship many orders to Illinois...

...but each order has only one carrier and one destination.

The primary key for the Shipping table consists of two fields: Carrier ID and Ship State/Province. Before Microsoft Access can correctly relate a shipping charge to an order, it must be able to find matching data for *both* fields. That's because a shipping charge is based both on the carrier that the customer chooses and the destination of the order.

Relate a multiple-field primary key to matching fields

Create a relationship between the Shipping and Orders tables so that Microsoft Access can automatically look up an order's shipping charge.

Relationships

Add Table

1   In the Database window, click the Relationships button on the toolbar.

The Relationships window appears, showing the layout you last saved.

2   From the Edit menu, choose Clear Layout and click OK to proceed.

3   Choose the Add Table button from the toolbar.

4   In the Add Table dialog box, select and add both the Shipping table and the Orders table to the Relationships window. Then close the Add Table dialog box.

5   In the Relationships window, drag the Carrier ID field from the Shipping field list to the Carrier ID field in the Orders field list.

When you release the mouse button, a Relationships dialog box appears. Check to be sure that the Carrier ID field is listed for both tables. If it is not, you can click the list box down arrow and select the proper field.

6 Click the cell under Carrier ID for each table, and then click the list box down arrow to select Ship State/Province.

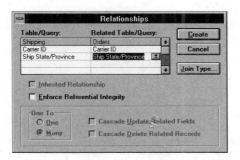

7 Choose the Create button.

The Relationship window displays the relationship between the two tables. To see the relationship more easily, you can drag the Orders table farther away from the Shipping table and drag the border of the Orders table downward to show both fields without having to scroll.

Note If Microsoft Access says that you can't relate the tables, close the Relationships dialog box, and then check the design of your Shipping table. Its primary key should consist of *both* the Carrier ID field and the Ship State/Province field. The Carrier ID field should have the Number data type, and its Field Size property should be set to Long Integer. The Ship State/Province field should have the Text data type. For help defining the table, see Lesson 7, "Attaching and Importing Data."

---

8 Double-click the Control-menu box on the Relationships window to close it. When Microsoft Access asks you if you want to save the layout, choose the Yes button.

Because the tables are now related, Microsoft Access can use the values in both tables to find information you ask for.

See how your relationships work

You've created one relationship between the Carriers and Shipping tables and another relationship between the Shipping and Orders tables. You can see how the relationships work when you need information that requires data from more than one table.

You have already learned to use a filter to request information from the Sweet database that meets specific criteria. With a filter, you were able to set criteria and display the selected data, but from only one table.

By using a *query*, you can take advantage of relationships between tables by drawing on information from two or more tables. In the following steps, you can see how related tables are used in a query. In Lesson 9, you create new queries and use the query grid to refine the selection of the information you want.

Use the Carrier ID and Ship State/Province fields in the Orders table to find the appropriate shipping charge for an order.

1   In the Database window, click the Query object button to display the list of queries, and then choose the New button.

2   In the New Query dialog box, choose the New Query button.

The Add Table dialog box and the Select Query window appear.

3   Add the Carriers, Shipping, and Orders tables to the query, and then close the Add Table dialog box. Adjust the size of the upper portion of the window so you can see the tables and relationships clearly.

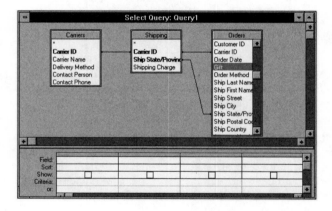

Microsoft Access uses the relationships you created to automatically join the tables in the query. You might need to rearrange the field lists so that you can see the join lines more easily.

4   Add these fields to your query grid in this order:

From the Orders table, the Order ID field

From the Carriers table, the Carrier Name field

From the Shipping table, the Shipping Charge field

5   Click the Datasheet View button on the toolbar to see the result of the query.

The related data appears from all three tables.

Datasheet View

Select Query: Query1		
Order ID	Carrier Name	Shipping Charge
404	Wild Fargo Carriers	$4.05
411	Wild Fargo Carriers	$4.25
408	Wild Fargo Carriers	$3.35
412	Grey Goose Expres	$4.86
407	Grey Goose Expres	$5.96
405	Grey Goose Expres	$4.86
410	Pegasus Overnight	$7.51
413	Pegasus Overnight	$8.01
402	Pegasus Overnight	$8.11
406	Pegasus Overnight	$8.11
409	Pegasus Overnight	$8.91

6   Close the query.

You won't use this query again, so you don't need to save it.

Identifying Many-to-Many Relationships

When you evaluate a relationship between two tables, it's important to look at the relationship from both sides. You might think at first that you have a one-to-many relationship when you actually have a *many-to-many* relationship. A many-to-many relationship occurs when one record in *either* table can have more than one matching record in the other table. In those cases, you need a third table that links the two tables before you can create the relationships.

The Boxes and Bonbons tables in the Sweet database are a good example. At first glance, you might think that boxes and bonbons have a one-to-many relationship, since one box can contain many different bonbons. But take a look at the relationship from the other side—the bonbons side. One bonbon can appear in more than one box.

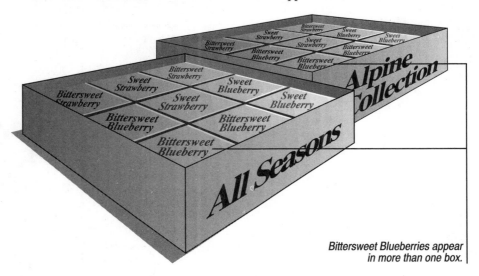

Bittersweet Blueberries appear in more than one box.

You'd have a problem if you tried to create a one-to-many relationship between the Boxes table and the Bonbons table. Which is the primary table in the relationship?

Suppose you made Boxes the primary table in the relationship. You'd add a Box ID field to the Bonbons table to hold the matching values. But in the record for the Bittersweet Blueberry bonbon, you'd have to enter box IDs for both the All Seasons and Alpine Collection boxes, since the Bittersweet Blueberry bonbon appears in both boxes. If you do that, Microsoft Access can't relate the Bittersweet Blueberry record with the right boxes—you can have only one value in each matching field. The same thing happens if you try putting a Bonbon ID field in the Boxes table.

Table: Bonbons		
Bonbon ID	**Box ID**	**Bonbon Name**
B01	SWEE, ROMA, NORT	Candlelight Ecstasy
B02	ALLS, BITT, SWEE, ALPI	Bittersweet Blueberry
B03	MARZ, AUTU	Marzipan Oakleaf

You can't have more than one value in a matching field for one record.

Table: Boxes		
Box ID	**Bonbon ID**	**Box Name**
ALLS	B02, B04, B05, M01, M09, M12	All Seasons
ALPI	B02, B04, M01, M12	Alpine Collection
AUTU	B03, M05, M08, W01	Autumn Collection

The solution is to create a linking table that contains the primary keys of both the tables you want to relate. In a linked table, you can add another field that is in neither of the original tables but gives you an additional piece of information relevant to both of the other tables. In the Sweet database, the linking table is called Box Details. The primary key of the Box Details table consists of Box ID and Bonbon ID—the primary keys of the two tables you're trying to relate. The Box Details table also contains a Quantity field, which tells you how many of each bonbon are in a box.

One box has a record in the table for each kind of bonbon it contains.

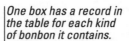

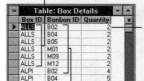

Table: Box Details		
Box ID	**Bonbon ID**	**Quantity**
ALLS	B02	2
ALLS	B04	2
ALLS	B05	2
ALLS	M01	2
ALLS	M09	2
ALLS	M12	2
ALPI	B02	4
ALPI	B04	5

The value in this field tells how many Bittersweet Blueberry bonbons are in the All Seasons collection.

One bonbon has a record in the table for each kind of box it's in.

Using Linking Tables

When you create a linking table, you don't add fields to it that really belong in one of the two related tables. For example, you might be tempted to add the Box Name field to the Box Details table. But that field is already in the Boxes table; it shouldn't be repeated. The only fields that belong in the Box Details table are those needed to define the link (Box ID and Bonbon ID) and any field whose data describes the relationship between the records in the other two tables. The Quantity field qualifies because its data relates to *both* of the other tables—it tells how many of each bonbon are in each box.

See how a linking table relates two other tables

The Boxes table has a one-to-many relationship with the Box Details table, and so does the Bonbons table. The Box Details table serves as a linking table between the two tables involved in the many-to-many relationship.

Relationships

1 In the Database window, click the Table object button, and then choose the Relationships button on the toolbar.

2 From the Edit menu, choose Clear Layout, and click OK to proceed.

Add Table

3 Choose the Add Table button from the toolbar.

The Add Table dialog box appears.

4 Add the Bonbons table, the Box Details table, and the Boxes table to the Relationships window, and then close the Add Table dialog box.

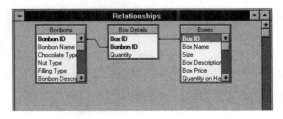

You can see the links between the tables.

5 Close the Relationships window, and click the No button in the message box.

One Step Further

Customers call Sweet Lil's to place orders for boxes of bonbons. The Sweet database includes an Orders table that contains a record for each order, with information such as when the order was placed, where it should be shipped, and how the customer paid for it. It also has an Employees table that includes a record for each employee, with information such as the employee's name, phone number, and date of hire.

So that you can easily find out the name of the employee who took an order, you will relate the Employees and Orders tables.

To create a relationship between the two tables, you relate the primary key field of the primary table to a matching field in the related table. However, there is no matching field, so you must add an appropriate field to the related table. First, evaluate the relationship between two tables, and then create a field to relate them.

Evaluate the relationship between the two tables

Relationships

1   Choose the Relationships button on the toolbar to display the Relationships window.

2   From the Edit menu, choose Clear Layout, and then choose the OK button to proceed.

Add Table

3   Click the Add Table button, and then add both the Employees table and the Orders table to the Relationships window.

4   Choose the Close button to close the Add Table dialog box.

5   Study the field list of each table to determine which is the primary table in the relationship (the table on the "one" side of a one-to-many relationship) and which is the related table. Drag the bottom of each field list, if necessary, to see all the fields at once.

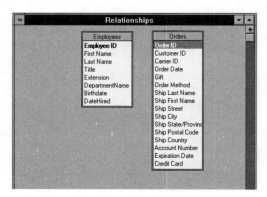

Consider that each employee can take many orders, but each order can only be taken by one employee.

6   Look at the primary key field in the primary table and see if there is a match in the related table.

In this case, the Employees table has Employee ID as its primary key, but the Orders table does not have a matching field, so a matching field needs to be created.

7   Double-click the Control-menu box on the Relationships window to close it. Choose the Yes button to save the layout of the Relationships window.

Create a matching field in the related table

To relate these two tables, you need to create a matching field between them. The matching field is based on the primary key of the primary table. The primary key of the primary table, Employees, is the Employee ID field. Create a matching field in the Orders table, and then relate the two tables.

1   In the Database window, select the Orders table, and then click the Design button to open the table in Design view.

2   In the Field Name column, add a new field called Employee ID, and set the Data Type to Number.

3   Close the Orders table, and save your changes.

4   Click the Relationships button, and view the Employees table and Orders table in the Relationships window.

5   Drag the Employee ID field in the Employees field list to the Employee ID field in the Orders field list.

When you release the mouse button, a Relationships dialog box appears. Check to be sure that the matching field is listed for both tables. If it is not, you can click the down arrow and select the proper field.

6   Choose the Create button.

The Employees table is now related to the Orders table. You see a line between the matching fields in the two tables.

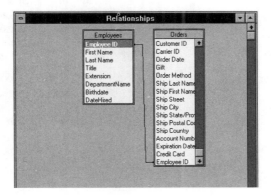

If You Want to Continue to the Next Lesson

▶ Double-click the Control-menu box on the Relationships window. Or, from the File menu, choose Close.

This closes the window, but it does not exit the Microsoft Access program.

If You Want to Quit Microsoft Access for Now

▶ Double-click the Control-menu box in the Microsoft Access window. Or, from the File menu, choose Exit.

This closes the table and exits the Microsoft Access program.

Lesson Summary

To	Do this	Button
Create a relationship between two tables	In the Database window, choose Relationships from the Edit menu or choose the Relationships button. In the Add Table dialog box, select the primary table from the Table/Query list, and choose Add. Select the related table, and choose Add. Close the dialog box. In the Relationships window, drag the common field from the primary table to the related table. Choose Create.	
Delete a relationship between tables	Open the Relationships window. Click the line linking the tables, and then press DELETE.	
Use a linking table to create a many-to-many relationship	Click the Add Table button. In the Add Table dialog box, select the tables, choose Add, and then close the dialog box. In the Relationships window, drag the field you want to relate from the primary table to the related table. Choose Create.	
Display a query	In the Database window, choose the Query object button. Select the query, and then choose the Open button. Click the Datasheet View button to see the results.	

For more information on	See in *Microsoft Access User's Guide*
Deciding what tables belong in your database	Chapter 2, "Designing a Database"
Setting relationships between tables	Chapter 8, "Changing and Customizing Tables"

For online information about	From the <u>H</u>elp menu, choose <u>S</u>earch and then type
Creating or deleting relationships between tables	relationships window
Using a linking table	relationships between tables

Preview of the Next Lessons

In Part 3, you'll learn about creating and using queries. You'll join tables, and add fields to a query, set criteria for a query, and sort query data. You'll create a parameter query, and use parameters to find a range of records and create a report. In the next lesson, you'll limit the records you see to those that meet your criteria, and you'll show totals and other calculations in a query.

Review & Practice

In the lessons in Part 2, you learned how to create tables, establish relationships, and work with related tables. If you want an opportunity to refine those skills before going on to Part 3, you can do so in the Review & Practice section that follows.

Part 2   Review & Practice

Before you begin to learn about asking questions of your database, you can use the steps in this Review & Practice section to practice the skills and techniques you learned in Part 2, "Expanding a Database."

Scenario

The Marketing department is planning for the next quarter. They will run advertising promotions for selected boxes of bonbons. You create and relate tables to keep track of their information. When you're finished, you delete an unneeded table from the database.

You will review and practice how to:

- Create a table.
- Create a relationship between two tables.
- Set a primary key in a table.
- Identify a many-to-many relationship.
- Create a linking table.
- Delete a table from a database.

Estimated practice time: 35 minutes

Step 1: Create a Table

The Marketing department wants to use Microsoft Access to keep track of advertising promotions for different boxes of bonbons and the Marketing employee who is responsible for each promotion. The promotion name will be unique to each project.

1   Create a new table that has fields for Employee ID, Promotion Name, Start Date, and Box ID.

2   Select Counter as the data type for the Employee ID field.

3   Enter a description for each field.

4   Set the Promotion Name field as the primary key.

5   Save the table with the name **Promotions**

6   Close the table and verify that the Promotions table is listed in the Database window.

For more information on	See
Creating a table	Lesson 6
Selecting a data type	Lesson 6
Setting a primary key	Lesson 6, Lesson 8

Step 2: Relate Tables with a One-to-Many Relationship

Each promotion will be handled by one employee, but one employee might handle more than one promotion. Create a one-to-many relationship between the Employees table and the Promotions table, where the Employee ID field is the matching field.

1 Determine which table is the primary table and which is the related table.

2 Use the Relationships window to create a relationship between the Employees table and the Promotions table.

3 Do not save the layout of the Relationships window when you close it.

For more information on	See
Understanding relationships between tables	Lesson 7
Displaying relationships in the Relationships window	Lesson 7

Step 3: Relate Tables with a Many-to-Many Relationship

The Marketing department is interested in the dates and locations of orders for certain boxes. The Orders table contains a record for each order, with information such as when the order was placed, where it should be shipped, and how the customer paid for it. The Boxes table contains a record for each box in the product line, with information such as the box name, size, description, and price. An order could include more than one kind of box, and a box could appear on more than one order.

How would you relate the Orders and Boxes tables so that you could easily find the names of all the boxes in an order?

1 Analyze the relationship between the Orders and Boxes tables from both sides.

2 Open the Order Details table, which is a linking table between the Orders and Boxes tables based on their primary keys. It also contains a Quantity field.

3 Close the Order Details table, and view the relationship between the Orders, Boxes, and Order Details tables in the Relationships window.

For more information on	See
Identifying a many-to-many relationship	Lesson 8
How a linking table works	Lesson 8

Step 4: Delete a Table from a Database

The Marketing Department has notified you that, for the next quarter, they will use an outside consultant for their promotions. Therefore, they do not need to track the promotions information in the Sweet database.

1   Delete the relationship between the Employees table and the Promotions table.

2   In the Database window, delete the Promotions table from the database.

For more information on	See
Deleting relationships	Lesson 8
Deleting a table from a database	Lesson 7

If You Want to Continue to the Next Lesson

▶   If you are not in the Database window, double-click the Control-menu box on the Relationships window. Or, from the File menu, choose Close.

This closes the window, but it does not exit the Microsoft Access program.

If You Want to Quit Microsoft Access for Now

▶   Double-click the Control-menu box in the Microsoft Access window. Or, from the File menu, choose Exit.

This closes the table and exits the Microsoft Access program.

3

Asking Questions and Getting Answers

Selecting the Records You Want

If your business changes from day to day, you'll frequently want to look at your data from different angles. Before calling your customers for a marketing campaign, you'll want to create a list of selected names and phone numbers. To review sales trends, you'll want to find out how many orders you received for a specific month. To facilitate express orders of supplies, you'll want to identify a contact person's name and phone number quickly.

In this lesson, you'll create a variety of queries that select the data you want. You'll also calculate total values using a query, and you'll use a query to answer a "what if" question.

Customer	State/Province	Gift	Order Date
Adams, Cathy	CA	Yes	23-Dec-92
Fogerty, Sam	CA	Yes	09-Dec-92
Harkin, Rory	CA	Yes	03-Dec-92
Kennedy, Brian	CA	Yes	10-Dec-92
Kimball, Mary	CA	Yes	23-Dec-92
Kimball, Mary	CA	Yes	02-Dec-92
Kumar, Andrew	CA	Yes	19-Dec-92
Lopez, Maria	CA	Yes	10-Dec-92

You will learn how to:

- Create a query based on a table or another query.
- Set criteria to get a set of related records.
- Sort data and hide a field in a query.
- Create a query that shows related data together.
- Join tables in a query, and summarize data.
- Change a field name in the datasheet.
- Show calculations in a field.

Estimated lesson time: 45 minutes

What Is a Query?

A *query* defines a group of records you want to work with. You can think of a query as a request for a particular collection of data, such as "Show me the names and phone numbers for our carriers with their shipping charges." The answer to the request is called a *dynaset*. The records in a dynaset can include fields from one or more tables.

Dynaset of the Shipping Charges query

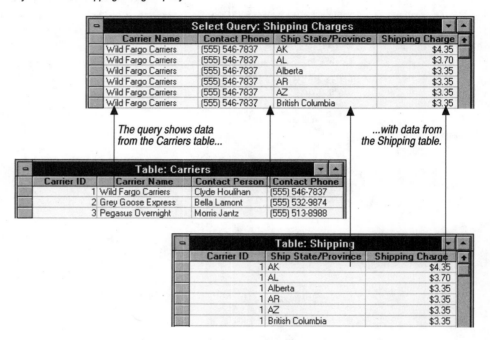

You might wonder why you don't simply include all the data you need in one large table. The answer holds the secret to the power of a relational database. When you create a separate table for each subject of data—for example, customers or products—the result is a system that provides extraordinary flexibility in how you can bring related data together.

You use queries in much the same way as you use tables. You can open a query and view its dynaset in a datasheet. You can base a form or a report on a query. You can also update the data in a query's dynaset and have the changes saved back to the table where the data is stored.

Due to the flexibility of queries, you might find that you use queries more often than tables. That's because you can use a query to sort data or to view a meaningful subset of all the data in your database. You can look at only the customers in your region, for example, instead of wading through all the customers in the Customers table, and you can see information about their purchases at the same time.

When you worked with a filter in Lesson 4, you found information from a single table. By using a query, you can ask questions of your data that requires information from more than one place in your database. You can also save the query to use again, and you can use an existing query to build a new query.

You can create one query that shows which customers bought which products, another query that shows which products sold best in Europe, and another that shows postal codes sorted according to product sales. You don't have to store the product information three times for the three different queries—each piece of information is stored once, in its table. With queries you can access the same information in many different ways.

What Is Graphical QBE?

In the Query window, you design a query by using a feature called *graphical query by example (QBE)*. With graphical QBE, you create queries by dragging fields from the upper portion of the Query window to the QBE grid. You place the fields in the QBE grid in the order you want them to appear in the datasheet. In this way, you use the QBE grid to show Microsoft Access an example of what you want the results of your query to look like.

After choosing fields, you use the QBE grid to zero in on the records you want.

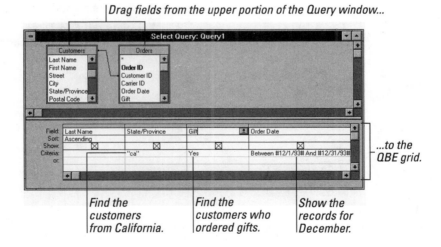

Drag fields from the upper portion of the Query window...

...to the QBE grid.

Find the customers from California.

Find the customers who ordered gifts.

Show the records for December.

Graphical QBE makes it easy to build on a query. Often, one question leads to another, and you find that you want to keep changing a query. For example, you might start by finding all your customers from California. Then, by making small changes to the QBE grid, you can find all the California customers who ordered gifts, and finally, all the California customers who ordered gifts in December. And you can keep going, refining the query until you get it just right.

In Lesson 8, you got a preview of working with a query when you created relationships for three tables, and then displayed data from all three tables at the same time. In this lesson, you learn to create queries, and then refine your requests for more specific data.

Start the lesson

▶ If Microsoft Access isn't started yet, start it and open the Sweet database. If the Microsoft Access window doesn't fill your screen, maximize the window.

Creating and Saving a Query

You're in charge of a telephone survey of Sweet Lil's customers in your sales region. Your region is New York state, so you'll use a query to get a list of the names and phone numbers of the New York customers. The information you need is stored in the Customers table.

Create a query

1   In the Database window, click the Query object button.

2   Choose the New button.

3   In the New Query dialog box, click the New Query button.

The Select Query window opens and displays the Add Table dialog box. You use this dialog box to select the tables (or queries) you want in your query.

4   Scroll downward in the Table/Query box, if necessary, until you see the Customers table.

5   Double-click the Customers table, and then choose the Close button.

In the upper portion of the Select Query window, a field list appears for the Customers table. The field list shows all the fields in the table. You use this list to select the fields you want to display in your query.

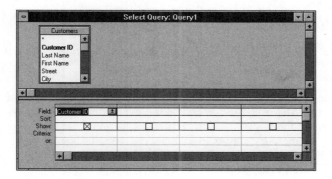

Add fields to a query

1 Drag the Customer ID field from the field list to the first cell in the Field row of the QBE grid.

2 Drag the Last Name, First Name, State/Province, and Phone fields to the QBE grid. When you finish, the QBE grid has five fields.

You might have to scroll to the right before you drag the Phone field into position.

Tip   Instead of dragging a field, you can double-click the field to move it into the next empty field cell in the QBE grid.

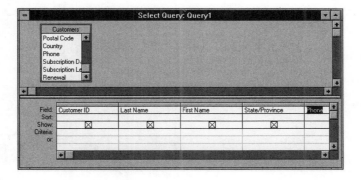

Save and name a query

1 From the File menu, choose Save.

2 In the Save As dialog box, type the name **NY Customers** and choose the OK button.

The name of the query appears in the title bar. Microsoft Access also adds this query to the list of queries in the Database window for you to use again.

Setting Criteria for the Records You Want

If you run the query now, you'll see records for all customers in the Customers table. But you're interested only in the customers from New York, so you'll set *criteria* to limit the result of the query to only those records for New York customers.

For more information, see the Appendix, "Using Expressions."

You set criteria for a query using an *expression*, a type of formula that specifies which records Microsoft Access should retrieve. For example, to find fields with a value greater than 5, you'd use the expression >5. You use an expression in a query in exactly the same way as in a filter, covered in Lesson 4.

Specify criteria

1   In the QBE grid, click in the Criteria cell below the State/Province field.

2   Type **NY** and press ENTER.

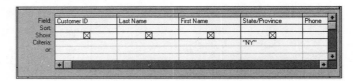

After you press ENTER, Microsoft Access automatically places quotation marks around what you typed, indicating that it is text.

Note   If you type text that contains commas or periods, Microsoft Access will not automatically place quotation marks around the text. You must type the quotation marks yourself to indicate that what you have typed is text, not an expression.

Run your query

Datasheet View

▶   Click the Datasheet View button on the toolbar to check the results of this query.

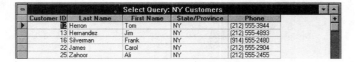

Microsoft Access displays the customers from New York state with their phone numbers.

Add more criteria

Now you have a list of customers in your sales region. But you want to call only your most recent customers—customers with customer IDs greater than 200. To find these customers, you'll add another criterion to the query.

Design View

1 Click the Design View button on the toolbar to switch to Design view.

2 In the Criteria cell below the Customer ID field, type the expression **>200**

By adding this criterion, you're now telling Microsoft Access, "Find customers who have customer IDs greater than 200 and who live in New York."

Field:	Customer ID	Last Name	First Name	State/Province	Phone
Sort:		Ascending			
Show:	☒	☒	☒	☒	
Criteria:	>200			"NY"	
or:					

For more information on operators, see the Appendix, "Using Expressions."

Note   The > (greater than) sign is called a comparison operator. Other operators you can use in expressions are < (less than), >= (greater than or equal to), and <= (less than or equal to).

3 Click the Datasheet View button to see the customers you're going to call.

Customer ID	Last Name	First Name	State/Province	Phone
249	Gunther	Paul	NY	(212) 555-4934
257	Petri	Laura	NY	(716) 555-0684
280	Kahn	Juliet	NY	(212) 555-9424
292	Singh	Rama	NY	(212) 555-4927
298	Hendricks	Louise	NY	(516) 555-2067

Select Query: NY Customers

Sorting in a Query

For more sorting examples, see Lesson 4, "Finding Information."

To make it easier to find a phone number for a specific customer, you can list the customers in alphabetical order. You'll change the NY Customers query so it sorts your customers by last name.

Sort records alphabetically

1 Click the Design View button on the toolbar to switch to Design view.

2 Click in the Sort cell below the Last Name field.

3 Click the down arrow, and select Ascending from the list to sort the records from A to Z.

4 Click the Datasheet View button to see the names in alphabetical order.

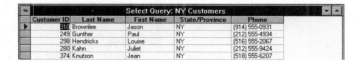

Customer ID	Last Name	First Name	State/Province	Phone
310	Brownlee	Jason	NY	(914) 555-0931
249	Gunther	Paul	NY	(212) 555-4934
298	Hendricks	Louise	NY	(516) 555-2067
280	Kahn	Juliet	NY	(212) 555-9424
374	Knutson	Jean	NY	(518) 555-6207

Select Query: NY Customers

Hiding a Field

In the NY Customers query, you don't really need to see the State/Province field in the datasheet because the query shows only the customers from New York. This field has to be included in the Design view of the query because you use it to set criteria. But you don't need to see this field repeated for every record in the dynaset. You'll use the Show box in the QBE grid to hide this field so it doesn't appear in the datasheet.

Hide a field

Design View

1 Click the Design View button on the toolbar to switch to Design view.

2 In the Show row below the State/Province field, click the Show box so that the X disappears.

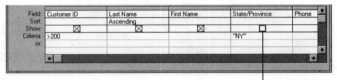

Click the Show box.

The query will use any criteria or sort information in this field, but will not show the field in the datasheet.

Datasheet View

3 Click the Datasheet View button on the toolbar.

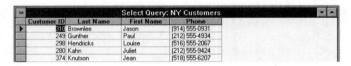

The State/Province field no longer appears.

4 From the File menu, choose Save Query to save the changes. Then close the query.

5 Scroll through the list of queries in the Database window, if necessary, and see that the query you created, NY Customers, is now included in the list.

Creating a Query Based on Related Tables

To associate data in different tables correctly, Microsoft Access uses matching values in equivalent fields in the two tables. To create a relationship between two tables, you draw a *join line* between two matching fields in the Relationships window. In most cases, the primary key from one table is joined to a field in another table that contains the matching values.

Lesson 8, "Relating Tables," showed you how to create relationships between tables. Now you can create a query based on tables that are related.

Lillian Farber, the president of the company, is analyzing the company's orders for the month before the holidays. She has asked you to give her a list of all orders that were placed in November. She wants to know the order IDs, the customers' names, and the dates of the orders.

Create a query using related tables

The information Lillian Farber needs is contained in two different tables, the Orders table and the Customers table. Create a new query using these tables.

1 In the Database window, click the Query object button, and then choose the New button.

2 In the New Query dialog box, click the New Query button.

The Select Query window opens and displays the Add Table dialog box.

3 Select the Orders table in the Table/Query box, and then choose the Add button.

4 Select the Customers table in the Table/Query box, and then choose Add again.

5 Choose Close to close the Add Table dialog box.

The field lists for the Orders and Customers tables are placed in the Select Query window. Notice that a join line automatically appears between the Customer ID fields in the two field lists. This is because a relationship already exists between these two tables.

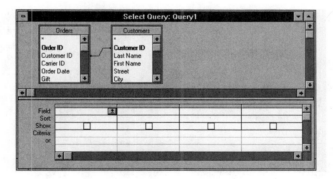

6 From the File menu, choose Save.

7 Name the query **Order Information**, and then choose OK.

Add fields from two tables to the query

You add fields from the related tables to the query.

1 Drag the Order ID, Customer ID, and Order Date fields from the Orders table to the QBE grid.

2 Drag the Last Name field from the Customers table to the QBE grid.

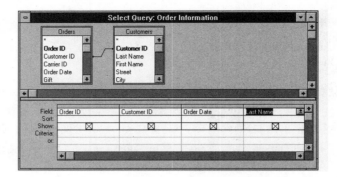

Specify criteria and check the results

You use an expression to select records during the month of November. This expression includes the *Between...And* operator.

1 In the Criteria cell below the Order Date field, type **Between 1-Nov-93 And 30-Nov-93** and then press ENTER.

The format of the date changes and number symbols (#) appear around the dates automatically. Because this is a long expression, you might want to widen the Order Date field in the QBE grid so you can see the entire expression after you've typed it.

2 To size the column to its "best fit," double-click the right border of the field selector at the top of the Order Date column in the query grid.

Note Microsoft Access uses the Date format for your country. To find out which country your computer is set up for, open the Windows Control Panel and double-click the International icon, which will display the Country setting as well as the Date and other formats.

Datasheet View

3 Click the Datasheet View button on the toolbar to see the orders for November.

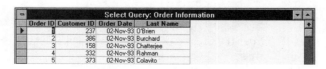

4   Save the query again, and then close it.

If you are prompted to confirm your changes, choose OK.

Joining Tables in a Query

As you have just seen, when you add related tables from the Sweet database to a query, join lines automatically appear between them in the Query window.

Join lines also appear automatically in a query for tables that do not have an existing relationship, but that do have a field with the same name and data type, and where one of the join fields is a primary key. In this case, the join lines indicate that the matching fields will relate the data for the purposes of the query, but a permanent relationship between them is not established.

If no relationship exists between the tables you want to use, and one is not automatically created when you add the tables to a query, you can still use related data by joining the tables in the Query window when you create the query. For the join to work, the tables must contain fields with matching data.

Note   When you draw a join line between two tables in the Query window, the join applies to that query only. If you want to use the same two tables in another query, you'll need to join them again in the new query.

Join two tables in a query

You need a quick way to look up the contact names of the suppliers of the ingredients for Sweet Lil's products.

The Ingredients table lists categories and types of ingredients that bonbons are made of, and it contains a field called "Source ID" that identifies where the ingredient is purchased. The Suppliers table has detailed information about the suppliers of ingredients for Sweet Lil's products, and it contains a field called "Suppliers ID." You can join these two fields in a query because they contain matching data.

1   In the Database window, click the Query object button, and then choose the New button.

The Suppliers table was added in Lesson 6, "Adding a Table."

2   Click the New Query button, add the Ingredients table and the Suppliers table to the query, and then close the Add Table dialog box.

3   Drag the Source ID field from the Ingredients field list to the Suppliers ID field in the Suppliers field list.

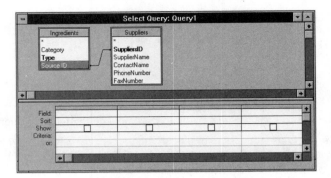

A join line connects the two fields to associate the data correctly between the two tables.

4 Drag the Category and Type fields from the Ingredients field list to the QBE grid.

5 Drag the Contact Name field from the Suppliers field list to the QBE grid.

6 Drag the Source ID field from the Ingredients field list to the QBE grid.

7 Under Source ID, set the Sort cell to Ascending.

View the datasheet

Datasheet View

1 Click the Datasheet View button to view the results of your query.

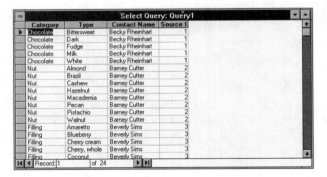

2 Scroll down the records to see the information in the Contact Name field change according to which supplier (Source ID) is used.

Save and name your query

1 From the File menu, choose Save Query.

The Save As dialog box appears.

2 Name the query **Ingredient Source**, and then choose the OK button.

3 Close the query.

4 To see your query in the Database window, scroll down the alphabetical list of queries.

Your query is saved in the Sweet database. You can open it anytime by double-clicking the query in the Database window. When you open the Ingredient Source query, Microsoft Access gets the most current data stored in the Ingredients and Suppliers tables and brings it together in the query's dynaset.

Summarizing Data

When you design a query, you can specify which fields to use for grouping records and which fields to use for totals (calculations). For example, you can calculate the total number of bonbons (the type of calculation) within each box (the group).

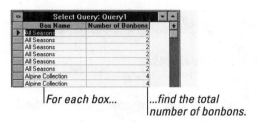

For each box... ...find the total number of bonbons.

You could begin a new query, but in this case you can use an existing query as the foundation of your new query.

You'll create a new query by modifying the existing Order Information query. The new query will find the total number of orders by country. Then you find the totals of each state or province in each country.

Use an existing query to create a new query

The Order Information query shows you a list of orders by customer. Often, you'll want more than just a list of orders; you'll also want to know the total number of orders placed by country or the total value of all boxes within one order. You can use Microsoft Access queries to perform these calculations for you.

1 In the Database window, click the Query button, and select the Order Information query.

2 Click the Design button in the Database window.

3 From the File menu, choose Save As.

4 Name the query **Total Orders by Country** and click the OK button.

The name of the query appears on the title bar of the query and also in the list of queries in the Database window.

Add and delete fields in a query

To specify the information you want, you need to change the fields included in the query.

1   Delete the Last Name field from the query by selecting the field selector at the top of the column, and then pressing DELETE.

2   Delete the Customer ID field and the Order Date field from the query.

3   Add the Country field from the Customers table to the query by dragging it on top of the Order ID field.

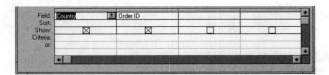

When you release the mouse button, the Country field becomes the first field listed in the query grid, and the Order ID field moves to the right.

Calculate totals in your query and group the results

Totals

1   Click the Totals button on the toolbar.

A row called Total appears in the QBE grid. Each box contains the designation "Group By."

2   Click the Total cell below the Order ID field, and then click the down arrow. From the list, select Count.

Click here.

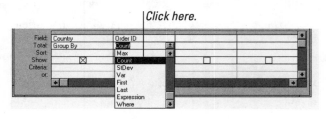

Since there is one order ID for each order, you are counting the number of orders. You're grouping by country, so the count will be the count of orders for each country.

3 Click the Datasheet View button to view the results of your query.

Datasheet View

The datasheet shows the total number of orders for each country. The second column automatically displays the name CountOfOrder ID.

Group totals by two fields

You'd like to investigate further. So far you have grouped the results of your query by country. But you also want to know how many orders you've received from each state or province within each country. You can group by a second field.

1 Click the Design View button on the toolbar to switch to Design view.

Design View

2 Add the State/Province field from the Customers table to the QBE grid. Place the field between the Country and Order ID fields.

"Group By" appears in the Total row.

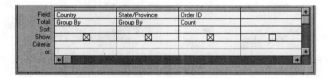

3 Click the Datasheet View button on the toolbar to switch to Datasheet view.

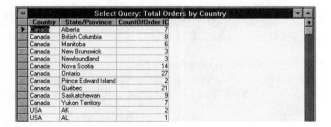

Microsoft Access groups first by country (because this is the first Group By field in the QBE grid), and then by state or province. The totals are calculated for each state or province within each country.

Changing a Name in the Datasheet

By changing the name of a field in a query, the datasheet shows a relevant column heading, and you can use the new field name for referring to the field in forms, reports, and other queries.

Change a field name

In the Total Orders By Country query, CountOfOrder ID is a generic field name assigned by Microsoft Access. You can easily change it to a more meaningful name, such as Total Orders.

Design View

1   Click the Design View button on the toolbar.

2   In the QBE grid, place the insertion point immediately to the left of the Order ID field name, and then click the mouse button. Type **Total Orders:** to the left of the field name. (Be sure to include the colon. A space after the colon is optional.)

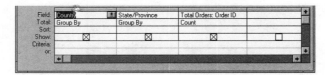

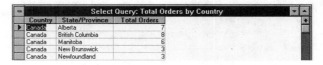

Datasheet View

3   Click the Datasheet View button on the toolbar to look at the query.

4   Save the query, and then close it.

Showing Calculations in a Field

When you're running a business, one of your most common questions is "What if?" Sweet Lil's is no exception. The chocolates are selling so well that the sales manager wants to know "What if I raise prices on our boxes by 5 percent?"

Since the tables in the Sweet database don't contain a field that shows prices raised by 5 percent, you'll use a query with a calculated field to answer this question.

Create the query

The new query is based on the Boxes table.

1   Create a new query, and then add the Boxes table.

2   Add the Box Name and Box Price fields to the QBE grid.

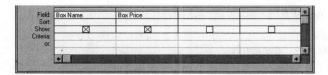

The query you've just created will display the current price for each box.

3 Click the Datasheet View button on the toolbar to look at the query.

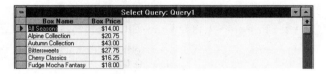

4 Save the query and name it **Raise Prices**

Add a calculated field

Now you'll add a calculated field that will show what prices would be if you raised them by 5 percent.

1 Click the Design View button on the toolbar, and place the insertion point in the empty Field cell to the right of the Box Price cell.

2 Type **[Box Price]*1.05** and press ENTER.

In an expression, the square brackets indicate that this is a field name. Brackets automatically appear around a single-word field, but here, you must type the brackets because the field name contains a space. For more details on using expressions in calculated fields, see the Appendix, "Using Expressions."

Multiplying by 1.05 is the same as raising the price by 5 percent. After you press ENTER, Microsoft Access adds a name for the field: Expr1. This is the name that will appear as the heading for this row in the datasheet.

3 To see the whole expression, double-click the right border of the field selector.

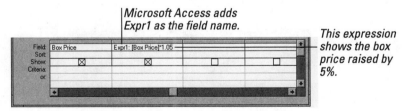

4 Click the Datasheet View button on the toolbar to see your results.

Change the name and format of the calculated field

Since Expr1 is a generic field name that doesn't describe your data very well, you will change the name of this field to "New price." You also want to show the new price information formatted as currency, and you want a description that readily explains what the new prices mean. You use the Properties sheet to customize the characteristics of your query.

Design View

1   Click the Design View button on the toolbar, and then click in the cell with the expression Expr1:[Box Price]*1.05.

2   Replace Expr1 with **New Price**

Properties

3   Click the Properties button to open the Field Properties box.

4   To change the display of the new price information, select the Format property and click the down arrow to display the list.

5   From the list, select Currency to format the prices with dollar signs and decimals.

6   Select the Description property, and type **Shows prices raised by 5%**

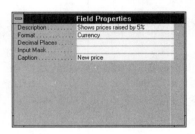

7   Close the Field Properties box.

Datasheet View

8   Click the Datasheet View button on the toolbar to see the new prices with the properties you specified.

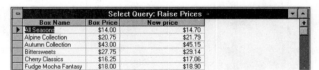

The new prices appear as currency, and you can see the New price caption at the top of the column. When you click in the New price field, the description appears on the status bar at the bottom of the datasheet window.

9   Save and close the query.

One Step Further

Since new bonbons are being added to Sweet Lil's collection, you want to create a new form to add information about the suppliers of additional ingredients. Because of the popularity of some adveritised specials, you'd like to have the phone number of a supplier readily available to confirm the express shipment of an ingredient order. You can use the Ingredient Source query as the basis for your new form.

First you'll add the Phone Number field from the Suppliers table to the Ingredient Source query for quick reference when you are working with ingredient orders. Then you'll delete the Source ID field from the query, and you'll create a new form to help you track ingredient information.

Add a field to a query

You want to be able to quickly find the phone number of a supplier's contact person in case you need to check the shipment of an ingredient.

1 Open the Ingredient Source query, and then click the Design View button on the toolbar.

2 Drag the Phone Number field from the Suppliers field list to the QBE grid and drop it on the Source ID field so that it is positioned between the Contact Name field and the Source ID field.

Delete a field from a query

Now that you can see the contact name and phone number in your query's dynaset, you don't need to see the Source ID number.

1 Click the field selector for the Source ID column, and then press the DEL key.

2 Save your changes to the query.

3 Click the Datasheet View button on the toolbar to see the results of the query.

Create a form based on a query

You could create your new form using the same technique you previously used to create the Shipping form—click the Form button in the Database window, and then choose the New button. But in this case, you'll use two shortcuts to create a quick form based on the Ingredient Source query.

New Form

1 With the Ingredient Source query open, click the New Form button on the toolbar.

The New Form dialog box appears with the Ingredient Source query already selected in the Select A Table/Query box.

2 Click the Form Wizards button.

3   Select AutoForm from the list and choose the OK button.

A single-column form appears that displays one record at a time, including the values from all fields of the records.

4   When you're finished reviewing the form, close it and save it with the name **Ingredient Source**

If You Want to Continue to the Next Lesson

▶ Double-click the Control-menu box on the Select Query window. Or, from the File menu, choose Close.

Be sure the Database window appears on your screen.

If You Want to Quit Microsoft Access for Now

▶ Double-click the Control-menu box in the Microsoft Access window. Or, from the File menu, choose Exit.

This closes the table and exits the Microsoft Access program.

Lesson Summary

To	Do this
Open a new query	In the Database window, click the Query object button. Choose the New button, and then choose the New Query button.
Add a table or query to a query	Open a new query. In the Add Table dialog box, double-click the table or query you want to add. Choose Close. To add a table after you have closed the Add Table dialog box, click the Add Table button on the toolbar.
Add a field to a query	Drag the field from the field list in the upper portion of the Query window to an empty Field cell in the lower portion of the Query window.

To	Do this	Button
Save and name a query	From the File menu, choose Save. In the Save As dialog box, type a name and choose the OK button.	
Set criteria	In the QBE grid, enter criteria in the Criteria cell for any field in the query.	
Sort the records in a query	In the QBE grid, click in the Sort cell for the field you want to sort, and select Ascending or Descending.	
Hide a field in a query	In the QBE grid, click the Show box under any field so that the X disappears.	
Find a range of data	In the QBE grid, enter criteria using the Between...And operator.	
Join tables in a query	From the Add Table dialog box, add the tables to the query, and then close the dialog box. The two tables must contain fields with matching values. Drag the matching field from one field list and drop it on the matching field in the other field list.	
Delete a field from a query	Click the field selector in the QBE grid to select the field, and then press DELETE.	
Calculate totals	Click the Totals button on the toolbar. Click in the Total cell for the field you want to calculate. Click the down arrow and choose a total function (such as Count).	Σ
Give a field a custom name	In the QBE grid, place an insertion point to the left of the field name. Then type a custom field name followed by a colon.	
Show calculations in a field	In the Field cell, add an expression that calculates a value.	
Change the properties of a field	Click in the cell with the properties you want to change, and then click the Properties button. Select a property and either type your data or choose an option if there is a list.	

For more information on	See in *Microsoft Access User's Guide*
Creating queries	Chapter 10, "Query Basics," and Chapter 11, "Designing Select Queries"
Joining tables in a query	Chapter 11, "Designing Select Queries"
Creating expressions	Chapter 11, "Designing Select Queries"

For online information about	From the __H__elp menu, choose __S__earch and then type
Creating queries	queries: creating
Adding or deleting fields and tables in a query	queries: adding fields queries: deleting fields queries: adding tables queries: deleting tables
Joining tables in a query	queries: joining tables in
Setting criteria in a query	queries: criteria
Changing field properties	queries: properties
Calculating in a query	queries: calculations

Preview of the Next Lesson

In the next lesson, you'll learn how to make queries easier to use. You'll create a query that displays a dialog box that prompts you for criteria. When you run the query, the criteria you enter will appear in the datasheet.

Creating User-Friendly Queries

How often do you ask the same types of questions about your data? A customer might ask for information about the contents of your 12-ounce boxes of candy, and later another customer might ask for information about the 8-ounce boxes. Similarly, a customer might ask how many boxes of each kind of candy you have in stock, and then want to know how many of each size you have. These requests might occur over and over again, and only the details differ. In this lesson, you will learn two ways to work with repetitive queries to make answering questions easier.

Instead of creating numerous queries to answer different but related questions, you can create a *parameter query*. A parameter query prompts you for criteria each time you run the query, so you can use the same query over and over again with a change in criteria. You'll find out how to create parameter queries, and then you'll create a report based on a parameter query.

To look at a large volume of data in a more readable format, you can create a *crosstab query*. A crosstab query selects the information you want and rearranges it in a spreadsheet format so that you can immediately pick out the answer to a question. A crosstab query can also calculate totals. You'll use a Query Wizard to create a crosstab query to see at a glance how many boxes you have in stock.

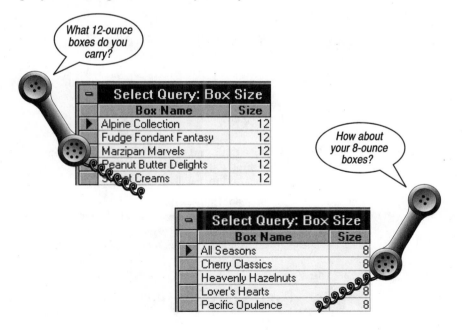

You will learn how to:

- Create a parameter query.

- Use parameters to find a range of records.

- Base a report on a parameter query.

- Use the Query Wizard to create a crosstab query.

Estimated lesson time: 20 minutes

What Is a Parameter Query?

A parameter query asks you to enter one or more parameters—or criteria—when you run the query. For example, a parameter query might ask you to enter a beginning and ending date. Microsoft Access runs the query using your parameters as criteria, and then displays the datasheet. Typically, you create a parameter query when you expect to run a query frequently, but you'll be using different criteria each time you run it.

When you run the query, Microsoft Access asks you for the criteria...

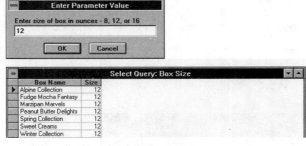

...and then displays the datasheet.

Parameter queries save time, and they're easy to use. Because the query displays dialog boxes that prompt you for criteria, you don't have to change the design of your query every time you want to use different criteria.

Parameter queries are especially helpful as the basis for reports. For example, suppose you run a sales report at the end of every week. You can create a parameter query that prompts you for the dates you're interested in. You fill in the dates you want and then they are automatically included in the report.

Start the lesson

▶ If Microsoft Access isn't started yet, start it and open the Sweet database. If the Microsoft Access window doesn't fill your screen, maximize the window.

Creating a Parameter Query

You're designing new boxes of bonbons, and you want to feature a different type of chocolate in each box. Today you might want to run the query to see a list of dark chocolate bonbons; tomorrow you might want to take a look at milk chocolates. You'll design a parameter query that asks you which type of chocolate you're interested in.

Create the query

The new query is based on the Bonbons table.

1   In the Database window, click the Query object button and then click the New button.

2   Click the New Query button to display the Query window and the Add Table dialog box.

3   Add the Bonbons table to the query, and close the Add Table dialog box.

4   Add the Bonbon Name, Chocolate Type, Bonbon Cost, and Bonbon Description fields to the QBE grid.

5   In the Sort cell below the Bonbon Name field, select Ascending to display the bonbon names in alphabetical order.

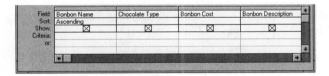

6   Save the query, and name it **Bonbon Information**

Set criteria with a parameter

Now that you've created a query and added fields, you're ready to specify criteria. To do this, you type the prompt that you want to appear in the dialog box when you run the query. Then you define the data type of the value that should be entered in the dialog box.

▶   In the Criteria cell below the Chocolate Type field, type **[Enter chocolate type]**

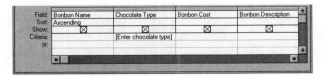

This is the prompt that appears in the dialog box when you run the query.

Define the parameter's data type

Define the data type of the parameter so that the data entered at the prompt will be the right kind. If someone tries to enter the wrong type of data in the query's dialog box, Microsoft Access displays a message and won't allow the query to proceed.

1 From the Query menu, choose Parameters.

2 In the first Parameter cell, type the same prompt as you entered in the Criteria cell, but without the brackets: **Enter chocolate type**

3 Press TAB to go to the Data Type cell.

The Query Parameters dialog box appears.

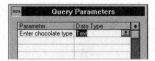

Note that the default data type is Text. This is the correct data type for the Chocolate Type field.

4 Choose the OK button to save the information and close the Query Parameters dialog box.

Run the parameter query

A parameter query prompts you for information anytime you open it from the Database window or display its datasheet.

Datasheet View

1 Click the Datasheet View button on the toolbar.

The Enter Parameter Value dialog box appears.

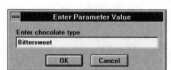

2 Type **Bittersweet** and choose the OK button.

The datasheet for the query displays the records for bittersweet bonbons.

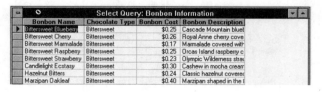

Using Parameters to Find a Range of Records

When you're running the Bonbon Information query, you might want to limit the bonbons to a specific cost range. To do this, you'll add two new parameters to the Bonbon Information query. These parameters will specify the lowest and the highest cost of bonbons that will appear in the datasheet.

Add a range of parameters

Before displaying the datasheet, Microsoft Access will need two parameters: the lowest cost and the highest cost. To add a range of parameters, you'll use the Between...And operator.

Design View

1   Click the Design View button on the toolbar.

2   Click in the Criteria cell below the Bonbon Cost field.

3   To be able to see the whole expression as you type it, press SHIFT+F2 to open the Zoom box.

4   Type **Between [Enter low cost] And [Enter high cost]** and choose the OK button.

5   Drag the right border of the field selector for the Bonbon Cost field to widen the field so that you can read the parameters you entered.

You have added two prompts: one for the lowest cost and one for the highest cost.

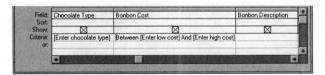

Define the parameters' data types

Define the data type of these parameters so that the data entered at the prompts will be the right kind.

1   From the Query menu, choose Parameters.

The Query Parameters dialog box appears.

2   In the second Parameter cell, type the prompt **Enter low cost** and press TAB to move to the Data Type cell.

The default data type, Text, appears. Since the Box Cost field has a Currency data type, you need to change the data type to Currency.

3   Click the arrow in the Data Type cell. Then select Currency in the drop-down list.

You might need to scroll up the list to find Currency.

4   In the third Parameter cell, type **Enter high cost** and press TAB. Change the data type to Currency.

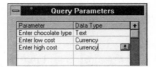

5   Choose the OK button.

6   From the File menu, choose Save to save the Bonbon Information query with the two new parameters.

Run the query

Now when you run the query, you'll be prompted for all three parameters, with a different dialog box for each.

Datasheet View

1   Click the Datasheet View button on the toolbar to run the query.

The Enter Parameter Value dialog box appears.

2   Type **Dark**, and choose the OK button.

The second dialog box prompts you for the low cost.

3   Type **.25** to find bonbons that cost a minimum of $0.25, and then choose the OK button. Notice that you don't need to type a dollar sign ($).

The third prompt appears.

4   Type **.35** to find bonbons with a maximum cost of $0.35, and then choose the OK button.

The datasheet displays the records for dark chocolate bonbons that cost between $0.25 and $0.35.

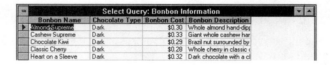

5   Close the query.

Basing a Report on a Parameter Query

Your research has shown that there's a huge market for moderately priced boxes that feature milk chocolate bonbons. So you're proposing a new line of boxes to Lillian Farber, the company president. As part of your presentation, you'll hand out an attractive report that lists milk chocolate bonbons that cost between $0.15 and $0.22.

You base the report on the Bonbon Information query. Because you want it to contain all the fields of the query, you can use the AutoReport Wizard to automatically create the report.

Create the report

For your report, you want the information about each bonbon displayed in a single-column list. In the New Report dialog box, you enter which table or query in the database contains the data you want to print in your report, and then you choose whether to start with a blank report or have a Report Wizard build your report for you.

1 In the Database window, click the Report object button, and then choose the New button.

The New Report dialog box appears.

2 In the Select A Table/Query box, click the down arrow, select the Bonbon Information query, and then click the Report Wizards button.

3 To answer the question about which Access Wizard you want to use, double-click AutoReport.

The Report Wizard automatically builds the report with the default choices, and then prompts you for the three parameters.

4 Enter the following parameters:

Chocolate type:	**Milk**
Low cost:	**.15**
High cost:	**.22**

A single-column report appears that includes all the values from all the fields and records of the Bonbon Information query.

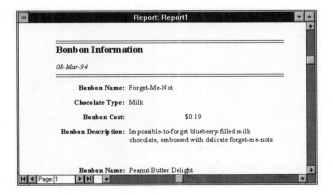

Zoom

5   To see what a page will look like when it is printed, click the Zoom button. Click the Zoom button again to see a close-up view of the report.

6   Save the report with the name **Bonbon Information**, and then close the report.

Creating a Crosstab Query

Every time a holiday approaches, orders start to pour in for specific boxes of candy. Customers want to know how many boxes you have on hand and also how many of each size. The questions are similar, but the names and sizes of boxes change. To respond to volume orders, you need a convenient way to see the total number of boxes for each bonbon collection you have in stock, in addition to how many boxes you have in each size.

You could study the Boxes table, and then create a number of queries to answer the questions, but a crosstab query can summarize your data in a compact, spreadsheet-like format. A crosstab query can show a large amount of information arranged in a way that is easy to review.

Use a Query Wizard to create a crosstab query

A Query Wizard creates a crosstab query for you, calculates the totals you need automatically, and displays the data in a readable format.

1   In the Database window, click the Query object button, and then click the New button.

2   Click the Query Wizards button.

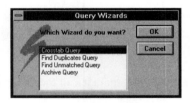

3   Select Crosstab Query from the list, and then choose the OK button.

The Crosstab Query Wizard window appears.

4   Select the Boxes table from the list, and then click the Next button.

5   Double-click the Box Name field to make it the leftmost column of the query, and then click the Next button.

6   Select the Size field to make its values the column headings, and then click the Next button.

7   Select the Quantity On Hand field for the data you want in the middle.

8   In the Functions list, select Sum.

9   Click the Finish button.

The datasheet for the crosstab query appears, showing the layout of the names and quantities of boxes, as well as how many of each size you have in stock.

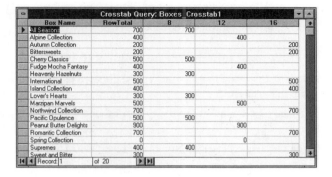

Box Name	RowTotal	8	12	16
All Seasons	700	700		
Alpine Collection	400		400	
Autumn Collection	200			200
Bittersweets	200			200
Cherry Classics	500	500		
Fudge Mocha Fantasy	400		400	
Heavenly Hazelnuts	300	300		
International	500			500
Island Collection	400			400
Lover's Hearts	300	300		
Marzipan Marvels	500		500	
Northwind Collection	700			700
Pacific Opulence	500	500		
Peanut Butter Delights	900		900	
Romantic Collection	700			700
Spring Collection	0		0	
Supremes	400	400		
Sweet and Bitter	300			300

If you want to change anything about the crosstab query, you can switch to Design view and modify it as you would any other query.

10   From the File menu, choose Save Query As, name the query **Boxes in Stock**, and then close the query.

One Step Further

To track rising costs, you are asked to query the Sweet database for costs of bonbons according to the type of nut used.

You can base the new query on the Bonbon Information query. You delete a parameter, and then you add a new parameter for Nut Type. You also change the order in which you want the parameters to appear when you run the query.

Create a new query based on an existing one

To use the Bonbon Information query as the basis for a new query, open it and save it with a new name.

1   In the Database window, select the Bonbon Information query, but do not open it.

2   Click the Design button.

3   From the File menu, choose Save As, and name the query **Nut Information**

Delete a parameter from the query

To delete a parameter from a query, delete the prompt from both the QBE grid and the Query Parameters dialog box.

1   In the Criteria cell below Chocolate Type, select the parameter including the brackets, and then press DELETE.

2 From the Query menu, choose Parameters to display the Query Parameters dialog box.

3 If it is not already selected, select "Enter Chocolate Type," and then press DELETE.

4 Choose the OK button to return to Design view.

Add a new field and a new parameter to the query

Add the Nut Type field to the query, and create a parameter that displays a prompt when the query is run.

1 Drag the Nut Type field to the QBE grid and drop it so that it is to the left of Bonbon Cost.

2 In the Criteria cell below Nut Type, type **[What type of nut?]**

3 Widen the cell so that you can read the whole parameter, if necessary.

You can save time by copying the parameter to the Query Parameters dialog box. By copying instead of typing you can also be sure that the text matches exactly.

4 Select **What type of nut?** not including the brackets. Press CTRL+C to copy the text.

5 From the Query menu, choose Parameters to display the Query Parameters dialog box.

6 Click in the first cell, and then press CTRL+V to paste the text.

7 Press TAB to go to the Data Type cell and verify that the data type is set to Text.

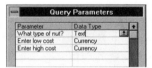

8 Choose the OK button to save the information and close the Query Parameters dialog box.

Run the query

Now you are ready to see the results of your new query.

Datasheet View

1 Click the Datasheet View button to run the query.

2 Answer the prompts by entering the following information:

Nut type:	**Hazelnut**
Low cost:	**.20**
High cost:	**.33**

Change the order of the parameters

The order in which the prompts appear depends on the order in which they are listed in the Query Parameters dialog box. You can change the query so that the prompts for the range of bonbon prices come before the prompt for the type of nut.

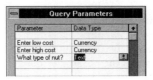

Design View

1 Click the Design View button on the toolbar.

2 From the Query menu, choose Parameters.

3 Select the parameter **What type of nut?** and press CTRL+X to cut the text.

4 Click in the cell below "Enter high cost" and press CTRL+V to paste the text.

Query Parameters	
Parameter	Data Type
Enter low cost	Currency
Enter high cost	Currency
What type of nut?	Text

5 Verify that the data type is set to Text, and then click OK.

6 Click the Datasheet View button to run the query with the parameters in the new order.

If You Want to Continue to the Next Lesson

▶ Double-click the Control-menu box on the Nut Information query, and then click Yes to save your changes. Or, from the File menu, choose Close.

This closes the query but it does not exit the Microsoft Access program.

If You Want to Quit Microsoft Access for Now

▶ Double-click the Control-menu box in the Microsoft Access window. Or, from the File menu, choose Exit.

This closes the table and exits the Microsoft Access program.

Lesson Summary

To	Do this
Set criteria with parameters	Display the query in Design view. In the Criteria cell below the appropriate field, type the prompt that will appear when you run the query. Enclose the prompt in square brackets.
Define the parameter	From the Query menu, choose Parameters. Enter the same prompt from the Criteria cell, but without the square brackets. Then select the data type. Click OK.
Run a parameter query	In the Database window, click the Query object button, and then click the Open button. Type a value in the Enter Parameter Value dialog box.
Base a report on a parameter query	Create a parameter query and save it. In the Database window, click the Report object button, and then click the New button. In the New Report dialog box, select the parameter query you just created. Click the Report Wizards button, and then double-click AutoReport. Enter any values for which you are prompted. The report appears.
Create a crosstab query	In the Database window, click the Query object button, and then click the New button. Click the Query Wizards button. Select Crosstab query and click OK. Select a table or query from the list and choose Next. Select fields for the row and column headings, and then select the field for the data in the middle. Select a function if you want. Choose Finish.

For more information on	See in *Microsoft Access User's Guide*
Creating parameter queries	Chapter 12, "Advanced Queries"
Creating crosstab queries	Chapter 12, "Advanced Queries"

For online information about	From the <u>H</u>elp menu, choose <u>S</u>earch and then type
Creating crosstab queries	queries: crosstab
	queries: Wizards
	crosstab queries
Creating parameter queries	queries: parameter

Preview of the Next Lessons

In Part 4, you'll learn to use controls to customize your forms. You'll create controls to show text and data, and you'll show a picture on a form. By using a Form Wizard, you'll be able to create a form based on two tables, and you'll create a combo box with a list of choices that will make your forms easier to use. In the next lesson, you'll add graphical controls to a form to make data entry quick and convenient.

Review & Practice

In the lessons in Part 3, you learned how to select records by using a query and how to adjust queries so that they answer complicated questions easily. The following Review & Practice section gives you an opportunity to gain more experience with building and fine-tuning your queries.

Part 3   Review & Practice

Creating queries is one of the fundamental ways you can unlock the power of a database. Before you go on to the next lesson to learn how to customize the forms you use, this Review and Practice section provides an opportunity to apply some of the techniques you have learned about querying for information.

Scenario

Sweet Lil's has asked its departments to gather data for a plan to increase their production while lowering their costs. The Marketing department wants to find out what products could be promoted to a wide group of customers who want to give high quality boxes of candy as gifts but are watching their budgets. The Shipping department has questions about the carriers and the shipping methods they have been using. Both departments ask you to help them design queries for the information they need.

You will review and practice how to:

- Create a query and set criteria.
- Sort information and find a range of data in a query.
- Create a query with related tables.
- Summarize data in a query.
- Set parameters in a query.
- Create a report based on a parameter query.

Estimated practice time: 25 minutes

Step 1: Create a query and set criteria

The Marketing department wants to focus on increasing the orders from customers who request boxes of candy that fall within a certain price range. They ask you to identify those boxes larger than the 8-ounce size, but with a price under $30.00.

1   Create a new query using the Boxes table.
2   Add fields to the query so that you can see the names, sizes, and prices of the possible boxes.
3   Create an expression that will find boxes with sizes larger than 8 ounces.
4   Create an expression that will find boxes costing less than $30.00. You don't need to enter the dollar sign in the expression.
5   Run the query.

6   Close the query without saving it.

For more information on	See
Creating a query and setting criteria.	Lesson 9
Using an expression in a query	Lesson 9 Appendix, "Using Expressions"

Step 2: Sort and find a range of data in a query

To move existing merchandise quickly, the company is planning a large-scale campaign to promote medium-priced assortments of bonbons ("Quality Everyone Can Afford"). You want to advertise only boxes that have prices between $17.00 and $25.00 inclusive and for which you have more than 200 boxes on hand. You'd like to list the boxes in alphabetical order.

1   Create a new query based on the Boxes table.

2   Add fields to the query to show the names, prices, and quantities of the boxes on hand.

3   Sort the query alphabetically by the names of the boxes.

4   Use an expression with comparison operators to find prices between $17.00 and $25.00, but do not include dollar signs. (Hint: Type **>=17 and <=25**)

5   Create an expression that shows only those boxes with quantities of more than 200 in stock.

6   Run the query.

7   Save the query with the name **Mid-Priced Boxes**, and then close the query.

For more information on	See
Sorting data in a query	Lesson 9
Finding a range of data	Lesson 9
Using an expression in a query	Lesson 9 Appendix, "Using Expressions"
Naming and saving a query	Lesson 9

Step 3: Create a query with related tables

The Shipping department staff has asked you to help compile some statistics for their quarterly budget report. They have a question about the services they have used from a particular carrier. Create a query that shows all orders shipped by air within the USA.

1   Create a new query and add the tables for Orders and Carriers.

You created the Carriers table in Lesson 6.

2   Add a field that shows the order identification numbers.

3   Add a field and criteria to the query that shows "USA" as the ship country.

4   Add a field and criteria to the query that shows the carrier name.

5   Add a field for the delivery method, and then type **Yes** in the criteria cell to show that air is the selected method.

6   Run the query.

7   Since all the results of your query are from the USA, you don't need to see USA in the dynaset. Return to Design view, and hide the Ship Country column.

8   Save the query with the name **Shipping USA**, and then close it.

For more information on	See
Creating a query with related tables	Lesson 9
Hiding a field in a query	Lesson 9

Step 4: Summarize data in a query

The Shipping department is now interested in how much money they have spent on shipping by air in the USA by carrier. Modify the Shipping USA query, which summarizes shipping charges by carrier, for destinations in the USA.

1   Add the Shipping table to the Shipping USA query.

You imported the Shipping table in Lesson 7. This table is already related to the other two, with a join line drawn from the Carrier ID field.

2   Add the Shipping Charge field to the query.

3   From the View menu, choose Totals to add the Total row to the query grid, and then select Sum from the list for the Shipping Charge total.

4 To set the query to search all carriers, delete "Pegasus Overnight" from the criteria cell under Carrier Name.

5 Since you don't need the Order ID field for this query, delete this field and then run the query.

6 Hide the columns for Ship Country and Air Delivery for a better view of the relevant data.

7 Close the query and save your changes.

For more information on	See
Summarizing data in a query	Lesson 9

Step 5: Add parameters to a query

Bob in the Shipping department has been using the Order Review query in the Sweet database so he can routinely check on orders for each customer. But the query always shows *all* the orders, and he would like to see orders only for a specific range of dates. Modify the Order Review query so Bob will be prompted for a beginning and ending date each time he runs the Order Review query.

1 Open the Order Review query in Design view.

2 Add a parameter to the Criteria cell below the Order Date field that will prompt Bob to enter information between one date and another date.

3 Open the Query Parameters dialog box and type the prompts.

4 Set the data type for the prompts to Date/Time to match the data type of the Order Date field.

5 Run the query and find orders between the dates of December 26, 1993 and December 31, 1993.

6 Save and close the query.

For more information on	See
Setting parameters in a query	Lesson 10

Step 6: **Create a report based on a parameter query**

To target customers for a "buy before the rush" promotion, the Marketing department has asked you to identify who ordered boxes of bonbons during the last two days before Christmas. The parameters you just added to the Order Review query are exactly what you need to get this information. You can use the Report Wizard to quickly create a report based on the Order Review query.

1 Use the AutoReport Wizard to automatically build a report for you, based on the Order Review query.

2 When prompted for dates, query for records between December 23, 1993 and December 24, 1993.

3 Look at both magnified and reduced views of your report.

4 Save your report and name it **Order Review**

For more information on	See
Creating a report based on a parameter query	Lesson 10

If You Want to Continue to the Next Lesson

▶ Double-click the Control-menu box on the Order Review report. Or, from the File menu, choose Close.

This closes the report, but it does not exit the Microsoft Access program.

If You Want to Quit Microsoft Access for Now

▶ Double-click the Control-menu box in the Microsoft Access window. Or, from the File menu, choose Exit.

This closes the table and exits the Microsoft Access program.

4 Customizing Your Forms

Using Controls to Show Text and Data

When you want a quick form with standard features, an automatic form that you create using Form Wizards is perfect. It is already formatted and prompts you for all the basic elements of a form. But what if you're looking for a form that provides a more custom fit? For example, you might want to add your own text, use colors to match your corporate look, or replace a standard field with a check box to make the form easier to use. All the tools you need are available in the Design view.

In this lesson, you'll learn how to add text and fields to a form, and you'll use the graphical tools available in Design view to enhance your form.

You will learn how to:

- Add a text label to a form.
- Change the size of text and the colors on a form.
- Add a field (bound control) to a form.
- Create a check box.
- Set the properties of a control.
- Align controls.

Estimated lesson time: 50 minutes

What Is a Control?

A *control* is a graphical object on a form or report that displays data, performs an action, or improves readability. The most common type of control used to display data from a field is called a *text box*. A text box can display text or numbers, and you can use it to type in new data or change existing data. Another type of control, called a *check box,* provides a graphical way to display Yes/No data. A third type of control, called a *label,* can display text that you use as a title for a form or to identify fields.

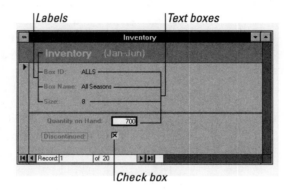

Microsoft Access provides many types of controls you can use to customize your forms, including lines, rectangles, and command buttons. It also provides controls that display lists of values, as well as pictures, graphs, or other objects.

Each control on a form is a separate object. This means that when you're working on the design of a form, you can select any control, drag it to another location on the form, resize it—even copy it onto the Clipboard and paste it onto a different form.

In addition, each control has a set of *properties,* such as its color and position on the form, that you can set to determine how the control looks and operates. In the previous illustration, for example, the Box Name text box has a gray background that matches the background of the form. In contrast, the Quantity On Hand text box has a white background. The background color of a text box is a property that you can set.

Start the lesson

▶ If Microsoft Access isn't started yet, start it and open the Sweet database. If the Microsoft Access window doesn't fill your screen, maximize the window.

Changing the Design of a Form

Before you create a form, it's a good idea to figure out the purpose of the form and plan how it should look and function. If other people will use the form, talk to them and find out how they'll use it. Will they change the data on the form or only view the data? Do they intend to print the form? What fields should the form include? How will you arrange the fields so the data is displayed most effectively? By planning your form carefully, you'll save time creating it.

Sweet Lil's is about to conduct its semi-annual inventory count. Herb, from the warehouse, stops by your office and asks you to design an online inventory form for him. He explains that his workers will use the form to update the quantity on hand of each box in inventory. "All we need on the form is the box ID code and the quantity on hand, so we can find the right box and update its quantity," says Herb. "Real simple. But can you make it look like all the other online forms? You know, with the blue and gray colors and everything?" You assure him that his inventory form will be exactly what he needs.

Create a form

You'll use a Form Wizard to create the basic form, and then switch to Design view to customize its appearance.

1   In the Database window, click the Form object button, and then click the New button.

The New Form dialog box appears. Since Herb's workers will use the form you're creating to change the data in the Quantity On Hand field in the Boxes table, you'll make Boxes the underlying table for the form.

2   In the Select A Table/Query list box, click the down arrow, select the Boxes table, and then click the Form Wizards button.

The first Form Wizards dialog box appears and asks which Wizard you want to use.

3   Double-click Single-Column.

The Form wizard then asks which fields from the Boxes table you want to include on the form.

4   Double-click the Box ID field and double-click the Quantity On Hand field to add them to the form. Then choose the Next button.

5   Select the Standard option for the form, and then choose the Next button.

6   For the title of the form, type **Inventory**, and then choose the Finish button.

The form opens in Form view. In Form view of a single-column form, you see the field name and the data from one record of the Boxes table.

7 From the File menu, choose Save Form. In the Form Name box, type **Inventory**, and then click OK.

Switch to Design view

You use Form view and Datasheet view to look at and change data. A form has one more view—Design view—that you use to look at and change the design of the form.

Design View

▶ Click the Design View button on the toolbar.

You might need to adjust the size of the Form window to display the information in the following illustration.

In Design view, you see the field
name instead of data in the field.

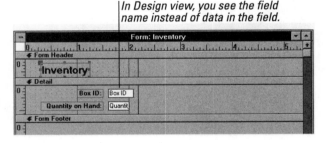

Notice that in Design view, the form is divided into three sections. When you're viewing data, the *form header* appears at the top of the window. In this form, the form header contains a label that shows the title of the form. The *detail* section makes up the main body of the form and contains the fields from the Boxes table. The *form footer* is empty, but you could add information to it that you want to appear at the bottom of the form when you're viewing data on screen and at the end of the form when you see it in print.

Adding a Label

A label is a control that contains text you want to display on the form. The text in the label doesn't come from a field; instead, you just type it right in the label control.

To add a label to a form, you use the Label tool in the *toolbox*. The toolbox contains a tool for every type of control you can use on a Microsoft Access form.

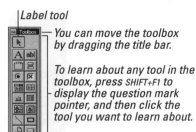

Label tool

You can move the toolbox by dragging the title bar.

To learn about any tool in the toolbox, press SHIFT+F1 to display the question mark pointer, and then click the tool you want to learn about.

When you switch to Design view for the first time, Microsoft Access displays the toolbox near the left side of the window. You can move the toolbox by dragging its title bar.

Toolbox

Note   If the toolbox isn't visible, click the Toolbox button in the toolbar.

Add a label

Label

Herb wants a label in the form header of the Inventory form that tells what period of time the inventory covers.

1   Click the Label tool in the toolbox.

2   Click in the form header to the right of the Inventory label.

Click inside this line, which marks the right edge of the form.

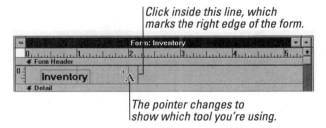

The pointer changes to show which tool you're using.

3   Type (**Jan-Jun**) in the label, and then press ENTER.

After you press ENTER, Microsoft Access selects the control. You can tell the control is selected because it has *sizing handles* around it. You can resize a control by dragging one of its sizing handles.

Sizing handles

You don't need to resize this control, but you might want to move it to a different position in the form header.

Move a control

If your new label covers part of the Inventory label, you can move the new label. You move a control by dragging it with the mouse.

1   Move the pointer over the edge of the selected label control.

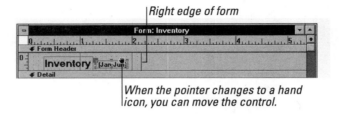

Right edge of form

When the pointer changes to a hand icon, you can move the control.

2   While the pointer is a hand icon, drag the control to the right, away from the Inventory label but still inside the right edge of the form. When the control is where you want it, release the mouse button.

Don't worry about aligning the labels exactly at this point—you'll learn about aligning controls later in this lesson.

Changing the Size of Text and Setting Colors

The toolbar that appears in Design view contains options you can use to set the size of text in a control and the colors used in a control.

These options appear when you select a control that contains text.

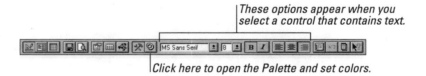

Click here to open the Palette and set colors.

For quick help on options on the toolbar, you can press SHIFT+F1, and then click the toolbar.

Change the text size and resize the label

If the toolbar isn't visible, the Built-In Toolbars Available option has been turned off. From the View menu, choose Options. In the General category, set the Built-In Toolbars Available option to Yes.

You'd like the text in your new label to be bigger than it is. To change the point size, you use the Font Size box on the toolbar.

1   Select the label and verify that the sizing handles are visible.

2   With your new label selected, set the Font Size box to 12 points. You can either type **12** in the box, or select 12 from the drop-down list.

Be sure the label is selected...

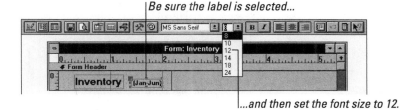

...and then set the font size to 12.

Note   If you click the label after it's already selected, Microsoft Access puts an insertion point inside the label so that you can edit its text. As long as the insertion point is inside the label, you can't change the point size. If that happens, click outside the label, and then click the label once to select it again.

After you change the text's font size, the label is no longer big enough to show all the text. There's a fast way that you can resize the control to make it fit the text perfectly.

3   From the Format menu, choose Size, and then choose To Fit.

Microsoft Access resizes the control so that it fits the new text size.

4   If necessary, move the label to create some space between it and the Inventory label.

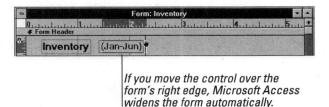

If you move the control over the form's right edge, Microsoft Access widens the form automatically.

Change a section's background color

Sweet Lil's corporate style calls for form headers to have a dark blue background with light gray text in the labels. Labels for fields are dark blue. To change your Inventory form so that it matches the corporate style, you'll select colors from the Palette. You use the Palette to change the appearance and colors of a control. To see an example of the corporate style, you can open the Bonbons form, then be sure to close the form.

1   Select the form header section of the Inventory form.

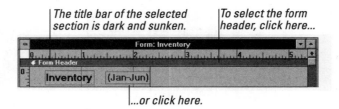

The title bar of the selected section is dark and sunken.

To select the form header, click here...

...or click here.

Palette

2 Click the Palette button on the toolbar. If the Palette covers a label, drag the Palette out of the way.

3 Select dark blue as the Back Color.

The background color of the form header changes to dark blue.

Change the color of text

You want to change the text in the labels in the form header to light gray. You can do both labels at once by selecting both controls.

1 Click the Inventory label to select it, and then hold down SHIFT and click the (Jan-Jun) label.

You can see handles on both labels indicating that they are both selected.

Click here...

...then hold down SHIFT and click here.

2 In the Palette, set the Back Color to dark blue and the Fore Color to light gray.

The colors of both labels are set to match.

3 Using the same method, change the Fore Color of the two labels for the Box ID and Quantity On Hand fields to dark blue.

Close the Palette and save your changes

You're finished changing colors for the time being, so you can close the Palette.

1   Close the Palette by clicking the Palette button on the toolbar.

2   From the File menu, choose Save to save your changes to the Inventory form.

Adding a Field (Bound Control)

When you want to display information from a field or add new data to a field, you use a *bound control*. A bound control is tied to a specific field in the underlying table or query. For example, the Box ID text box on the Inventory form is bound to the Box ID field in the Boxes table. In Form View, the control displays the box ID codes that are stored in the Box ID field.

After looking over the form you designed, Herb comes back with a request for modifications. His workers think the form would be easier to use if it displayed the box name and size as well as the box ID. Also, Herb says he needs a Discontinued field on the form so the workers can mark which boxes were discontinued during the past six months. You'll add three bound controls to the Inventory form, one for each of the three fields.

Make room for a new field

The detail section of the Inventory form that you created with the Form Wizard is only big enough for its two text boxes. You need to make room for the new fields.

1   Drag the lower border of the detail section downward to make the section taller.

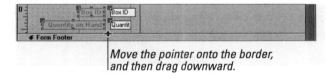

Move the pointer onto the border, and then drag downward.

Don't worry about its exact size for now; you can always adjust it again later if you need to.

You'll put a text box bound to the Box Name field right under the Box ID text box. You need to move the Quantity On Hand text box downward to make room.

2   If the Box ID and Quantity On Hand labels are both still selected, click on the form outside the labels to cancel the selection. Then drag the Quantity On Hand field to the lower portion of the detail section.

Notice that when the pointer becomes a hand icon, the Quantity On Hand label is *attached* to the text box—if you move one, the other moves as well.

Tip To move a text box without moving its label, position the pointer over the upper-left corner of the text box. The pointer changes to a pointing finger. Now drag the text box. It moves separately from its attached label. The special, larger handle on the upper-left corner of a control is called a *move handle*. You can use it to move either a control or its attached label independently.

Add a field

First, you'll add a text box that's bound to the Box Name field in the Boxes table. The easiest way to add a bound control to your form is to drag the field from the *field list* to the form. The field list lists the name of every field in the form's underlying table or query.

Field List

1 If the field list isn't visible, click the Field List button on the toolbar.

The field list includes every field in the Boxes table, which you selected as the Inventory form's underlying table. If the field list covers up part of your form, you can drag it to a new location.

2 Drag the Box Name field from the field list to the spot on the form where you want the field (not its label) to be.

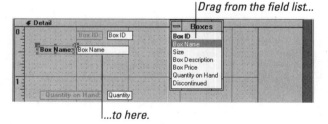

Drag from the field list...

...to here.

Microsoft Access creates a new text box where you drop the field, and it creates a label to the left of the field. Your new text box is bound to the Box Name field in the Boxes table.

3 Move the Quantity On Hand field upward so that it is just below the Box Name field.

Form View

4 Click the Form View button on the toolbar.

In Form view, the text box displays the name of the current box of chocolates. If you want, scroll through a few records to see the data in the text box change.

Design View

5 Click the Design View button on the toolbar to return to Design view.

Change the default appearance of a control

You probably noticed that the text in the label for the Box Name control is black. You can change it to blue to match the other controls; but what you'd really like is for Microsoft Access to automatically give every new label on this form blue text. You can do that by changing the default properties of labels.

Palette

1   To change the Fore Color of the Box Name label, click the label, and then click the Palette button on the toolbar. Set the Fore Color to dark blue.

Now you can use this label to determine how you want all new labels on this form to look.

2   With the Box Name label selected, from the F̲ormat menu, choose C̲hange Default.

Any new label on the form will now have dark blue text.

3   Close the Palette.

Add more fields

Add the Size and Discontinued fields to the form.

1   In the field list, click the Size field, and then hold down CTRL and click the Discontinued field.

2   Drag the two fields to the detail section of the form, and drop them below the Quantity On Hand field but above the bar for the Form Footer section. Notice that the labels for the new controls are dark blue.

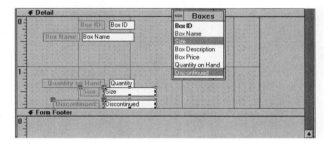

When you drop the fields on the form, Microsoft Access automatically makes the detail section taller if necessary to fit the two controls in the section.

3   Switch to Form view to see how your form looks. If some of the fields are hidden from view, from the W̲indow menu, select Si̲ze To Fit Form to view the complete form.

4   Switch back to Design view.

5   Rearrange the fields on the form so that Box ID, Box Name, and Size are on top, and Quantity On Hand and Discontinued are on the bottom, with a space between the two sets of fields.

Creating a Check Box

The Discontinued field in the Boxes table has a Yes/No data type. It displays the value of Yes or No in a text box. You realize you can make your form more graphical and easier to use by replacing the Discontinued text box with a check box. That way, the person using the form can simply click the check box to indicate that a box has been discontinued.

Create a check box

First you'll delete the Discontinued text box and its attached label. Then you'll replace it with a check box that's bound to the Discontinued field in the Boxes table.

1   Click the Discontinued text box to select it, and then press DELETE.

Be sure none of the other fields are selected; otherwise, they will also be deleted. Microsoft Access deletes both the text box and its attached label.

Tip   If you select the attached label and press DELETE, Microsoft Access deletes only the label. You can still delete the text box by selecting it and pressing DELETE.

Check Box

2   Click the Check Box tool in the toolbox.

3   From the field list, drag the Discontinued field from the field list to the lower portion of the detail section.

When you release the mouse button, Microsoft Access creates a check box that's bound to the Discontinued field.

Tip   If your check box's label says something like "Field19" instead of "Discontinued," that means it's not bound to the Discontinued field. Delete the label and the check box, and then try again. Be sure to select the Check Box tool first, and then drag the Discontinued field from the field list.

---

4   Switch to Form view and click the new check box to see how it works. Click it again to clear it, and then switch back to Design view.

Setting Properties

When you move a control or change its color, you're setting and changing properties of the control. You can set some properties, such as color and text size, by using tools on the toolbar. But to see and set all the properties of a control, you can use a *property sheet*.

There are two kinds of fonts: screen fonts, which display characters on the screen, and printer fonts, which you use to print your documents. You might want to use printer fonts if your printer has an installed font that is not in your software program. If you set the Layout For Print property setting to Yes, the toolbar displays the fonts and point sizes available for the printer you selected using the Print Setup command on the File menu.

Each control on a form has its own set of properties that determine how the control looks and operates. For example, the Control Source property of a bound control is the name of the field the control is bound to. You can bind the control to a different field simply by changing its Control Source property.

Each form section also has its own set of properties. When you changed the background color of the form header section, for example, you were changing one of that section's properties.

And finally, the form as a whole has a set of properties that relate to how the entire form looks and operates. For example, if you plan to print a form, you can set its Layout For Print property to Yes. Then Microsoft Access uses printer fonts instead of screen fonts for all text and data on the form.

To display the property sheet, you can click the Properties button on the toolbar. A quick alternative method is to double-click the object whose properties you want to display (if it's not an OLE object, such as a picture or graph).

You're ready to adjust the position of the controls on the Inventory form so that they line up with each other, and to use a property to further change the look of your form. First you'll set the GridX and GridY properties of the form so that it is easier to align the controls horizontally and vertically. Then you'll use the grid to position the controls precisely. Finally, you'll use a Property Builder button to change the border color of a text box.

Display form properties

Make changes to the properties in the property sheet.

1   Double-click the form background, outside the right edge of the form, or click the Properties button on the toolbar. Drag the property sheet to a convenient location on your screen.

Properties

*If you don't see the
right edge of the
form, enlarge the
window by dragging
the right border.*

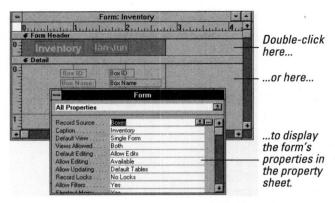

Double-click
here...

...or here...

...to display
the form's
properties in
the property
sheet.

The property sheet displays the properties of the form when the form is selected.
After the property sheet is open, you can display the properties of an individual
control or a section of the form by clicking on the form or section.

2 Display the properties for different controls and form sections to see how the
property sheet works. For example, click the Box ID text box to display its
properties, and then click the label attached to this text box to display the label's
properties. Click in the detail section (but not on a control) to display the section's
properties.

*For quick help on any
property, click the
property in the
property sheet, and
then press F1.*

3 After looking at a few different sets of properties, click the form background again
(outside the right edge) to display the form's properties.

Tip In a large form, you might find that the sections take up all the space on your
screen, and you don't have any form background to click to select the form. In these
cases, you can select the form by choosing Select Form from the Edit menu.

Change the grid settings

The grid marks on a form are small dots that show positions for alignment.

1 If you don't see the grid marks on your form, from the View menu choose Grid.

2 In the property sheet for the form, scroll downward until you see the GridX and
GridY properties.

The Form Wizard that created this form set each of these properties. These grid
settings make it easy for you to move controls by very small amounts using the
mouse. You'll change the fineness of the grid settings. Higher numbers indicate
greater fineness.

3 Look at the ruler above the form's header. If your default unit of measurement is
inches, change the GridX property to 8. If it's centimeters, change the property
to 3.5.

4 Change the GridY property to 10 (or 4 for centimeters).

5   Click outside the GridY box.

The new grid settings appear on the form.

Use a Property Build button to set properties

Some of the properties on the property sheet have a Build button that assists you in setting the property. When you select a property with a *builder*, you'll see the Build button (with three dots on it) to the right of the property box. A builder helps you perform a task for the selected item.

To make it easier to focus on the most important piece of information in the form, you can change the Border Color and Border Width properties to make the information stand out.

1   In the Inventory form, select the Quantity On Hand text box to display its property sheet.

2   In the property sheet, click in the Border Color text box to display the Build button to the right.

Build

3   Click the Build button.

The Color dialog box opens, giving you a choice of standard or custom-designed colors.

4   Click the dark blue color and then click OK.

5   Press ENTER to make the change and move to the next property.

The Border Color text box now displays the code number associated with the dark blue color that you selected for the Quantity On Hand text box.

6   To further emphasize the Quantity On Hand information, click the down arrow for the Border Width property and select **2 pt** from the list.

The Quantity On Hand text box has a more prominent border.

Aligning Controls

Microsoft Access provides a variety of tools that help you align controls. To align controls as you add and adjust them, you can use the rulers on the top and right side of the form in Design view, the grid itself, or the Snap To Grid command. To adjust controls after you've added them, you can use the Align command on the Format menu.

Turn on Snap To Grid

It's easier to align controls to the grid when Snap To Grid is on. To see whether this command is on, you'll look at it on the Format menu.

1   Choose the Format menu.

2   If Snap To Grid is not checked, choose it. If there is already a check mark next to Snap To Grid, close the menu.

Align controls vertically to the grid

You'll align the controls vertically so that there's one vertical *grid subdivision* between controls. There should be space between the controls. You should not see any of the dots that define the grid.

1   Select the Box ID text box and move it slightly in any direction.

Because the Snap To Grid command is on, the control moves from one grid point to another.

2   Move the Box Name text box so that there's one vertical subdivision between it and the Box ID text box. Then move the Size control so that there's one vertical subdivision between it and the Box Name text box.

3   Align the Quantity On Hand and Discontinued controls at the bottom of the detail section so that there's one subdivision of vertical space between them.

Align controls horizontally

Next you'll align the controls so that their left edges line up.

1   Click the first label (but not the text box itself), hold down SHIFT, and then click the remaining labels for all five controls on the form.

2· From the Format menu, choose Align, and then choose Left from the submenu.

The left edges of the labels align.

3   Select the Box ID, Box Name, and Size text boxes (the top three text boxes).

4   From the Format menu, choose Align, and then choose Left from the submenu.

The left edge of the text boxes align.

5   Align the left edges of the Quantity On Hand text box and the Discontinued check box.

6   Switch to Form view to see how your changes look, and then switch back to Design view and save the form.

One Step Further

Your Inventory form is coming together—just a few more adjustments and it will be perfect.

Make the background for a text box invisible

You want the data in the Box ID, Box Name, and Size text boxes to appear in Form view as though they're directly on the form background, not in a box. This is a visual cue to the people using the form that they don't change the data in these fields. The Palette has all the tools you need.

1   Select the Box ID text box, and then hold down SHIFT while selecting the Box Name and Size text boxes.

Palette

2   Click the Palette button on the toolbar.

3   Click the light gray color on the Palette as the Back Color.

4   To make the border invisible, click the lower Clear button on the Palette so that it appears depressed.

The border will still be visible in Design view.

5   Switch to Form view to see how the form looks with data on it.

Left-align number data in a text box

Sweet Lil's boxes come in three sizes: 8 ounces, 12 ounces, and 16 ounces. By default, Microsoft Access right-aligns the numbers in a text box. You'd rather have the number in the box appear left-aligned so that it lines up with the text in the Box ID and Box Name text boxes.

1   Switch to Design view.

2   Select the Size text box.

You can change the alignment in the property sheet or with a toolbar button. The alignment buttons are available on the toolbar only when an object containing text is selected on the form. If you don't see the buttons, be sure the Size text box is selected.

You'll use the Left Alignment button, but you'll see the change take place in the property sheet.

3   In the Size text box property sheet, scroll downward until you see the Text Align property.

Left Alignment

4   Click the Left Alignment button on the toolbar.

Notice that the Size text box is left-aligned and that the Text Align property box now displays Left

5   Close the property sheet.

6   To see how a number in the box looks, switch to Form view.

Draw a line on a form

Sweet Lil's corporate style uses a heavy gray line to separate groups of fields. The gray lines on the form help group related fields visually. You'll draw a line between the first three fields and the last two fields on the Inventory form.

1   Switch the Inventory form to Design view, and verify that the Palette is open.

2   Open the Bonbons form to see an example of the heavy gray dividing lines. Then close the Bonbons form and select the Inventory form.

3   Select the Line tool in the toolbox.

Line

4   Below the Size field, drag across the form to create a line as wide as the form.

5   Use the Palette to set the line's width to 2 pt and Border Color to dark gray.

6   To make the window fit the form exactly, switch to Form view, and then from the Window menu, choose Size To Fit Form.

Tip   If the Size To Fit Form command isn't available on the Window menu, check to see if your form is maximized. If it is, click the Restore button in the upper-right corner of the title bar so that your form is no longer maximized, and then choose the Size To Fit Form command.

---

7   Save the Inventory form.

If You Want to Continue to the Next Lesson

▶   Click the Control-menu box on the Inventory form. Or, from the File menu, choose Close.

This closes the form, but it does not exit the Microsoft Access program.

If You Want to Quit Microsoft Access for Now

▶   Double-click the Control-menu box in the Microsoft Access window. Or, from the File menu, choose Exit.

This closes the table and exits the Microsoft Access program.

Lesson Summary

To	Do this	Button
Create a form	In the Database window, click the Form object button, and then choose the New button. In the Select A Table/Query list box, select the table on which to base the form. Select the wizard you want, and then select the fields from the table to include on your form. Select a format and title for the form, and then choose the Finish button.	
Name and save a form	From the File menu, choose Save Form. Name your form, and then click OK.	
Add a label to a form	Click the Toolbox button to display the toolbox. Click the Label tool in the toolbox, and then click on the form to place the label. Type the text you want to appear in the label.	A

To	Do this	Button
Move a control	Move the pointer over the edge of the control until the hand icon appears. Drag the control where you want it.	
Change the size of text displayed in a control	Select the control and be sure the sizing handles are visible. Then change the size in the Font Size box on the toolbar.	
Resize a label so it exactly fits its text	Select the label. From the Format menu, choose Size, and then choose To Fit.	
Change an object's color or a line's width	Select the object, and then click the Palette button to open the Palette. Select the Fore Color or Back Color and line width you want.	
Add a field (bound control) to a form	Click the Field List button on the toolbar to display the field list, and then drag the field from the field list to the form.	
Change the default properties of a type of control	Select a control that has the properties you want for the new default properties. From the Format menu, choose Change Default.	
Create a check box bound to a Yes/No field	Select the Check Box tool in the toolbox, and then drag the Yes/No field from the field list to the form.	
Display the property sheet	Select the object whose properties you want to display, and then click the Properties button on the toolbar. *or* Double-click the object to display its properties.	
Set properties	Display the property sheet. Locate the property you want to change, and then type over or modify the value in the property box. If a Build button appears when you click in the property box, click the button, and then make your changes.	
Turn on Snap To Grid	From the Format menu, choose Snap To Grid, if it is not already selected.	

To	Do this
Align controls	Be sure Snap To Grid is on, and then drag one or more controls to align them. *or* Select one or more controls. From the Format menu, choose Align, and then choose from the submenu.

For more information on	See
Adding controls to a form	Chapter 15, "Designing Forms" in *Microsoft Access User's Guide*
	Chapter 16, "Customizing Forms" in *Microsoft Access User's Guide*
Setting the properties of controls	Chapter 5, "Customizing Your Form" in *Microsoft Access Getting Started*
	Chapter 15, "Designing Forms" in *Microsoft Access User's Guide*
Aligning controls	Chapter 5, "Customizing Your Form" in *Microsoft Access Getting Started*
	Chapter 16, "Customizing Forms" in *Microsoft Access User's Guide*

For online information about	From the <u>H</u>elp menu, choose <u>S</u>earch and then type
Adding controls	controls: adding
Customizing controls	controls: customizing
Aligning controls	controls: aligning
Changing properties of a Control	controls: properties
Using the grid	grid

Preview of the Next Lesson

In the next lesson, you'll learn how to add pictures to your form's design and how to add a control bound to a field that contains pictures or other OLE objects.

Using Pictures and Other Objects

A picture might be worth a thousand words—but only if it's where people can see it. You can put pictures, graphs, and other objects created in other applications on your Microsoft Access forms and reports. For example, you can put your company's logo on a report next to a graph showing company sales. In addition, you can store objects in tables in your database and display the objects on a form similar to the other data in the table.

In this lesson, you'll learn how to put a picture on a form, and you'll learn how to create a control that displays objects stored in a table.

You will learn how to:

- Add a picture to a form.

- Add a control (object frame) that displays an object from a record.

- Make an object that's stored in a table fit in its frame.

Estimated lesson time: 20 minutes

Understanding OLE

An *OLE object* is any piece of information created with a Windows-based application that supports *object linking and embedding* (OLE). With the OLE features in Microsoft Access, you can place OLE objects—such as pictures, sounds, and graphs—on your forms and reports, and you can store objects as data in your tables. In addition, OLE makes it easy to edit these objects directly from the form or report.

When you place an object on a form or report, it's displayed in a control called an *object frame*. Microsoft Access provides two kinds of object frames—unbound and bound. A *bound object frame* displays a picture, graph, or any OLE object that is stored in a table in a Microsoft Access database. An *unbound object frame* is not bound to a table, such as a picture created and stored in Microsoft Paintbrush.

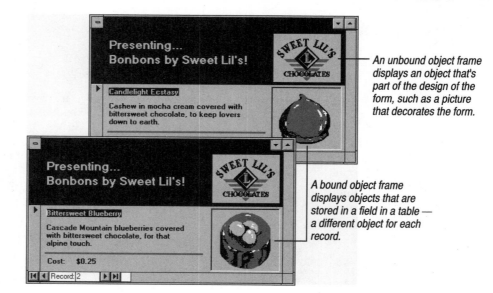

An unbound object frame displays an object that's part of the design of the form, such as a picture that decorates the form.

A bound object frame displays objects that are stored in a field in a table — a different object for each record.

You can either embed or link an object in an object frame. When you *embed* an object, Microsoft Access stores the object in your database file. You can easily modify the object from within Microsoft Access. If the object came from another file, only the embedded object in your database is changed, not the object in the original file.

On the other hand, when you *link* an object, Microsoft Access doesn't put the object in the object frame; instead, it creates a link to the object's source file (the file in which the object was created) in the frame. You can still look at the object and make changes to it on the form or report, but your changes are saved in the object's source file, not in your database file.

In this lesson, you'll create an unbound object frame and embed a picture in it. You'll also create a bound object frame that displays pictures stored in the Bonbons table. You won't be linking any objects in this lesson. For more information about linking, see Chapter 19, "Using Pictures, Graphs, and Other Objects," in the *Microsoft Access User's Guide.*

Start the lesson

▶ If Microsoft Access isn't already started, start it and open the Sweet database. If the Microsoft Access window doesn't fill your screen, maximize the window.

Adding a Picture to a Form

An outside vendor wants to package Sweet Lil's bonbons in his own products, and it's your job to present the bonbons to him in their best light. In your presentation to the vendor, you'll use an online form that displays information about each of Sweet Lil's bonbons. The Sweet database already has a form called Presenting Bonbons with some of the right data on it, but the form could use a little more visual appeal.

Open a form in Design view

You'll start by adding Sweet Lil's logo to the form header of the Presenting Bonbons form. To add a picture to the design of the form, you must be working in Design view.

1 Click the Form object button in the Database window.

The Presenting Bonbons form is near the bottom of the Forms list.

2 Select the Presenting Bonbons form, and then choose the Design button.

The form opens in Design view.

3 If the form window isn't large enough to display all of the detail section, resize it to make it bigger.

Add a picture

The Sweet Lil's logo is in a Paintbrush file named LOGO.BMP. You'll add an unbound object frame to the form header of the Presenting Bonbons form, and then embed the logo in the frame.

Object Frame

If the toolbox isn't displayed, from the View menu, choose Toolbox. If the Toolbox command isn't on the View menu, be sure you're in Design view.

1 Click the Object Frame tool in the toolbox to create space for an unbound object. (Be sure you do not click the Bound Object Frame tool, which looks similar.)

If you clicked in the form header, the unbound object frame would appear in the default size. Since the default size is a lot bigger than Sweet Lil's logo, you'll draw the control instead.

2 Drag the pointer to create a square-shaped control that fits in the form header beside the title.

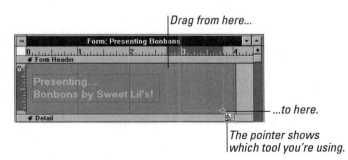

Drag from here...

...to here.

The pointer shows which tool you're using.

Don't worry about the exact size of the square; you can adjust it later after the picture is embedded.

If you wanted to draw the logo now, you'd double-click Paintbrush Picture, and Paintbrush would start with an empty drawing area.

When you release the mouse button, the Insert Object dialog box appears.

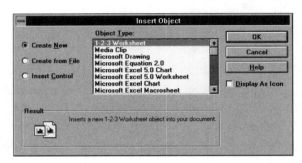

Since your logo already exists in a file, you'll tell Microsoft Access which one to use.

3   Select the Create From File option.

A box appears for you to type in the name of the file you want to use.

The LOGO.BMP file was copied to your PRACTICE directory when you copied the practice files to your hard disk.

4   If the File box does not show the PRACTICE directory, use the Browse button to locate the directory.

5   Double-click LOGO.BMP, and then click OK.

The logo is embedded into the object frame on your form.

6   From the Format menu, choose Size, and then choose To Fit.

The object frame is sized so that it fits the logo perfectly.

Look at the picture in Form view

The logo will appear on the form of each record.

Form View

1   Click the Form View button to see how the logo looks with a record of data.

2   Move from record to record on the form.

Because the logo is embedded in the design of the form, it appears on the form background for every record.

3   Switch back to Design view.

Start Paintbrush to edit the picture

As you saw when you worked with properties in Lesson 11, a handy way to display the properties of most controls is to double-click the control. But when you double-click a Paintbrush picture, Microsoft Access starts Paintbrush instead of displaying the property sheet.

1   Double-click the logo.

Paintbrush starts and displays the logo in its window. If you want, you can use Paintbrush to change the logo, but you don't have to make changes to continue with this lesson.

2   When you're finished looking at or editing the picture, from the File menu of Paintbrush, choose Exit & Return To Presenting Bonbons.

If you changed the picture, Paintbrush asks if you want to update it in Microsoft Access. You can update the picture with your changes (choose Yes) or discard your changes (choose No). Because the picture is embedded rather than linked, changes you make are saved only in the picture on the form, not in the LOGO.BMP file.

Tip   To display the properties of an unbound object frame, first select the frame, and then click the Properties button on the toolbar.

Adding a Control That Displays a Picture from a Record

The Bonbons table includes a field named Picture that contains pictures of Sweet Lil's bonbons. You'll add a control to the detail section of the Presenting Bonbons form that displays the pictures in Form view.

Add a bound object frame to a form

Your control will be bound to the Picture field, so you'll use the Bound Object Frame tool.

Bound Object Frame

1   Select the Bound Object Frame tool in the toolbox.

Tip   Here's an easy way to remember which tool is for the bound object frame and which is for the unbound object frame. Notice that the picture on the tool for the bound object frame includes some letters at the top, similar to an attached label. You can think of those letters as the name of the field that the control is bound to. When you create a bound object frame, Microsoft Access adds an attached label to the frame, just as it does when you create a text box.

---

2 Drag the pointer to create a square-shaped control that fits in the right side of the detail section.

When you release the mouse button, Microsoft Access creates a bound object frame with an attached label. You don't need the label, so you'll delete it.

3 Click the attached label, and then press DELETE.

Bind the object frame to the Picture field

In Lesson 11, you learned how to create a control that's bound to a field by dragging the field from the field list to the form. Now you'll learn another way to bind a control to a field—by setting the Control Source property of the control.

1 If the property sheet isn't displayed, double-click the new bound object frame to display its properties. If the property sheet is displayed but shows the properties for another control, click the bound object frame.

You will bind the object frame to the Picture field, that contains the pictures of the bonbons.

2 In the property sheet, select the Control Source box, click the down arrow, and then select Picture from the list of fields.

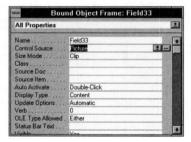

Look at the data

Do you know why a picture of a bonbon didn't appear in the bound object frame after you bound it to the Picture field? The answer is clear when you think about which view of the form shows the data from the table. You're looking at the form in Design view, but the pictures of bonbons aren't part of the form's design. They're part of the data in the Bonbons table.

1 Switch to Form view and, if necessary, move to the first record.

The picture for Candlelight Ecstasy appears as the first bonbon in the table.

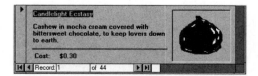

2   Move to the next record in the table.

Now the control displays the picture for Bittersweet Blueberry.

Edit the picture

You use the same method to modify a picture in a bound control as in an unbound control—except that you do it in Form view, where the data is displayed, rather than in Design view.

For steps on adding a new bonbon, including its picture, to the Bonbons table,see Lesson 2, "Getting the Best View of Your Data."

1   In Form view, double-click the picture of the Bittersweet Blueberry bonbon.

Paintbrush starts and displays the picture in its window. If you want, you can use Paintbrush to change the picture, but you don't have to make changes to continue with this lesson.

2   When you're finished looking at or editing the picture, from the File menu in Paintbrush choose Exit & Return To Presenting Bonbons.

If you changed the picture, Paintbrush asks if you want to update it in Microsoft Access. Choose Yes to update the picture with your changes, or choose No to discard your changes. If you update the picture, your changes are saved in the Bonbons table.

3   Look at a few more records, and then switch back to Design view.

Only the first five bonbons and a few bonbons that appear later in the table have pictures. In the other records, the Picture field is empty.

Making an Object from a Table Fit in a Frame

If the pictures of bonbons don't fit in your bound object frame exactly, you might see an empty white area on the edge of the frame (showing that the frame is too big), or the frame might cut off a portion of the picture (showing that it's too small).

With an *unbound* object frame, such as the logo in the form header, you can choose commands from the Format menu to fit the picture exactly to the frame. However, this doesn't work for a *bound* object frame, because the objects displayed in the frame could be different sizes. In the Bonbons table each picture is the same size, but bound objects don't have to be the same size. You could have a tiny picture in one record and a very large one in the next.

To choose the best way to display an object in its bound object frame, you set the frame's Size Mode property. The Size Mode property has three possible settings:

- *Clip* displays as much of the object as will fit in the frame with no changes to the size of the object and no distortions. This is the default setting.

- *Stretch* enlarges or shrinks the object to fit the size of the frame. This might distort the proportions of the object, especially if its size is quite different from the frame's size.

- *Zoom* enlarges or shrinks the object to fit the frame as well as it can without changing the proportions of the object.

Scale the picture to fit the control

Because your frame is close to the same size as the pictures in the Bonbons table, you can set the Size Mode property to Stretch, and each picture will fit the frame with a minimum of distortion.

1   In Design view, set the Size Mode property of the bound object frame to Stretch.

2   Switch to Form view.

Microsoft Access scales the picture so that it fits in the frame perfectly.

3   Switch back to Design view.

Give the object frame a sunken appearance

Give the object frame for the Picture field one more visual touch.

Palette

1   With the object frame selected, click the Palette button on the toolbar, if it is not already selected.

2   In the Palette, click the Sunken Appearance button.

Click here to give the frame a sunken look.

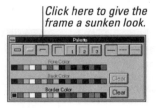

3   Switch to Form view to see how the form looks now.

4   To size the form's window so it fits the form, from the <u>W</u>indow menu, choose Si<u>z</u>e To Fit Form.

The form looks great—you're ready for your presentation.

5   Save the Presenting Bonbons form, and then close it.

One Step Further

So far, all the examples in this lesson use pictures that were created and saved before you put them on your form. You can also create an object at the same time you embed it. You'll embed your own drawing of a bonbon in the Picture field in the Bonbons table.

Add your own bonbon picture

Pictures of bonbons are stored in the Bonbons table. You can use the Presenting Bonbons form to add your own picture of a bonbon to the table.

1 Open the Presenting Bonbons form in Form view. Go to a record that doesn't have a picture (such as the sixth record).

2 Click the empty Picture field, and then from the Edit menu, choose Insert Object.

3 In the list box, double-click Paintbrush Picture.

4 Paint your picture of a bonbon, or just put a piece of sample text in a box (for example, **Delicious!**), and then close Paintbrush to return to Microsoft Access.

Your picture or text appears in the object frame.

Tip   Because the control's Size Mode property is set to Stretch, the entire Paintbrush work area is scaled to fit in the control. For that reason, your picture might appear very small. Either change the Size Mode property to Clip before choosing Insert Object, or paint a larger picture.

---

5 Save your changes.

The picture you drew in the Bonbons table is saved.

If You Want to Continue to the Next Lesson

▶ Double-click the Control-menu box on the Presenting Bonbons form. Or, from the File menu, choose Close.

This closes the form, but does not exit the Microsoft Access program.

If You Want to Quit Microsoft Access for Now

▶ Double-click the Control-menu box in the Microsoft Access window. Or, from the File menu, choose Exit.

This closes the table and exits the Microsoft Access program.

Lesson Summary

To	Do this	Button
Add an unbound object frame to a form or report	In Design view, select the Object Frame tool in the toolbox. Draw an object frame on the form. To create a new object, double-click the type of object you want in the Insert Object dialog box. If the object already exists in a file, choose the Create From File option and type or select the name of the file.	
Size an unbound object frame to fit the object it contains	In Design view, select the object frame. From the Format menu, choose Size, and then choose To Fit.	
Add a bound object frame to a form or report	In Design view, select the Bound Object Frame tool in the toolbox. Draw an object frame on the form. Set the Control Source property of the object frame to the name of the field that contains the objects. To view, edit, or add objects, switch to Form view.	
Modify a Paintbrush picture on a form or report	For an unbound object, double-click the object in Design view. For a bound object (stored in a table), double-click the object in Form view. Make your changes, and then from the File menu, choose Exit & Return.	
Scale an object so it fits in a bound object frame	In Design view, set the Size Mode property of the bound object frame to Stretch.	

For more information on	See in *Microsoft Access User's Guide*
Using OLE objects on forms and reports	Chapter 19, "Using Pictures, Graphs, and Other Objects"

For online information about	From the Help menu, choose Search and then type
Adding a bound frame to a form	object frame: bound
Adding a unbound frame to a form	object frame: unbound
Fit objects in a frame	pictures: scaling and sizing

Preview of the Next Lesson

In the next lesson, you'll learn how to create a form that shows information from two tables at the same time. The form will show information about both the customer and each order the customer has placed.

Showing Related Records on a Form

Arranging and presenting data efficiently are keys to making a database easy to use. A customer's phone number is in one table; the orders that the customer placed are in another. When you call the customer, you want to see a list of the customer's orders along with the customer's name and number.

You can design your forms to display data any way that it is most useful to you. In this lesson, you'll learn how to create a form that shows one record at the top (such as a customer's record) and related records in a subform at the bottom (such as a record for each order the customer placed). You'll also learn how to create a command button that opens another form with information that you need.

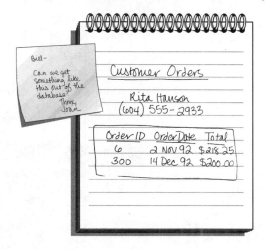

You will learn how to:

- Create a form with a subform.
- Create a command button that opens a form.

Estimated lesson time: 20 minutes

Creating Two Forms That Work Together

You might want to work with a form that requires information from more than one table, or from a table and a query. To do that, you use a form with a *subform*. A subform is a form within a form. By using a subform, you can combine information so that you don't have to switch back and forth between separate tables or forms.

In most cases, the subform is linked to the main form, so that it shows records that are related to the record on the main form. For example, the Boxes form in the Sweet database shows information about a box of bonbons. The subform, which lists the bonbons in the box, is linked to the main form.

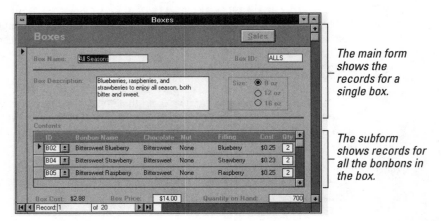

The main form shows the records for a single box.

The subform shows records for all the bonbons in the box.

A subform is saved as a separate form in the database. The form that appears as the subform on the Boxes form is named Boxes Subform. If you open this form separately, apart from the Boxes form, it shows all the bonbons in the database.

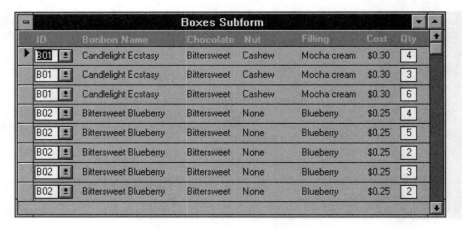

In this lesson, you'll create a form that shows customer information on the main form —the customer's name and phone number—and displays a list of the customer's orders on a subform. If one customer placed ten orders, you'll see all ten orders listed under the customer's name.

Start the lesson

▶ If Microsoft Access isn't started yet, start it and open the Sweet database. If the Microsoft Access window doesn't fill your screen, maximize the window.

Creating a Form with a Subform

The easiest way to create a form with a subform is to use the Main/Subform Form Wizard. This Form Wizard creates both forms and makes them work together. It can even link the two forms automatically as long as both of these conditions are met:

- The main form is based on a table.

For details about creating relationships between tables, see Lesson 8, "Relating Tables."

- The subform is based on a table that's related to the main form's table; or the subform is based on a table or query that contains a field with the same name and data type as the primary key of the main form's table.

In the example you create in this lesson, the main form is based on the Customers table, so the first condition is met. The primary key of the Customers table is the Customer ID field.

The subform is based on a query named Orders With Subtotals that also includes a Customer ID field, so the second condition is met. This query contains information about a customer's orders that you want to display on the subform.

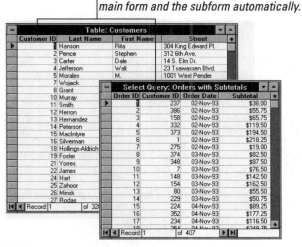

Microsoft Access uses the Customer ID fields in the underlying table and query to link the main form and the subform automatically.

Note   If the two conditions for automatically linking a main form and a subform are not met, you can still link the two forms yourself. Both the underlying table or query for the main form and the underlying table or query for the subform must still contain *linking fields*—fields that have the same value for linking records. For details on linking the forms yourself, see Chapter 17, "Creating Forms Based on More Than One Table" in *Microsoft Access User's Guide*.

Start the Main/Subform Form Wizard

When you use a Form Wizard to create a form with a subform, you need to select the underlying table or query for both the main form and the subform. You select the underlying table or query for the main form in the New Form dialog box. Later, as you work with the Main/Subform Form Wizard, you'll select the underlying table or query for the subform.

1   In the Database window, click the Form button to display the list of forms, and then choose the New button.

The New Form dialog box appears.

2   In the Select A Table/Query box, select the Customers table, and then choose the Form Wizards button.

3   In the list of Form Wizards, select Main/Subform, and then choose OK.

Enter information in the Form Wizard dialog boxes

When you use a Form Wizard, you work with a series of dialog boxes. Each of the following steps tells you what to enter in each dialog box. After completing each step through step 4, choose the Next button to go to the next dialog box.

1   Under View, select the Queries option. From the list, select the Orders With Subtotals query as the underlying query for the subform.

Be sure to choose the Next button after each step through step 4.

2   Add these fields to the main form in this order: First Name, Last Name, State/Province, and Phone.

3   Add these fields to the subform: Order ID, Order Date, and Subtotal.

4   Select the Standard look for the form.

5   Change the title of the form to **Customers and Orders**, and then choose the Finish button.

You will see a message about saving the subform. Microsoft Access creates two forms: the main form and its subform. The subform must be named and saved before Microsoft Access can put it on the main form.

6   Choose the OK button when you see the message. Type **Customers and Orders Subform** for the name, and then press ENTER.

Microsoft Access creates the Customers And Orders form, and the form opens.

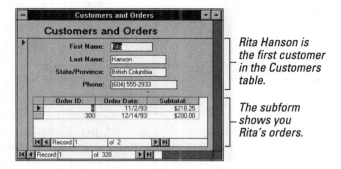

Rita Hanson is
the first customer
in the Customers
table.

The subform
shows you
Rita's orders.

See how the form works

The subform is automatically linked to the main form. To see how this works, look at some other customer records.

1   Go to the next customer record, using the navigation buttons at the bottom of the Form window.

The records in the subform change to display the current customer's orders.

Design View

2   On the toolbar, click the Design View button to switch to Design view.

In Design view, you can see the controls on the main form and one large control for the subform. The subform control has properties that link the records on the subform to the appropriate record on the main form.

3   If the property sheet isn't displayed, click the Properties button on the toolbar to display it.

Properties

4   Select the control for the subform to display its properties.

These matching
fields link the record
on the main form
with the record on
the subform.

5   Click outside the subform control to cancel the selection.

A subform doesn't have to be seen in Datasheet view. To see and modify the subform itself, you'll need to open it in Design view.

6   Double-click the subform control to open the subform in Design view.

Notice that the Form Wizard put a text box on the form for each field you selected from the subform's underlying query. The Form Wizard also set the form's Default View property to Datasheet. Datasheet view is appropriate for this subform because it displays all the related records in a list.

7 Close the subform.

8 Save and close the main form, and name it **Customers and Orders**.

Creating a Command Button to Open a Form

You can add a command button to a form to automatically open another form that contains information you want to check.

The Operations department wants a fast way to tell what the shipping charge is for a particular order. You use the Command Button Wizard to add a button to the Customers And Orders form. By using the button, you can open the Shipping form and look up the cost of each shipper to a particular destination.

Create an Open Form command button with a Wizard

The Customers And Orders form contains all the information about what each customer has ordered.

1 Open the Customers And Orders form in Design view.

2 In the toolbox, click the Control Wizards tool, if it isn't selected. (The tool is selected if it looks like the button is pressed down.)

Control Wizards

3 In the toolbox, click the Command Button tool.

Command Button

4 Click the location on the Customers And Orders form, such as in the header, where you want to place the upper-left corner of the button.

The first Command Button Wizard dialog box appears.

5 In the Categories box, select Form Operations.

6 In the When Button Is Pressed box, select Open Form, and then choose the Next button.

Choose a form to open

The Shipping form has the details about what shippers charge for each destination. After completing each step through step 4, choose the Next button to go to the next dialog box.

1 Select the Shipping form.

You created the Shipping form in Lesson 7.

2 Select the "Open the form and find specific data to display in it" option.

3 To show which fields contain matching data, select the State/Province field from the Customers And Orders table, select the Ship State/Province field from the Shipping table, and then click the double-arrow button.

4 Select the Text option, select the text "Open Form," and then type **Ship Charge**

5 Name the button **Ship Charge,** and then click the Finish button.

The Customers And Orders form appears in Design view including the new Ship Charge command button.

Use the command button

The Ship Charge command button is ready to use.

1 Switch to Form view.

2 Click the Ship Charge command button to open the Shipping form.

Notice that the state or province destination in the record showing on the Customers And Orders form matches the destination of the Shipping form.

3 Go to another record on the Customers And Orders form.

4 Click the Ship Charge command button.

The record on the Shipping form changes to show the shipping charge for the new destination.

5 Save the Customers And Orders form, and then close both the Customers And Orders form and the Shipping form.

One Step Further

The First Name and Last Name text boxes on the Customers And Orders form are bound to the First Name and Last Name fields in the Customers table. But suppose you want to show a customer's first name and last name together in one text box.

To do that, you use a *calculated* control. A calculated control is tied to an expression instead of a field. The expression can combine text values from more than one field in the underlying table or query, or it can perform calculations on values from the fields.

For more information about expressions, see the Appendix, "Using Expressions."

To tie a text box to an expression, you type the expression in the text box in Design view. Always start the expression with an equal sign (=).

Add and delete controls

You'll replace the First Name and Last Name text boxes on the Customers And Orders form with one text box that shows both names. Start by deleting the two bound text boxes.

1 Open the Customers And Orders form in Design view.

2 Select the First Name and Last Name controls at the same time by holding down SHIFT, and then clicking each text box.

3 Press DELETE to delete the First Name and Last Name text boxes and their labels.

4 In the toolbox, click the Text Box tool to add an unbound text box to the form.

Text Box

5 Click in the Detail section where you want the upper-left corner of the text box (not its attached label) to be.

A text box appears that is not bound to any field in the Customers table. It has a generic label such as "Field10."

Tie a text box to an expression

A text box that is bound to a field displays the field name in Design view. To bind a text box to an expression instead, you type the expression in the box. You'll use the "&" operator in the expression to display one text value followed by another.

1 Move the pointer over the text box. When the pointer turns into a vertical line, click in the text box.

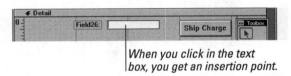

When you click in the text box, you get an insertion point.

2 Type =**[First Name]** & " " & **[Last Name]** in the text box, and then press ENTER.

Be sure to start the expression with an equal sign, and put a space between the two quotation marks in the expression so that there's a space between the first and last name.

This expression tells Microsoft Access to...

=[First Name] & " " & [Last Name]

...display the value in the First Name field... | *...followed by a space...* | *...followed by the value in the Last Name field.*

In an expression, you place brackets around field names and double quotation marks around a space or other text characters.

Form View

3 Click the Form View button on the toolbar to switch to Form view and see the results.

The full name appears in the text box.

4 Switch back to Design view.

Enhance the form's appearance

When you added the text box to the form, Microsoft Access gave it a default label, such as Field10. You'll replace the text in the label with something more descriptive.

1   Click the text box's attached label to select it, and then position the pointer over the label until it turns into a vertical line.

2   Double-click the generic label to select it.

3   Replace the text in the label with **Customer Name**

The size of the label adjusts to fit the new text.

4   Switch to Form view. From the Window menu, choose Size To Fit Form so that the window fits the form.

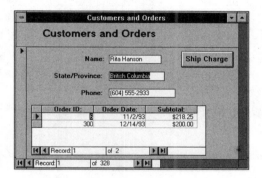

5   Save the form.

If You Want to Continue to the Next Lesson

▶   Double-click the Control-menu box on the Customers And Orders form. Or, from the File menu, choose Close.

This closes the form, but it does not exit the Microsoft Access program.

If You Want to Quit Microsoft Access for Now

▶   Double-click the Control-menu box in the Microsoft Access window. Or, from the File menu, choose Exit.

This closes the table and exits the Microsoft Access program.

Lesson Summary

To	Do this	Button
Create a form with a subform	In the Database window, click the Form object button and then click the New button. Select the table or query that contains the data you want on the main form. Choose the Main/Subform Form Wizard. Answer the questions in the Form Wizard dialog boxes.	
Create an Open Form command button with a Wizard	Click the Control Wizards button in the toolbox, and then click the Command Button tool. Click on the form to position the button. In the Categories box, select Form Operations and then select Open Form from the list of actions. Then follow the directions in the Button Wizard dialog boxes.	
Use a command button on a form	Click the command button in Form view.	

For more information on	See in *Microsoft Access User's Guide*
Creating a form with a subform	Chapter 17, "Creating Forms Based on More Than One Table"
Using Form Wizards	Chapter 17, "Creating Forms Based on More Than One Table"
Creating a Command Button	Chapter 16, "Customizing Forms"

For online information about	From the Help menu, choose Search and then type
Creating forms with subforms	subforms: creating
Creating a command button	command button: creating

Preview of the Next Lesson

In the next lesson, you'll learn how to make your forms easier to use by providing choices in lists and option groups.

Making Data Entry Easy and Accurate

The information you get from your database is only as good as the data you put into it. Forms are where most information is added into your database. Ensuring that the entries on a form are accurate is essential if you are to get the information you need from your database. By making forms easy to use and by preventing certain types of data from being changed, you can help to make data entry go faster and reduce the possibility of errors.

When looking up customer information on a form, you might find it easier and friendlier to identify the customer by a name rather than by a number. If you can pick the name from a list instead of typing it, that's even more convenient and it ensures that the value entered in the table is correct. But Microsoft Access can find a customer's information faster if you give it the customer's ID number instead of the name. How do you design your form so that it is easy to use, finds information as quickly as possible, and guarantees that the data you enter is accurate?

The answer is to design a list box or combo box on your form that lets you select a name but that tells Microsoft Access the ID number associated with the name. In this lesson, you'll learn how to create a combo box that displays customer names in a list, and then stores the selected customer's ID number in a field.

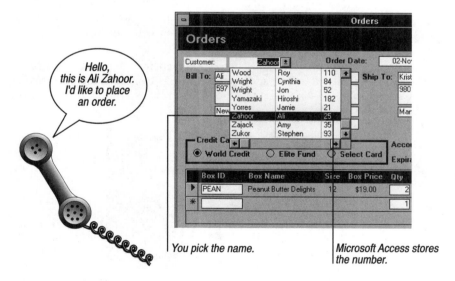

You pick the name.

Microsoft Access stores the number.

Even with forms that allow you to select items from a list, there are still ways that errors can be made. When writing today's date, you might accidentally put down the previous year instead of this year. When viewing data on a form, you could inadvertently change or erase a value in a field. How do you protect your data from everyday mistakes like these?

In this lesson, you'll learn how to display a value such as today's date automatically, so you don't have to type it yourself. You'll design a control so that it automatically displays a message if you enter invalid data in it. You'll also learn to set a property so that data is required in a field.

You will learn how to:

- Create a combo box control.
- Base a combo box on a query.
- Change the tab order of controls on a form.
- Set an initial (default) value for a control.
- Require data in a field.
- Validate data entered in a control.

Estimated lesson time: 40 minutes

How Controls and Properties Protect Your Data

Choosing data from a list in a combo box or a list box makes data entry fast and accurate. By changing the properties of a table or form to limit the information that can be entered into a field, you can also also make entering information easy and safe from error.

Microsoft Access has two types of controls that provide a list of choices you can scroll: list boxes and combo boxes. Because looking up a value in a list is often easier and quicker than remembering the value you want, these controls can make your forms easier to use and can prevent mistakes.

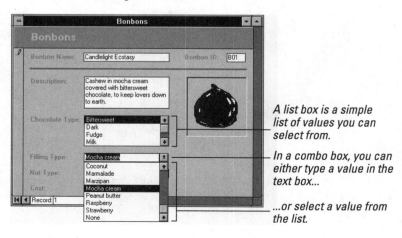

A list box is a simple list of values you can select from.

In a combo box, you can either type a value in the text box...

...or select a value from the list.

The list in a list box or combo box consists of a number of rows of data. Each row can have one or more columns. You specify which column contains the data you want stored in the field, and you can use other columns to display data, such as full names, that help you pick the right row. A list can be based on a table or a query.

To further protect your data, you can give a control a default value, which appears automatically in a field.

In addition to setting a default property, you can set properties that will:

- Describe what data is correct for a control by setting the control's Validation Rule property.

- Display a message that tells you how to fix an incorrect entry by setting the control's Validation Text property.

- Prevent changes from being made to data on a form by setting the form's Default Editing and Allow Editing properties.

Start the lesson

▶ If Microsoft Access isn't already started, start it and open the Sweet database. If the Microsoft Access window doesn't fill your screen, maximize the window.

Creating a Combo Box

When operators take new telephone orders for Sweet Lil's chocolates, speed and accuracy are their top priorities. To make their job easier, you plan to make several enhancements to the online form they use.

Currently, operators enter the ID number of the customer placing the order in a text box on the Orders form. You'll replace the text box with a combo box that shows a list of customer names as well as their ID numbers.

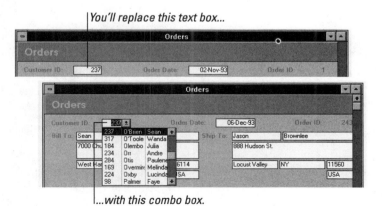

You'll replace this text box...

...with this combo box.

In many cases, the best way to define the list is to create a separate query that selects and arranges the data just the way you want it to appear in the list. Then you can tell Microsoft Access to use the fields in the query as columns in the list.

Look at the Customer List query

In this case, you want the list to show the last name, first name, and ID number of each of Sweet Lil's customers. You could create a new query that includes these fields, but the database already contains a query named Customer List that has exactly the data you want. Before creating your combo box, take a look at the Customer List query you'll use to define the rows that will be displayed in the combo box's list.

1 In the Database window, click the Query object button, and then open the Customer List query in Design view.

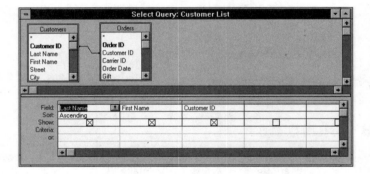

As you can see, this query is based on the Customers table and the Orders table. The Customer ID field links the two tables.

2 Look at the Customer List query in Datasheet view to see how the information appears.

3 Close the Customer List query.

Delete a text box

Before adding the combo box, make room for it by deleting the Customer ID text box and its label.

1 Click the Form object button, and then open the Orders form in Design view.

2 If the Orders form window is too small for you to see all its controls, resize the window to make it larger.

3 Click the Customer ID text box, and then press DELETE.

The Customer ID text box and its label are deleted.

Create a combo box bound control

Your combo box on the Orders form will be bound to the Customer ID field in the Customer List query. When an operator selects a customer from the combo box list on the form, Microsoft Access will store the customer's ID number in the bound field in the table.

Toolbox

Field List

Control Wizards

Combo Box

To create a bound combo box, you select the Combo Box tool in the toolbox and then drag the field you want from the field list to the form. The Combo Box Wizard will guide you through the creation process.

1   Be sure the toolbox and the field list are visible. If the toolbox isn't visible, click the Toolbox button on the toolbar. If the field list isn't visible, click the Field List button on the toolbar.

2   Be sure the Control Wizards button is selected in the toolbox.

3   In the toolbox, click the Combo Box tool.

Now when you drag the Customer ID field from the field list, Microsoft Access creates a combo box that's bound to the field.

4   Drag the Customer ID field from the field list to just above the First Name field on the form.

When you release the mouse button, the first Combo Box Wizard dialog box appears.

Create a combo box list

The Combo Box Wizard guides you through the creation of the combo box list for your form. Click the Next button after each of the following steps, through step 6.

1   In the first Combo Box Wizard dialog box, be sure the option is selected that will look up values in a table or query.

2   Under View, select the Queries option, and then select the Customer List query.

3   From the Available Fields list, move the Customer ID, Last Name, and First Name fields for the columns in your combo box.

4   Double-click the right edge of each column header to adjust the column width to its best fit.

5   Select Customer ID as the column which contains the data you want to store in your table.

6   Be sure that the option to store the value in the Customer ID field is selected.

7   Customer ID automatically appears as the choice for the label for your combo box. This is the label you want, so click the Finish button to complete the combo box.

The Orders form has a combo box bound to the Customer ID field.

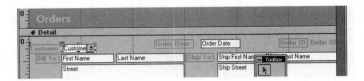

Use the combo box

You can immediately see how using the combo box makes looking up a customer's ID easy.

1   Switch to Form view.

2   Click the down arrow on the combo box and select any name from the list.

The customer ID number appears in the Customer ID field.

Place a control in the right tab order

When you switched to Form view, the Order Date field was automatically selected. To make the Customer ID field selected whenever you open the form, you can change the tab order of the Orders form. The *tab order* of a form is the order in which the insertion point moves through fields when you tab from field to field in Form view.

When you create a new control, Microsoft Access puts the new control last in the tab order of the form, regardless of where you place the control on the form. You'll edit the tab order of the form so that the new Customer ID combo box you just created is first in the tab order, not last.

1   Switch to Design view, and then select the Customer ID combo box control, if it is not already selected.

2   From the Edit menu, choose Tab Order.

The Tab Order dialog box appears.

3   Scroll downward in the list of controls until you see the Customer ID control, which is last in the list.

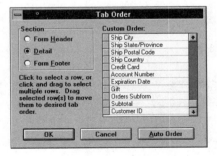

4   Click in the left column to select the Customer ID control, and then drag it to the top of the list.

5 Choose the OK button.

Now your new control is first in the tab order, where it belongs.

6 Switch to Form view to test the tab order.

7 Save the Orders form.

Setting an Initial (Default) Value for a Control

Customer orders are the heart of Sweet Lil's business—a mistake on an order can mean lost revenue and lost customers. You plan to enhance the Orders form so that it will help ensure that the data on the form is correct. You'll give the form's Order Date text box a default value so that the operators don't have to type the date themselves.

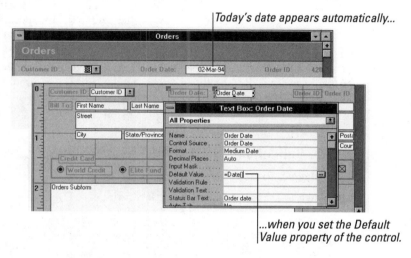

Today's date appears automatically...

...when you set the Default Value property of the control.

You can set the Default Value property either to an expression or to a constant value, such as text or a number. In this case, you'll set it equal to an expression that includes the Date function. The Date function is a small program that retrieves the current date from the system clock in your computer.

Display today's date in a text box

Enter the expression in the property sheet of the Orders form.

1 Switch to Design view for the Orders form.

2 If the property sheet isn't displayed, click the Properties button on the toolbar. Then click the Order Date text box to display its properties.

Properties

3 In the Default Value property box, type the expression **=Date( )**

4 Switch to Form view.

Since Microsoft Access enters the default value when you start a new record, you'll go to a new record to see your property setting work.

5 Click the Last Record and Next Record navigation buttons at the bottom of the form to move to a new blank record.

A new record appears with today's date in the Order Date text box.

Validating Data Entered in a Control

You've seen how to make data entry easier and more accurate by setting default values. You can also protect your data by adding a validation rule to a control. A validation rule checks the data that you enter in the control against a rule that you define. You can create an error message that automatically appears if the data doesn't meet the rule's requirements so that incorrect data won't be saved in your table.

For example, operators enter the expiration date of the customer's credit card in the Expiration Date text box on the Orders form. If the date entered has passed, you can display a message alerting the operator that the card has expired. You do this by setting a validation rule that requires the date entered to be greater than or equal to today's date. You'll also write an error message that tells the operator what to do if the card has expired.

Set the Validation Rule and Validation Text properties

Make changes to the Order form's property sheet.

1 Switch to Design view for the Orders form.

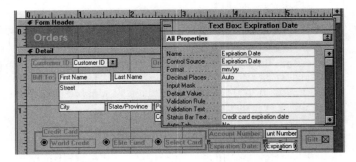

2 Display the properties of the Expiration Date text box.

3 In the Validation Rule property box, type the expression **>=Date( )**

4   Click in the Validation Text property box. Since the message you will type is long, press SHIFT+F2 to display the Zoom box so that you can see all your text as you type.

5   Type the following message:

Credit card has expired! Choose the OK button, and then press Esc. Pick a different card or cancel the order.

Your validation text message can be up to 255 characters long.

6   Choose the OK button to close the Zoom box.

Type the
validation
message
here.

Test your validations

Now try to enter an expired date and see what happens.

1   Switch to Form view, and move to the first record.

2   In the Expiration Date text box, change the value to **11/93**

3   Press TAB.

Your error message appears.

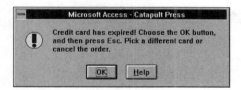

4   Choose the OK button to clear the message.

5   Press ESC to replace 11/93 with the original value in the text box.

Now you can enter a different credit card or cancel the order.

6   Save and close the Orders form.

Requiring Data Entry in a Field

Setting properties on a form makes forms easier to use and more accurate. But they control only the individual form where you made the settings. You might want the data in a field always to follow certain rules, no matter what form uses it. To do this, you can set the properties in the table that contains the field you want to affect.

If you had set the Validation Rule and Validation Text properties on the Orders table instead of on the Orders form, all forms containing the Expiration Date field would contain the same validation rules. You can still change or delete the validation rule on an individual form if you want.

The Required property is another field property you can set in a table that affects all forms using that field. If the Required property is set to Yes, you *must* enter a value in that field or any control bound to that field.

For example, when you use the Subscription form, you might want to require that a customer's address always contains a postal code so that shipping isn't delayed.

Set the Required property

The Subscription form is based on the Customers table, so you will set the Required property of the Customers table. While you're changing the design of the Customers table, you can't open the Subscription form in Form view. However, you can open it in Design view.

1   In the Database window, click the Table object button and open the Customers table in Design view.

2   Click in the Postal Code field.

3   In the Field Properties section of the table design, change the Required field to **Yes**

From now on, you cannot save a record with a *null value*, meaning that this field must contain information.

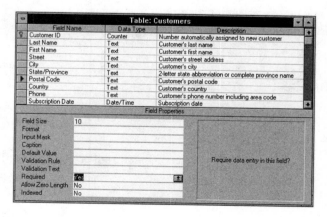

4   Close the Customers table.

5   Choose the Yes button to save the changes.

A message appears asking if you want to check the existing data to be sure it follows the new validation rule. If you don't check the data, you could have records that have null values in this field.

6   Choose the Yes button to test the existing data with the new rule.

If any records violate the rule, another message box appears to warn you.

Test the Required property

Try to enter a record in a form, without a postal code.

1   In the Database window, click the Form object button, and then double-click the Subscription form to open it in Form view.

2   Enter the following record:

Matthew Wilson
1876 Parker Lane
Wilshire, MD

3   Leave the Postal Code field blank and tab to the next field.

4   Select the option boxes for 6 months and Renewal.

5   Try to tab to a new record.

A message appears telling you that this field cannot be a null value, which means that it cannot be empty.

6   Choose the OK button.

7   Enter a postal code of **17634** for the current record.

8   Close the form.

One Step Further

Besides being able to protect your data from incorrect entries, you can set properties of forms so that data cannot be entered at all. To do this, you make a form read-only and you make the menu choice for making edits unavailable.

Make a form read-only

The Presenting Bonbons form in the Sweet database is used in presentations of Sweet Lil's product line to outside vendors. To prevent inadvertent changes to the data, you'll make the form read-only, so that it is not possible to make any changes to data on the form.

1   Open the Presenting Bonbons form in Design view.

Properties

2 If the property sheet isn't visible, click the Properties button on the toolbar.

3 To display the form's property sheet, click inside the Form window but outside the border of the form.

4 Set the form's Default Editing property to Read Only.

5 Switch to Form view and try to change data on the form, such as the bonbon name or the cost.

You can't edit, add, or delete records now.

Disallow editing of a form permanently

While you are in Form view, you can choose the Allow Editing command from the Records menu to allow edits to occur. Change the property settings so that changing data is not possible in Form view.

1 Click the Records menu. Notice that the Allow Editing command is black, which means it is available.

2 Choose Allow Editing.

Notice that a check mark appears. Editing is now possible again. You might not want a data entry person to select this option from the menu.

You can make the Allow Editing choice unavailable by setting another property.

3 Switch back to Design view, and then set the Allow Editing property of the form to Unavailable.

This affects the Allow Editing command on the Records menu in Form view.

4 Switch to Form view, and then click the Records menu. Notice that the Allow Editing command is not available.

This prevents anyone who is entering data in Form view from making changes to your data. If you change your mind, you can switch to Design view, and then reset the properties.

5 Save the Presenting Bonbons form.

If You Want to Continue to the Next Lesson

▶ Double-click the Control-menu box on the Presenting Bonbons form. Or, from the File menu, choose Close.

This closes the form, but it does not exit the Microsoft Access program.

If You Want to Quit Microsoft Access for Now

▶ Double-click the Control-menu box in the Microsoft Access window. Or, from the File menu, choose Exit.

This closes the form and exits the Microsoft Access program.

Lesson Summary

To	Do this	Button
Use a Wizard to create a combo box bound to a field	In the form's Design view, click the Control Wizard button and the Combo Box tool in the toolbox. Then drag the field from the field list to the form. Answer the questions in the Wizard dialog boxes.	
Use a combo box on a form	In Form view, click the down arrow on the combo box and select from the list.	
Put a control in the right tab order	In a form's Design view, select the Edit menu, and then choose Tab Order. Drag the fields into the order you want.	
Display today's date in a text box for new records	In the form's Design view, set the text box's Default Value property to this expression: **=Date( )**	
Set an initial (default) value for a control	In the form's Design view, set the control's Default Value property. You can set the property to text, a number, or an expression.	
Check the value entered in a control, and then display a message if it's incorrect	In the form's Design view, set the control's Validation Rule and Validation Text properties.	
Require that data is entered in a field	In the table's Design view, set the Required property to Yes.	

For more information on	See in *Microsoft Access User's Guide*
Creating combo boxes	Chapter 15, "Designing Forms"
Setting default values and validation rules for controls on a form	Chapter 15, "Designing Forms"
Setting field properties in a table	Chapter 8, "Changing and Customizing Tables"

For online information about	From the <u>H</u>elp menu, choose <u>S</u>earch and then type
Creating combo boxes	combo box: creating
Setting default values for controls on a form	control properties
Setting validation rules for controls on a form	validation: rules and text
Requiring that data is entered in a field	requiring data entry

Preview of the Next Lessons

In Part 5 you'll learn how to use a Report Wizard to create a quick report. You'll also learn how to modify the report in Design view to show groups of records. You'll create a report that includes groups and subtotals for each group. Then you'll customize the report by adding descriptive text for each group, calculating a percentage for each group, and changing the sort order.

Review & Practice

In the lessons in Part 4, you learned to customize forms with controls, such as buttons and pictures. You created a combo box to make data entry easier, and you learned how to ensure the accuracy of your data. The Review & Practice section that follows gives you a chance to practice some of the ways you can customize your forms.

Part 4   Review & Practice

Now that you know how to add controls to a form, you can make other forms in the Sweet database easier to use, and at the same time ensure the accuracy of the data that goes on them.

Scenario

Word has traveled throughout Sweet Lil's about the capability of making forms more usable. Several departments have realized that when forms are easier to use information can be entered and retrieved more quickly. In addition, easy-to-read forms are good presentation tools for company meetings and for customers. You agree to enhance several forms to improve company communications.

You will review and practice how to:

- Add a label to a form.
- Add a bound control to a form.
- Add a picture to a form.
- Create a form with a subform.
- Create a command button.
- Create a combo box on a form.
- Set properties to protect your data.

Estimated practice time: 30 minutes

Step 1: Add a Label to a Form

The Marketing department would like to make it easy to identify and work with data that is collected on a form. Add a label to the Boxes Sales form to make it more descriptive, and change a color on the form to make it better looking.

1 Open the Box Sales form in Design view.

2 Use the Label tool from the toolbox to create a label control in the header of the form.

3 Type **4th Quarter** in the label.

4 Use the Palette to change the foreground color to light gray to match the form's title.

5 Resize the label so that the text is easy to read.

For more information on	See
Adding a label to a form	Lesson 11
Changing the size of a control	Lesson 11
Using the Palette	Lesson 11

Step 2: Add a Bound Control to a Form

It would be convenient to see the box size as you enter data about Sweet Lil's bonbons. You add a bound control to the Boxes Sales form to easily see the weight of each box of candy. You then make the new bound control match the format of the others on the form. You also change the field's name so that if you ever refer to it in another form or query it has a logical name.

1   Make room on the Boxes Sales form to place a new field just below the box name field and above the gray line that separates the main form and the subform.

2   Drag a field from the Field List to create a bound control for the size of the box.

3   Since the largest size box is 12 ounces, resize the new Size text box so that it is an appropriate size for up to two digits.

4   Change the Caption property of the Size label to **Box Size**

5   Switch to Form view to check your enhancements. If necessary, adjust the label size.

6   In Design view, select the Box Size label and change its Fore Color property to dark blue.

7   Change label's Name property to **Box Size** instead of the default field number.

8   Close the Boxes Sales form and save your changes.

For more information on	See
Adding a bound control to a form	Lesson 11
Setting the properties of a control	Lesson 11

Step 3: Add a Picture to a Form

The Human Resources department has learned that you can add pictures to forms in the Sweet database. They plan to add employees' photographs in the future, but for now, they want to upgrade the Employees form with the company logo.

1   Open the Employees form in Design view.

2   Use the Object Frame tool to create space for the logo in the form's header.

3   Embed the LOGO.BMP file from the PRACTICE directory into the object frame.

4   Size the logo to fit in the frame, and then look at the picture in the frame in Form view.

5   Return to Design view and set the Name property to Company Logo.

6   Close the form and save your changes.

For more information on	See
Adding a picture to a form	Lesson 12
Sizing an embedded object	Lesson 12

Step 4: Create a Form with a Subform

The Shipping department would like to be able to see at a glance what a carrier charges for a particular destination.

Create a form with a subform to check the list of charges for each shipper.

1   Create a new form based on the Carriers table.

2   Use the Main/Subform Form Wizard to create a subform based on the Shipping table.

3   Add the Carrier ID, Carrier Name, and Delivery Method fields to the main form.

4   Add the Ship State/Province and Shipping Charge fields to the subform.

5   Name the main form **Carriers Charges** and the subform **Ship Charge Subform**

6   Close both forms.

For more information on	See
How two forms work together	Lesson 13
Creating a form with a subform	Lesson 13

Step 5: Create a Command Button

The Presenting Bonbons form is being well received as a tool to show bonbons to vendors. But some people immediately want more information about each bonbon. You create a command button on the Presenting Bonbons form to open the Bonbons form.

1   Open the Presenting Bonbons form in Design view.

2   Create a command button on the Presenting Bonbons form using the Command Button and Control Wizards tools.

3   Set the command button to open the Bonbons form with specific data in it.

4   Select the Bonbon Name field as the field that contains matching data.

5   Type **Bonbon Details** as the text on the button. Give the same name to the button.

6   Switch to the Form view of the Presenting Bonbons form to try the new button.

7   Close both forms and save your changes to the Presenting Bonbon forms.

For more information on	See
Creating a command button	Lesson 13

Step 6: Create a Combo Box on a Form

The Orders Subform contains a text box in which operators type the ID code of the box the customer wants. The control is bound to the Box ID field in the Order Details table. It would be easier for operators if they could select the code from the list and if they could see the full name of the box. The Box List query displays fields the way you would like the combo box to appear.

1   Open the Orders Subform form in Design view.

2   Delete the Box ID text box in the detail section.

3   Use tools from the toolbar to replace it with a combo box bound to the Box ID field, and then start the Combo Box Wizard.

4   Define the list so that it displays the values from the Box List query.

5   Delete your new combo box's attached label and resize the combo box so that it fits in the space.

6   Set the tab order of the subform so that the Box ID combo box is first.

7   Close the Orders Subform and save your changes.

8   Open the Orders form and test the combo box. Then close the Orders form.

For more information on	See
Creating a combo box on a form	Lesson 14
Setting the tab order of a form	Lesson 14

Step 7: Set Properties to Protect Your Data

You want to create a number of different order forms, all feeding data to the Orders table. You want the current date to appear on every form, and you want to be sure that a credit card's expiration date must be a future date.

1 Open the Orders table in Design view to set default values affecting the Order Date control.

2 Set the Default Value property of the Order Date field so that the field's default value is today's date.

3 Select the Expiration Date field, and then set its Validation Rule property so that the date entered into this field cannot be a date in the past.

4 Type a message for the Validation Text property to inform the person entering the data that the expiration date is invalid and to instruct them what to do.

5 Save the Orders table.

For more information on	See
Setting default values for a control	Lesson 14
Validating data entered in a control	Lesson 14

If You Want to Continue to the Next Lesson

▶ Double-click the Control-menu box on the Orders table. Or, from the File menu, choose Close.

This closes the form, but it does not exit the Microsoft Access program.

If You Want to Quit Microsoft Access for Now

▶ Double-click the Control-menu box in the Microsoft Access window. Or, from the File menu, choose Exit.

This closes the table and exits the Microsoft Access program.

Part

5 Customizing Your Reports

Creating a Quick Detail Report

How do you get a quick report that shows off your data in print? You might want a sales report to take to a meeting right away or an attractive list of products for a prospective customer. Ideally, you'd like to create a great-looking report in a few minutes—a report that looks like it was designed by a professional.

A Report Wizard can do most of the work for you. As you have done with other wizards, you can answer a series of questions to build a professional-looking report. You can use the report as is, or you might want to touch it up and add a few custom details.

In this lesson, you'll learn how to create a simple detail report with a Report Wizard. You'll preview the report, and then switch to Design view to make a few changes.

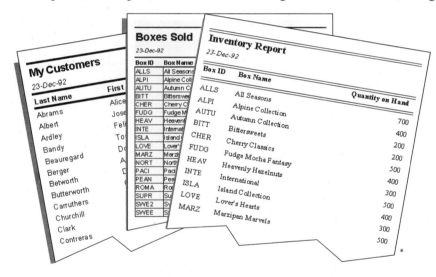

You will learn how to:

- Use a Report Wizard to create a detail report.
- Preview and print a report.
- Understand and change the design of a report.
- Show groups of records by hiding duplicates.

Estimated lesson time: 30 minutes

What Is a Detail Report?

Although you can print a table or query directly, you can take a little more time and create a report that presents your information in an easier-to-read, more professional-looking format. A *detail report* displays the same essential information you see when you print a table or query, but it contains additional elements, such as *report headers*, *page headers*, and *page footers*.

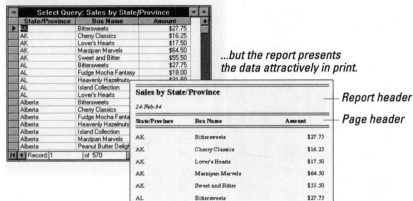

The query displays the raw data...

...but the report presents the data attractively in print.

Report header

Page header

In this lesson, you'll create a detail report. In the following lesson, you'll learn how to create a *grouped report*, which combines your data into groups and calculates totals or other information for each group.

As you learned in Lesson 5, the fastest way to create a report is with a Report Wizard. A Report Wizard places fields on the report and presents the data in one of several presentation styles. After you've created the report, you can customize it.

Start the lesson

▶   If Microsoft Access isn't started yet, start it and open the Sweet database. If the Microsoft Access window doesn't fill your screen, maximize the window.

Creating a Detail Report

Sweet Lil's is planning new advertisements that promote the most popular boxes of bonbons. At a meeting with other people from the Marketing department, you plan to hand out a report that shows sales by state or province. You don't need anything elaborate—just an easy-to-create, easy-to-read report.

Decide which Report Wizard to use

The two reports in the following illustration show the differences between a Single-Column and a Tabular report. The Single-Column report displays the data in one long column, while the Tabular report uses a more compact format and presents the data in a table.

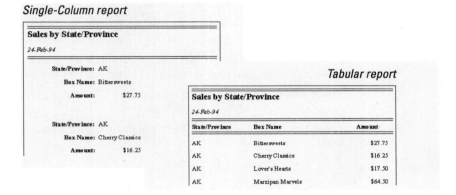

Single-Column report

Tabular report

Begin a new report

The Sales By State/Province query in the Sweet database contains the records you need for this report.

1   In the Database window, click the Report object button, and then choose the New button.

The New Report dialog box appears.

2   In the Select A Table/Query box, select the Sales By State/Province query.

3   Choose the Report Wizards button.

4   In the Report Wizards dialog box, select Tabular, and then choose the OK button.

The first dialog box appears.

Enter information in the Report Wizard dialog boxes

When you use a Report Wizard, you go through a series of dialog boxes. Each of the following steps shows you how to enter information in one dialog box. The first dialog box lists the available fields from the Sales By State/Province query, and asks which fields you want to include on the report.

1   Add all three available fields to the report, and then choose the Next button.

2   When you're asked which fields you want to sort by, add State/Province first, and then add Box Name. Then choose the Next button.

This means that the report will first sort the state and province names alphabetically, and then it will sort the box names within each state or province.

3   When you're asked what style you want for your report, verify that Executive is selected, and then choose the Next button.

4   Leave the title unchanged, and then click the Finish button to see how your report will look when you print it.

Your report appears in Print Preview.

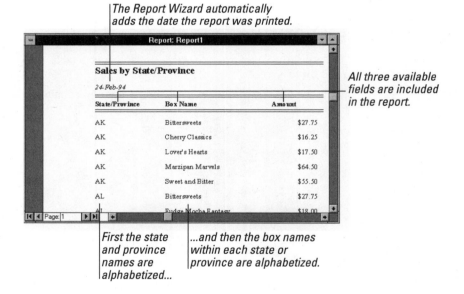

The Report Wizard automatically adds the date the report was printed.

All three available fields are included in the report.

First the state and province names are alphabetized...

...and then the box names within each state or province are alphabetized.

5   Check which view you have of your report by clicking the File menu and looking at the list.

Print Preview has a check mark next to it.

Note   The look of the text in your report might differ from that in the illustration, depending on the printer that is selected.

6   Save the report, and name it **Sales by State/Province**

Previewing and Printing a Report

By previewing your report, you can make sure you've designed it the way you want before you print it. After you create the Sales by State/Province report, the report is magnified.

Change the picture size in Print Preview

Use the magnifying glass pointer to switch between viewing data in a magnified view and seeing the layout of the entire page.

1   To see the whole page, click anywhere on the report.

A reduced view appears so that you can see the whole page.

2   To return to viewing data, click the report again.

Move from page to page

Move around the report to see how the information is laid out.

▶   Use the navigation buttons at the bottom of the window to page through your report.

Print the report

If your system is set up for printing, try printing the report now. Since this is a long report, you will print a sample page to view the report.

1   From the File menu, choose Print.

2   Click the Pages option.

3   To print just the first page, in the From box, type **1**, and in the To box, type **1** again.

4   Choose the OK button.

Exploring the Design of the Report

As you preview the report, you can see how Microsoft Access displays the records from your query along with added information that makes the report easier to read. If you page through this report, you'll see:

■   A *report header* at the top of the first page of the report that includes the title of the report and today's date.

■   A *page header* at the top of every page of the report that displays the heading for each column of data.

- The *detail* area, between the page header and the page footer, displays the records from the Sales by State/Province query, which you selected as the report's underlying query when you created the report.

- A *page footer* at the bottom of every page of the report. In this case, the page footer shows the page number.

- A *report footer* at the very end of the report. For this report, the report footer shows the total sales amount.

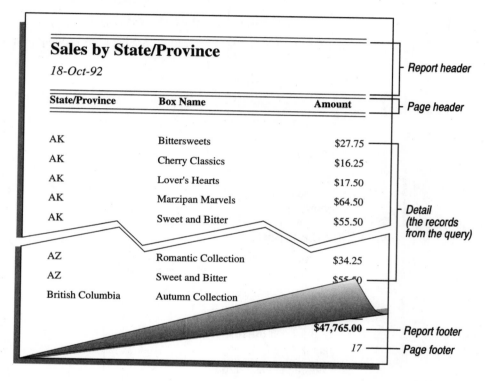

Return to Design view

Design view is a blueprint for the report.

Close Window

1   When you have finished previewing or printing the report, click the Close Window button on the toolbar, and then close the Report window.

2   Be sure that the Sales By State/Province report is selected in the Database window, and then click the Design button.

The report appears in Design view.

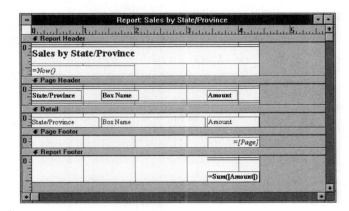

3 If the Report window is too small for you to see all the controls, resize the window to make it larger.

In Design view, the different sections represent the elements you saw in Print Preview. The report design shows how to display each element when you preview or print the report. The detail section in Design view shows how the records from the underlying table or query should look. When you look at the report in Print Preview, you'll see many records, each formatted as shown in Design view.

Note   When you have the report open in Design view, you can print by choosing Print from the File menu. You can also print a report from the Database window. First select the report, and then click the Print button.

Move the design tools out of the way

When you switch to Design view, the toolbox and the property sheet might cover up part of the report. You'll use these design tools to customize your report. For now, though, you might want to move them so you can see the report better.

Toolbox

1 If the toolbox is not visible, click the Toolbox button on the toolbar. If the property sheet is not visible, click the Properties button on the toolbar.

2 Drag the title bars of the toolbox and the property sheet to move them to a more convenient location.

Properties

Identify the elements created by the Report Wizard

These are some of the tasks a Report Wizard does for you:

- Creates the sections on your report.

- Places the data and other information in the appropriate sections.

- Aligns the columns and adds some decorative lines to create an attractive report.

- Selects fonts and font sizes for all the text on the report.

- Adds today's date to the report header.

- Adds an expression to calculate the total in the report footer.

You can build a report from scratch that contains all of these elements. But you can often save hours if you start with a Report Wizard, and then customize the report after the Report Wizard creates it.

When you created the Sales By State/Province report, the Report Wizard did a lot of work behind the scenes.

▶ Based on the above list, find each item on your report that the Report Wizard created for you automatically.

Customizing the Design of a Report

It took only a short time to create this report, and it attractively presents the data you need for your meeting. There are a few minor things you'd like to change, though. Working in Design view, you'll:

- Change the text in the Amount label so it's more descriptive, and move the label so it lines up better with the sales values below it.

- Add some information to the page footer.

Change the label in the page header

1 In the Page Header section, select the Amount label.

2 Move the pointer to the left of the word "Amount" so the pointer appears as an I-beam, and then click the mouse button.

3 Type **Sales** followed by a space, and then press ENTER.

Move the label

1 Drag the Sales Amount label to the right edge of the white area under Page Header.

2 Click the Print Preview button on the toolbar to see how your changes will look on the printed report.

Print Preview

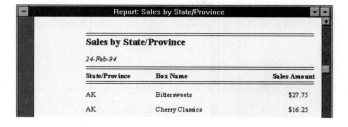

The Sales Amount label now appears directly above the sales values.

Add more information to the page footer

To help other Marketing personnel understand the purpose of the report, you'll add a footer to each page of the report.

Close Window

1 Click the Close Window button on the toolbar to switch to Design view.

2 In the toolbox, click the Label tool.

Label

3 Click in the left-hand side of the Page Footer section to add the label.

4 In the new label, type **Data for Marketing Quarterly Meeting**, and then press ENTER.

The label appears in bold type—the default font style for labels in this report. You want the label to be italic and not bold, like the page number in the page footer.

Bold

5 While the label is still selected, click the Bold button on the toolbar to cancel bold formatting for the text.

6 Click the Italic button on the toolbar to make the text italic.

Italic

7 Click the Print Preview button on the toolbar to view the report.

You'll see the page footer at the bottom of every page.

Hiding Duplicates to Show Groups of Records

What's wrong with the report? When you look down the left side, you see the name of the state or province repeated over and over. You only need to see each name once for each group. In Lesson 16, you'll learn how to create a grouped report, which will solve this problem. But for the report you're working on now, there's another quick way to fix this.

As the report is now, Microsoft Access displays data for the State/Province field even if this field contains duplicate values. You can change the Hide Duplicates property for the State/Province text box so that duplicate values are shown only once.

Hide the duplicate values

Close Window

1 Click the Close Window button on the toolbar to switch to Design view.

2 In the detail section, select the State/Province text box.

3 In the property sheet, change the setting of the Hide Duplicates property to Yes.

Print Preview

4 On the toolbar, click the Print Preview button to switch to Print Preview.

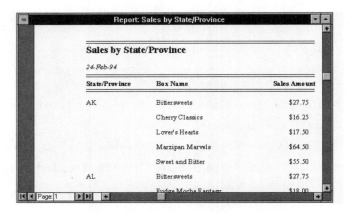

Each state or province appears only once on the report.

5   Save the report and close it.

One Step Further

An international gourmet food company is interested in ordering large quantities of individual bonbons from Sweet Lil's. The international company's representative wants a report that shows all of Sweet Lil's bonbons categorized by chocolate type. Since the representative wants it immediately, you want to make a report as fast as possible.

In Lesson 10, you used the AutoReport Wizard to create a report based on a query. You can create this new report even more quickly by using the AutoReport button on the toolbar, then you can customize the AutoReport feature to choose the type of report you use most often.

Create a report with the AutoReport button

1   In the Database window, select the Chocolate Types query.

AutoReport

2   Click the AutoReport button on the toolbar.

A report based on the Chocolate Types query is created automatically and appears in Print Preview.

3   Click the report to see a whole page at once.

The report is in Executive style. You would like a slightly different look for the report.

4   Since you want to change how an AutoReport is formatted, close the report but do not save it.

Change the default format of an AutoReport

You can set a default format so that the AutoReport is in the style you want.

1   From the File menu, choose Add-ins, and then choose Add-in Manager.

2   Select Form And Report Wizards from the list of add-ins.

3   Choose the Customize button.

The Customize Add-in dialog box appears.

4   Select Customize AutoReport, and then choose OK.

The AutoReport Style dialog box appears.

5   Select the Presentation style.

You can experiment with other settings and see how the sample report changes under the magnifying glass change.

6   Choose OK and then, in the Add-in Manager dialog box, click the Close button.

7   Click the AutoReport button on the toolbar.

Your report now appears in Presentation style. All new reports you create with AutoReport will be in the Presentation style unless you change the default again.

8   Save the report with the name **Chocolate Types**

Customize your report

To further improve the appearance of the report, you adjust it so that each type of chocolate appears only once.

1   On the toolbar, click the Close Window button to switch to the Design view of the Chocolate Types report.

2   In the detail section, select the Chocolate Type text box.

3   In the property sheet, change the setting of the Hide Duplicates property to Yes.

Print Preview

4   On the toolbar, click the Print Preview button to switch to Print Preview to see your changes.

5   Save the report.

If You Want to Continue to the Next Lesson

▶   Double-click the Control-menu box on the Chocolate Types report. Or, from the File menu, choose Close

This closes the report, but it does not exit the Microsoft Access program.

If You Want to Quit Microsoft Access for Now

▶ Double-click the Control-menu box in the Microsoft Access window. Or, from the File menu, choose Exit.

This closes the table and exits the Microsoft Access program.

Lesson Summary

To	Do this	Button
Create a tabular detail report using a Report Wizard	Click the Report object button, and then choose the New button. Select the underlying table or query, and then choose the Report Wizards button. Select the Tabular Report Wizard and answer the questions in the dialog boxes. Don't select any grouping for the report.	
Preview a report	In the Database window, select the report, and then click the Print Preview button on the toolbar. *or* In Design view, click the Print Preview button on the toolbar.	
View the design of a report	In the Database window, click the report, and then choose the Design button.	
Print a report	In the Database window or in Print Preview, click the Print button on the toolbar. *or* In Design view, choose Print from the File menu.	
Hide duplicates in the detail section	In Design view, select the control for which you want to hide duplicates. In the property sheet for this control, set the Hide Duplicates property to Yes.	

For more information on	See
Creating a report	Chapter 9, "Creating Reports and Mailing Labels," in *Microsoft Access Getting Started*
	Chapter 20, "Report Basics," and Chapter 21, "Designing Reports," in *Microsoft Access User's Guide*

For online information about	From the <u>H</u>elp menu, choose <u>S</u>earch and then type
Creating a report	reports: creating
Customizing a report	reports: design

Preview of the Next Lesson

In the next lesson, you'll learn how to create a report that includes groups and subtotals for each group. Then you'll customize the report by adding descriptive text for each group, calculating a percentage for each group, and changing the sort order.

Creating a Grouped Report

Your data becomes more meaningful when it's grouped, or divided into categories. When you're looking at regional sales patterns, for example, you don't want to see just a long list of sales data—what you'd rather see is a list of sales for each region. What would be even better is a list of sales with a subtotal for each region so that you can see at a glance where your sales are strongest.

Using Report Wizards, you can design grouped reports that make your data easier to understand. In this lesson, you'll create a report that groups your data and automatically calculates subtotals for each group. Then you'll create another grouped report that calculates a percentage, and you'll change the sort order of that report and add customized page numbering.

You will learn how to:

- Create a grouped report.
- Customize the group header.
- Use an expression in the group footer.
- Print groups together.
- Change the sort order.
- Add customized page numbering.

Estimated lesson time: 30 minutes

What Are Groups and Totals?

A *group* is a collection of similar records. By creating a grouped report, you can often improve your reader's understanding of the data in the report. That's because a grouped report not only displays similar records together, it also shows introductory and summary information for each group.

In the following report, the records are grouped by state or province. The state of Alaska (AK), for example, makes up the first group.

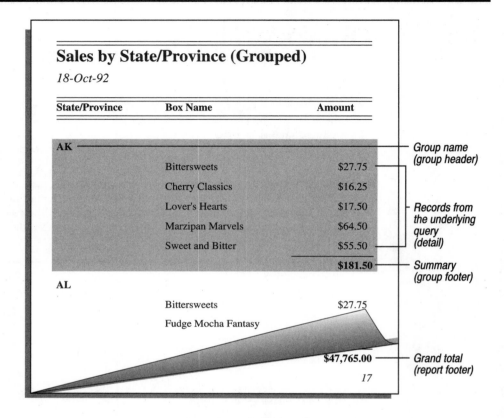

The *group header* (AK, in this case) identifies or introduces the group. The *detail* section, the body of the group, displays the appropriate records from the underlying query. The *group footer* summarizes the data for the group, showing the total sales for Alaska. The *report footer* at the very end of the report includes the grand total for the sales from all states and provinces.

In this lesson, you'll use the Groups/Totals Report Wizard to create grouped reports. This Report Wizard is a real time-saver. It asks how you want to group records in your report, and then it adds the group header and group footer sections for you. It even adds the expressions that perform the subtotal and total calculations.

Start the lesson

▶ If Microsoft Access isn't started yet, start it and open the Sweet database. If the Microsoft Access window doesn't fill your screen, maximize the window.

Creating a Grouped Report

Sweet Lil's new Marketing manager plans to expand sales through a mail order campaign. You'll start this process by sending a mail order advertisement only to people in the states and provinces where your products have been most successful.

What you'd like to see is a report that shows the total sales for each state and province so that you can decide where to send the advertisement. The quick detail report you created in Lesson 15 shows a list of sales, but it doesn't show you the totals for each state and province.

To get the report you want, you'll create a new report using the Groups/Totals Report Wizard. In this report, you want to see sales totals for each state and province, so you'll choose State/Province as the field to group by. You'll choose options that calculate both a sum and a percentage of the total for each state or province. The Sales By State/Province query in the Sweet database provides the records you need.

Begin a new report

Create a new report based on a query.

1 In the Database window, click the Report object button, and then choose the New button.

2 In the Select A Table/Query box, select the Sales By State/Province query, and then click the Report Wizards button.

3 Select Groups/Totals from the list of wizards, and choose the OK button.

Enter information in the Report Wizard dialog boxes

Now that you've selected a Report Wizard, you'll go through a series of dialog boxes. Each of the following steps shows you how to enter information in one dialog box.

1 Add all three available fields to the report, and then choose the Next button.

2 When you're asked which fields to group by, double-click the State/Province field, and then choose the Next button.

Because you're selecting State/Province as the field to group by, your report will show totals for each state and province. Grouping by State/Province also means that your report will display the states and provinces in alphabetical order.

3 When you're asked how you want to group data, choose the Next button to accept the default, Normal grouping.

Normal means that each group will consist of one state or province.

4 When you're asked what fields to sort by, double-click the Box Name field, and then choose the Next button.

This means that the box names for each state and province will appear in alphabetical order.

5 When you're asked what type of look you want, be sure Presentation is selected, and then choose the Next button.

6 Change the title of the report to **Sales by State/Province (Grouped)**

7 Notice that the check box to calculate percentages is already selected. This is what you want, so click the Finish button. Your report appears in Print Preview view.

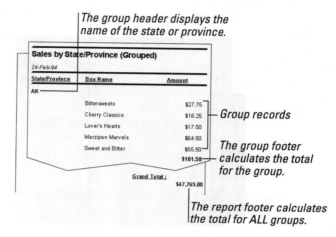

The group header displays the name of the state or province.

Sales by State/Province (Grouped)

24-Feb-94

State/Province	Box Name	Amount
AK		
	Bittersweets	$27.75
	Cherry Classics	$16.25
	Lover's Hearts	$17.50
	Marzipan Marvels	$64.50
	Sweet and Bitter	$55.50
		$181.50

Group records

The group footer calculates the total for the group.

Grand Total : $47,765.00

The report footer calculates the total for ALL groups.

8 Save the report, and name it **Sales by State/Province (Grouped)**

Check the report in Design view

Switch to Design view to compare the two views.

Close Window

1 Since you have just created this report with a Report Wizard, click the Close Window button on the toolbar to switch to Design view.

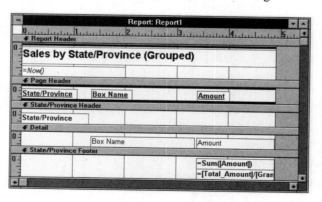

2   If the Report window is too small, resize it so you can see more of the controls on the report. You might need to move the toolbox, property sheet, or Palette out of the way for a better view of the report.

When you look at the report in Design view, notice that the Report Wizard has added these elements:

- **An expression that displays the current date**   At the top of the first page, today's date appears in the report header.

- **A group header and a group footer**   The Report Wizard has added a group header and a group footer for the State/Province group. In Design view, they're identified as the State/Province Header and the State/Province Footer. In more complex reports, you might have several group headers with different names.

- **Expressions that calculate totals**   Notice that the expression for totals in the State/Province footer is exactly the same as the expression in the report footer: =Sum([Amount]). When you place an expression in the State/Province footer or the State/Province header, it performs calculations for the records in each State/Province *group*. When you place an expression in the report footer or the report header, it calculates a value for *all records* in the report.

- **Expressions that calculate percentages**   The expression for percentage in the State/Province footer is =[Total_Amount]/[Grand Total_Amount]. It divides the value in each State/Province text box by the value in the Grand Total text box at the end of your report.

- **An expression that adds a page number**   At the bottom of each page, the current page number appears automatically in the page footer.

Customizing the Group Header

Now you can skim through your report easily and find the figures you're interested in. For your mail order campaign, you'll choose only those states and provinces with the highest percentages of sales.

You'd like to see at a glance what percentage of total sales is brought in by each state and province, and you'd like to display this information next to the name of the state or province.

Move a text box

Move the text box with the percentage expression to the group header for better visibility.

▶   Drag the text box with the expression =[Total_Amount]/[Grand Total_Amount] into the State/Province header and place it above the Amount text box of the Detail section.

You might have to stretch the right side of the text box to display all the text.

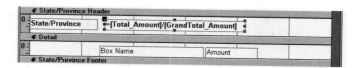

Add a label to the text box

Create a descriptive label for the percentage text box.

Label

1 Click the Label tool in the toolbox.

2 Click to the left of the percentage text box that you just moved into the State/Province header. Be sure to leave some room for the label box to expand for the text you want to type.

3 Type **Percentage of Sales** in the label box. If the label box and a text box overlap, move the boxes until they are properly aligned.

4 Switch to Print Preview to review your work.

Using an Expression in the Group Footer

You'd like to make it easier to skim the report and find the total sales figure for each state or province, so you'll add some text to identify each sales total. For example, to the left of the Alaska total, you'd like to see "Sales for AK."

To add this text, you'll use a text box with an expression so that the appropriate name for each state or province is filled in automatically.

The toolbox includes both a Label tool and a Text Box tool. Since you're adding descriptive text, you might think you'd use a label. But a label can contain only words, while a text box can contain an expression that performs a task for you.

Add a text box in the State/Province footer

1 Switch to Design view by closing the Print Preview window.

2 In the toolbox, click the Text Box tool.

Text Box

3 Click near the middle of the State/Province footer to add the text box.

4 Click in the text box you've just added to place the insertion point, and then type the following expression: **="Sales for " & [State/Province]**

For more information on expressions, see the Appendix, "Using Expressions."

Be sure to start the expression with the equal sign (=), and leave a space before the second quotation mark. If you don't leave a space, your label will contain text like this: Sales forAK.

The words in the quotation marks will appear on your report exactly as you type them. The & symbol means "followed by." The information in brackets is taken automatically from the State/Province field, and will change for each location.

5 Press ENTER.

6 Make the text box wide enough to accommodate long state or province names, and move it so it's roughly in the following position.

Change the format of the text box

Bold

Now you'll emphasize the text box with bold text.

1 Be sure the text box is still selected, and then click the Bold button on the toolbar.

Print Preview

2 Click the Print Preview button to see the report.

3 Save the report.

Changing the Sort Order

In the advertisement you send to a particular state or province, you want to feature boxes of bonbons that are best-sellers in that region.

When you originally created your report, you grouped by the State/Province field and then sorted by the Box Name field. Now you'd like to change the sort order. Within each state or province, you'd like to see a list of boxes starting with the box that brought in the most money and ending with the one that brought in the least. In other words, you want to sort by the Amount field rather than the Box Name field, and you want to sort in descending order.

You'll create a report like the following illustration.

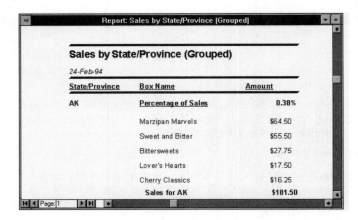

When you create reports with a Report Wizard, you're asked about how you want to group and sort your data. If you decide to change sorting or grouping after you've created a report, you don't have to start from scratch and run the Report Wizard again. Instead, you can use the Sorting And Grouping box to make the changes.

Open the Sorting And Grouping box

1   Switch to Design view for the Sales By State/Province (Grouped) report.

Sorting And Grouping

2   Click the Sorting And Grouping button on the toolbar.

The Sorting And Grouping box appears.

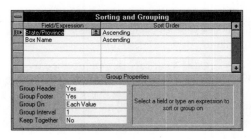

You can see the settings that were established when you answered the Report Wizard's questions.

The Field/Expression column shows fields that are used either for grouping and sorting or for sorting only. To the left of the State/Province field is the Grouping icon, which tells you that this field is used for grouping and sorting. The Box Name field doesn't have this icon, so you can tell it is used solely for sorting.

Change the sort order

Using the Sorting And Grouping box, you'll specify Amount instead of Box Name as the second field to group by.

1 In the Field/Expression column, click the Box Name cell, and then click the arrow to display a list of fields.

2 Select the Amount field from the list.

The Amount field replaces the Box Name field.

3 Click the Sort Order cell to the right of the Amount field, and then click the arrow.

4 Select Descending from the list.

By selecting Descending, you're asking Microsoft Access to display the box sales for each State or Province starting with the highest amount and working down to the lowest.

5 Close the Sorting And Grouping box, and then switch to Print Preview.

Your report should now show the boxes listed in descending order of sales, similar to the report shown previously under "Changing the Sort Order."

Printing Groups Together

You notice that some of the groups in the report begin on one page and finish on another. You can avoid a page break in the middle of a group by setting the Keep Together property in the Sorting And Grouping box.

Sorting And Grouping

1 In Design view, click the Sorting And Grouping button on the toolbar.

2 Click the Keep Together property.

3 Click the down arrow and select Whole Group from the list.

4 Close the Sorting And Grouping box, and then preview the report.

A complete group now appears on the same page, except where the group itself is bigger than a full page.

Adding Custom Page Numbers

When you created the Sales By State/Province (Grouped) report with the Report Wizard, an expression for a page number was automatically added to the design of your report. You can customize this page numbering to produce a format for the first page that would read, "Page 1 of 10." The Page property in a text box relates the current page number to the total number of pages in the report. The Page property is available only when you preview or print a report, so it doesn't appear in the list of properties on the property sheet.

Create a new text box

1   Switch to Design view.

2   Select the text box in the page footer containing the page number expression, and then press DELETE.

Text Box

3   Use the Text Box tool on the toolbar to place a new text box on the right side of the page footer.

Enter page numbers using the Expression Builder

In the Control Source property, create an expression that prints page numbers in the format, "Page 1 of 10."

Properties

Build

1   Be sure the property sheet is visible. If it is not, click the Properties button on the toolbar.

2   Click in the Control Source property, and then click the Build button to the right of the property box.

The Expression Builder appears.

3   From the first column, select Common Expressions.

4   In the middle column, select Page N of M.

The expression for this type of page numbering appears in the third column.

5   Choose the Paste button.

A copy of the expression appears in the upper text box, allowing you to edit the expression if you wish.

6   The expression is just as you want it, so choose the OK button.

The expression appears in the Control Source property box.

7   Click in the page footer text box.

The expression appears.

8   Preview your report, and examine the new footer.

9   When you have finished previewing it, save and close the Sales By State/Province (Grouped) report.

One Step Further

For quick identification of listings in a report, you can group items by the first letter of their names and print the letter in a group header. First you'll create a quick report based on the Customer List query, and then you'll change the properties in the Sorting And Grouping box to add a letter at the beginning of each alphabetic group of customer last names.

Create a new report

AutoReport

1   In the Database window, select the Customer List query without opening it.

2   Click the AutoReport button on the toolbar.

3   Close the report to switch to Design view.

Set the Sorting and Grouping properties

Sorting And Grouping

1   Be sure the Sorting And Grouping box is visible. If it is not, click the Sorting And Grouping button on the toolbar.

The first cell of the Field/Expression column will contain the instructions for starting a new group each time the first letter of the last name changes.

2   Click the first cell of the Field/Expression column, and then select Last Name from the list.

The second cell of the Field/Expression column will contain the instructions for sorting the names within each group alphabetically.

3   Click the second cell of the Field/Expression column, and then select Last Name from the list.

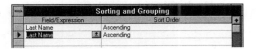

4   Set the properties in the Sorting And Grouping box to match those in the following table.

Field/ Expression	Sort Order	Group Header	Group Footer	Group On	Group Interval	Keep Together
Last Name	Ascending	Yes	No	Prefix Characters	1	With First Detail
Last Name	Ascending	No	No	Each Value	1	No

By choosing Prefix Characters for the Group On property, and 1 for the Group Interval, you will see only the first letter of each group's last name. By choosing

With First Detail for the Keep Together property, a group will not be restricted to one page, but will be allowed to run over a page break.

Use an expression in the group header

Now that you have set the properties, you need to create a text box and an expression to display the result.

1   Create a text box for the Last Name Header of the report and delete the attached label.

Center-Align Text

2   Position the text box in the center of the header, and then click the Center-Align Text button on the toolbar to center the text within the text box.

3   Enter the expression **=Left([Last Name],1)** in the text box, to print only the first letter of the name at the beginning of each new group, and then press ENTER.

The Left function with the number 1 extracts one character from the Last Name field, beginning on the left. In this case you will see the one letter that begins all the last names of each group.

4   Use the Palette to set the Back Color of the text box to light gray and the Fore Color to dark blue.

5   Preview the report and then save it with the name **Customer List (Grouped)**

If You Want to Continue to the Next Lesson

▶ Double-click the Control-menu box on the Customer List (Grouped) report. Or, from the File menu, choose Close.

This closes the report, but it does not exit the Microsoft Access program.

If You Want to Quit Microsoft Access for Now

▶ Double-click the Control-menu box in the Microsoft Access window. Or, from the File menu, choose Exit.

This closes the table and exits the Microsoft Access program.

Lesson Summary

To	Do this	Button
Create a grouped report	In the Database window, click the Report object button, and then choose the New button. Select a table or query, and then click the Report Wizards button. Select the Groups/Totals Report Wizard, and then answer the questions in the dialog boxes.	
Change the sort order in a report	Display your report in Design view. Click the Sorting And Grouping button on the toolbar. In the Field/Expression column, select the field for which you want to change the sort order. Then select Ascending or Descending in the Sort Order cell for this field.	
Print groups together	Display your report in Design view. Click the Sorting And Grouping button on the toolbar. Set the Keep Together property to Whole Group. Close the box.	
Add custom page numbers	In Design view, place a text box for the page number. Click the Properties button to display the property sheet. Click in the Control Source property, and then click the Build button. Select Common Expressions, and then select Page N of M. Choose Paste, and then click OK. Click in the page footer text box to display the expression. Preview your report.	

For more information on	See in *Microsoft Access User's Guide*
Creating reports	Chapter 20, "Report Basics," and Chapter 21, "Designing Reports"
Creating grouped reports	Chapter 22, "Sorting and Grouping Data"
Using expressions in reports	Chapter 23, "Using Expressions in Reports"

For online information about	From the <u>H</u>elp menu, choose <u>S</u>earch and then type
Creating grouped reports	reports: grouping data
Expression Builder	Expression Builder

Review & Practice

In the lessons in Part 5, you learned to customize reports. By using the Groups/Total Report Wizard, you were able to organize the information on the reports in meaningful ways. You tailored the design of the reports and changed the sort order to be more useful. The Review & Practice section which follows gives you a chance to practice some of these methods.

Part 5   Review & Practice

The ability to store and retrieve information quickly and efficiently are two primary reasons to use an online database. Equally important is the ability to print out the information in useful and attractive reports. In this Review & Practice section, you have an opportunity to apply the techniques you learned for creating and enhancing grouped reports.

Scenario

As your reports are circulated throughout the company, the staff begins to realize that you can print the information they need in a format that is attractive and easy to use. More requests for specialized reports arrive on your desk, including one from Lillian Farber, the company president.

You will review and practice how to:

- Create a detail report and hide duplicate entries.
- Create a grouped report.
- Use an expression to describe group totals.
- Change the sort order.
- Print groups together.
- Add custom page numbers.

Estimated practice time: 20 minutes

Step 1: Create a Detail Report and Hide Duplicates

You have been asked to create a report that lists the contact names and phone numbers for the suppliers of ingredients for Sweet Lil's bonbons. The Ingredient Source query contains the information you want.

1   Use the Tabular Report Wizard to create a detail report based on the Ingredient Source query.

2   Add all the fields to the report.

3   Sort within groups by Category and Type.

4   Select the Presentation style for your report.

5   Title the report **Ingredient Source**

6   Preview the report.

7   In Design view, set the Hide Duplicates property of the Category text box (under the Detail section) to Yes to avoid printing duplicate entries.

8   Preview the report again.

9   Close the report and save it with the name **Ingredient Source**

For more information on	See
Using a Report Wizard	Lesson 15
Hiding duplicate entries	Lesson 15
Previewing a report	Lesson 15

Step 2: Display the Cost of Bonbons in Each Box

Lillian Farber, the company president, wants to reduce box costs again. She wants a report that lists the bonbons in each box along with the cost of each bonbon. She also wants to know the total cost of the bonbons in each box.

Use a Report Wizard to make a report that shows the information Lillian wants.

1   Create a new report using all the fields in the Bonbons By Box query. Use the Groups/Totals Report Wizard and show all fields.

2   Group by Box Name and use Normal grouping.

3   Sort by Bonbon Name.

4   Select the Presentation style for your report, in Portrait orientation.

5   Give your report the title **Cost of Boxes** and do not calculate percentages of the total.

6   Preview the report.

7   Save the report, and name it **Cost of Boxes**

For more information on	See
Creating a grouped report	Lesson 16

Step 3: Describe the Group Totals and Change the Sort Order

Make it easier for Lillian to skim the Cost Of Boxes report by adding a descriptive line, reading "Total Cost," next to the total amount for each box. Change the second sort field so that the bonbons within each box are sorted by cost.

1   In Design view, use the Text Box tool to create a text box in the Box Name footer, and place it to the left of the Summary text box.

2 In the text box, type the expression **="Total Cost for " & [Box Name]**

3 Widen the box and make the text bold.

4 In the Sorting And Grouping box, change the second field to group by Cost Of Bonbons in descending order.

5 Preview, and then save the report.

For more information on	See
Using an expression in a report	Lesson 16
Changing the sort order	Lesson 16

Step 4: Print Groups Together and Add Custom Page Numbers

Two more steps make the report more convenient to use: keeping each list of bonbons together on a page, and adding page numbering that includes the report's total page count.

1 In the Sorting And Grouping box, select the Box Name expression, and then select Whole Group for the Keep Together property.

2 In the Page footer, delete the text box that now contains the page number expression, and create a new one.

3 In the property sheet, use the Build button in the Control Source property to set the page numbering style so that the word "Page" and the page number appear.

4 Preview the report.

5 Save and close the Cost Of Boxes report.

For more information on	See
Printing groups together	Lesson 16
Adding custom page numbers	Lesson 16

If You Want to Quit Microsoft Access for Now

▶ Double-click the Control-menu box in the Microsoft Access window. Or, from the File menu, choose Exit.

This closes the table and exits the Microsoft Access program.

Appendix

Using Expressions

No matter what type of work you're doing with Microsoft Access, you'll most likely need to use expressions. For example, you might want to calculate a subtotal on a report or design a query that asks for all products that cost $10. Or, you might want to filter a form so that you see only the records for your sales region. In all these cases, you need to create an expression. This appendix provides guidelines for writing expressions and examples of common expressions.

What Are Expressions?

Expressions are formulas that calculate a value. For example, the following expression multiplies the box price by 1.1 (which is the same as raising the price by 10 percent):
=[Box Price] * 1.1

An expression can include *functions*, *identifiers*, *operators*, *literal values*, and *constants*. The following expression contains most of these elements.

$$=\overbrace{\text{Avg}}^{\text{Function}}(\underbrace{[\text{Box Price}]}_{\text{Identifier}})\overset{\text{Operator}}{-}\underset{\text{Literal}}{5}$$

Functions help you perform specialized calculations easily. For example, you can use the **Avg** function to find the average of values in a field or the **Sum** function to find the total of all values in a field.

Identifiers refer to a value in your database, such as the value of a field, control, or property. For example, [Order Date] refers to the value in the Order Date field.

Operators specify an action (such as addition) to be performed on one or more elements of an expression. Operators include familiar arithmetic operators, such as **+**, **−**, *****, and **/**, as well as other operators, such as **=**, **<**, **>**, **&**, **And**, **Or**, and **Like**.

Literals are values that Microsoft Access uses exactly as you enter them. For example, the number 25 and the text value "San Francisco" are literals.

Constants represent values that don't change. For example, the constant **Null** always means a field that contains no characters or values. A constant might also be **True**, **False**, **Yes**, or **No**.

Guidelines for Entering Expressions

When you enter an expression, in some cases Microsoft Access inserts characters for you automatically. For example, Microsoft Access might insert brackets, number signs, or quotation marks. The examples in this appendix show how to type the entire expression, rather than having Microsoft Access supply additional characters.

Follow these general guidelines when you're entering an expression.

Element	How to enter	Example
Identifier	Enclose field names and control names in brackets.	[Order Date]
	Use a period (.) to separate the name of a table from a field in the table.	[Boxes].[Box Price]
	If an expression needs to get values from a different database object, use an exclamation point (!) to separate the type of object (Forms), the name of the form (Boxes), and the name of the control on the form (Boxes ID).	=Forms![Boxes]![Boxes ID]
Date	Enclose dates in number signs (#).	#10-Oct-94# #10/10/94#
	Number signs automatically appear around a date/time value you type in a validation expression or in a criteria expression for a field whose data type is Date/Time.	
Text	Enclose text in quotation marks.	"California" "British Columbia"
	If the text doesn't contain a space or punctuation, you can type the text without quotation marks, and the marks will appear automatically.	
Number	Don't enter a currency symbol ($) or a comma for separating thousands.	8934.75 (not $8,934.75 or 8,934.75)

Creating Expressions with the Expression Builder

When you want to create a common expression quickly, or when you want help in creating an expression, you can use the Expression Builder. You can start the Expression Builder from places where you would often write an expression, such as in a property sheet or in a criteria cell in the QBE grid.

Build

In a property sheet, first you click the property box where you want an expression, and then you click the Build button next to the box.

In the Query window, you use the right mouse button to click where you want an expression, and then you choose Build from the shortcut menu. If the property box or query cell where you start the Expression Builder already contains a value, that value is automatically copied into the Expression box.

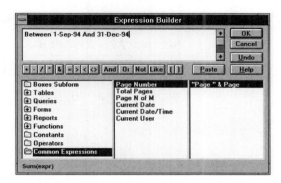

When the Expression Builder appears, you can select types of expressions, field names, and operators, and then paste them into the Expression box. You can also type in any elements you want. To accept the expression you built, choose OK.

Using Expressions in Forms and Reports

You use expressions in forms and reports to get information that you cannot get directly from the tables in a database. For example, you can create expressions that calculate totals, add the values from two fields, or set a default value for a field.

Calculated Control Expression Examples

When you want a form or report to calculate a value, you can create a calculated control that gets its value from an expression. You add the control to your form or report, and then you type an expression directly in the control (frequently a text box) or in the Control Source property box for the control.

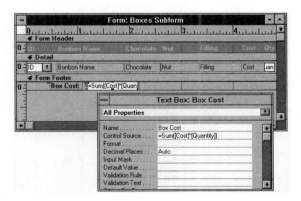

When you type expressions in calculated controls, be sure to include an equal sign (=) to the left of the expression. For example: **=[Salary] * 2**

When you type a long expression in a property box, you might want to press SHIFT+F2 to display the whole expression at once.

The following table shows some common expressions used for calculated controls.

Expression	Microsoft Access displays
=[Quantity]*[Box Price]	The product of the Quantity and Box Price field values.
=[First Name] &" "& [Last Name]	The values of the First Name and Last Name fields, separated by a space.
=[Bonbon Cost]*1.5	The value in the Bonbon Cost field multiplied by 1.5 (adds 50 percent to the Bonbon Cost value).
=Date()	Today's date.
=Page	The page number of the current page.
"Page " & Page & " of " & Pages	The page number of the current page followed by the total number of pages.
="Sales for "& [State/Province]	The text "Sales for " followed by the value in the State/Province field.
=[State/Province Total]/ [Grand Total]	The value from the State/Province Total control divided by the value from the Grand Total control.
=Sum([Bonbon Cost])	The sum of the values in the Bonbon Cost field.
=[Orders Subform] .Form![Order Subtotal]	The value from the Order Subtotal control on the Orders subform. (You use this expression on the main form that contains the Orders subform. To see how to use the expression, refer to the Subtotal control on the Orders form.)
=DatePart("yyyy", [Order Date])	Only the year portion of the date.

Validation Expression Examples

You can set validation rules for a field on a form to make sure that you enter the right type of data into the field. To specify a rule, you type an expression in the Validation Rule property box for the control.

The following table shows some typical validation expressions.

Expression	When you enter data, it must
>=Date()	Be a date that's either today's date or some date in the future.
Between 10 And 100	Be a value between 10 and 100, inclusive.
"USA" Or "Canada"	Match USA or Canada.
Like "[A–Z]##"	Include one letter followed by two numbers (for example, B23).

Using Expressions in Queries and Filters

You use expressions in queries and filters to specify criteria. In queries, you can also use expressions to create fields that are based on a calculation. You don't have to include an equal sign to the left of a query or filter expression.

Criteria Expression Examples

When you're designing a query or filter, you use expressions as criteria. These criteria tell Microsoft Access which records you want to see. You enter criteria for a field into the Criteria cell for that field. For example, to find people with customer IDs greater than 100, you'd type the expression **>100** in the Criteria cell for the Customer ID field.

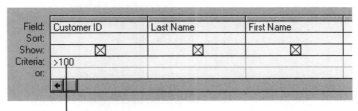

Type query criteria expressions in the Criteria cell in the Query window.

The following examples show some frequently used criteria expressions that you might use in a query based on the Orders table in the Sweet database.

Field	Criteria expression	Query finds orders
Customer ID	89	For the customer whose ID is 89.
Customer ID	>=60	For customers with IDs greater than or equal to 60.
Ship City	"Seattle" Or "New York"	For Seattle or New York.

Field	Criteria expression	Query finds orders
Ship State/Province	Not "Ontario"	For all states and provinces except Ontario.
Ship Last Name	Like "Mc*"	For names beginning with "Mc."
Ship Last Name	Like "J*son"	For names beginning with "J" and ending in "son."
Carrier ID	Null	That have no value in the Carrier ID field.
Order Date	Between 1-Dec-94 And 15-Dec-94	Placed during the first 15 days of December 1994.
Ship Last Name	Like [C] & "*" *(for parameter queries only)*	For last names starting with "C."

Calculated Field Expression Examples

You can use expressions to create new query fields. You enter the expression into a Field cell in the QBE grid.

Type calculated field expressions in the Field cell in the Query window.

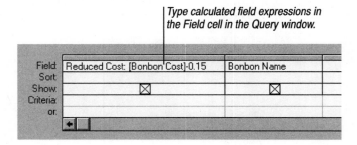

The following examples show some common calculated field expressions.

Name and expression	Microsoft Access displays
Sale Price: [Box Price] * 0.8	The values of the Box Price field multiplied by 0.8 (reduces the values by 20 percent).
Sale Price: CCur([Box Price] * 0.8)	The values of the Box Price field reduced by 20 percent and formatted as currency values (for example, $2,345.50).
Extended Price: [Order Details].[Quantity]* [Boxes].[Box Price]	The product of the Quantity field in the Order Details table and the Box Price field in the Boxes table.

For More Information

Although this appendix shows examples of expressions in forms, reports, queries, and filters, you can also use expressions in tables, macros, and modules. You'll find extensive information on expressions in the Microsoft Access documentation.

For more information on	See in *Microsoft Access User's Guide*
Expressions in forms and reports	Chapter 18, "Using Expressions in Forms," and Chapter 23, "Using Expressions in Reports"
Expressions in queries and filters	Chapter 10, "Query Basics," and Chapter 11, "Designing Select Queries"

For online information about	From the Help menu, choose Search and then type
Creating or entering expressions	expressions: creating expressions: entering
Entering expressions in forms and reports	expressions: as properties
Entering expressions in queries and filters	expressions: in queries/filters expressions: examples
Using Expression Builder	expression builder

Glossary

This glossary contains definitions of terms used in *Microsoft Access 2 for Windows Step by Step*. For definitions of additional database terms, see the online glossary in Microsoft Access Help. (From the Help menu choose Contents, and then choose the Glossary button.)

attached table   A table stored in a file outside the open database but from which Microsoft Access can access records. You can add, edit, and delete records in an attached table, but you can't modify the table's structure.

AutoForm Wizard   A tool that automatically creates a form that displays the values of all the fields and records of the selected table or query.

AutoReport Wizard   A tool that automatically creates a report using all the fields in the selected table or query. The report appears in the Print Preview window.

bound control   A control that's tied to a specific field in the underlying table or query so that it can display data from the underlying field. *See also* unbound control.

bound object frame   An object frame that displays objects that are stored in a field in a table. In Form view and in reports, you see a different object in the object frame for each record. *See also* unbound object frame.

calculated control   A control on a form or report that is tied to an expression rather than a field. A calculated control can combine text values from fields in the underlying table or query, or it can perform calculations on values from the fields.

calculated field   A field defined in a query that displays the result of an expression rather than stored data. The value is recalculated each time a value in the expression changes.

check box   A control that provides a graphical way to display Yes/No data. When a check box is selected, an X appears in the box.

Clipboard   The temporary storage area used by Microsoft Windows to store text, graphics, and other data. You transfer data to the Clipboard by choosing Cut or Copy from the Edit menu. You transfer data from the Clipboard by choosing the Paste command from the Edit menu.

combo box   A control, similar to both a list box and a text box, in which you type a value or select a value from a list.

command button   A control that runs a macro, carries out an event procedure, or calls an Access Basic function. A command button condenses related tasks into a single step. Command buttons are sometimes referred to as push buttons.

Command Button Wizard   A tool that helps you add a command button to a form.

constant   A value that doesn't change. For example, the constant *Null* always means a field that contains no characters or values. Other constants might be *Yes* or *True*.

control   An object on a form or report that displays data, performs an action, or decorates the form or report.

Control-menu box   The box in the upper-left corner of an application window or other window that contains a short horizontal line. You click the Control-menu box to open the Control menu, which contains commands to move, resize, and close the window. As a shortcut, you can double-click the Control-menu box to close a window or application.

criteria   A set of limiting conditions, such as "Denmark" or > 3000. You can use criteria in creating queries or filters to show a specific set of records.

Cue Cards   An online coach that walks you through the most common Microsoft Access tasks as you work with your own data. To use them, from the Help menu, choose Cue Cards.

data   The information stored in tables in a database. In Microsoft Access, data can be text, numbers, dates, pictures, or other OLE objects.

data type   An attribute of a field that determines what kind of data it can hold.

database   A collection of data related to a particular topic or purpose. A Microsoft Access database file can contain tables, queries, forms, reports, macros, and modules.

database object buttons   Buttons in the Database window that you can click to display a list of objects of the same type. For example, you click the Form button to display a list of all the forms in your database.

database objects   Tables, queries, forms, reports, macros, and modules.

database window   The window that is displayed when you open a Microsoft Access database. It contains the Table, Query, Form, Report, Macro, and Module object buttons, which you can click to display a list of all objects of that type in the database.

Datasheet view   A view that displays multiple records in a row-and-column format, enabling you to view many records at the same time. Datasheet view is available for tables, queries, and forms.

Design view   A view you use to design tables, queries, forms, and reports.

detail section   A section of a report or form used to display the records from the underlying table or query.

drag and drop   The ability to drag an object onto another to perform an action. For example, in the Query window, you can drag a field from the field list to the QBE grid to add the field to your query. To drag an object, position the pointer over the object, hold down the mouse button while you move the mouse, and then release the mouse button when the object is positioned where you want it.

dynaset   The set of records that results from running a query or applying a filter.

embed   To insert an object into a form or report by using commands from the Edit menu, you can use the Insert Object command to create a new object, or you can insert an existing OLE object using the Copy and Paste commands. After the object is embedded, you can edit it. If the object comes from another file, only the embedded object in your database is changed when you modify it. *See also* link.

expression   A formula that calculates a value. You can use expressions in forms, reports, tables, queries, and macros, and modules. For example, in queries you use expressions (such as >100) in criteria to specify which records Microsoft Access should retrieve.

Expression Builder   A tool that can help you create an expression. It is available wherever you want to enter the expression, for example, in many property boxes or in the Field or Criteria rows of a query. The Expression Builder contains a list of common expressions from which you can select.

external table   A table outside the open Microsoft Access database.

field   A category of information, such as Last Name or Address. On a form, a field is an area where you can enter data. A field is represented as a column in a datasheet.

field list   A small window that lists all the fields in the underlying table or query. You use field lists in the Design view of a form, report, or query, in the Filter window, and in the Relationships window.

field selector   A small box or bar at the top of a datasheet column that you can click to select an entire column.

filter   A set of criteria you apply to records to show a subset of the records or to sort the records.

filter grid   The grid in the lower portion of the Filter window. You use it to define the filter.

foreign key   A field (or fields) in a related table that contains the values that match the values in the primary key field in the primary table.

form   A Microsoft Access database object on which you place controls for entering, displaying, and editing data in fields.

Form view   A view that displays the data one record at a time in fields on a form. Form view is convenient for entering and modifying information in a database.

Form Wizards   Tools that help you create a variety of forms by asking you questions and then creating a form based on your answers.

function   A routine that performs a specialized calculation. For example, you can use the Avg function to find the average of values in a field.

group   A collection of similar records in a report.

group footer   Text and/or graphics that appear at the bottom of a group in a report. For example, a group footer can display the total sales for the group.

group header   Text and/or graphics that appear at the top of a group in a report. A group header typically displays the group name.

Groups/Totals Report Wizard   A tool that organizes data into groups that are displayed in a tabular format. You can calculate a subtotal for each group and a grand total for all groups. Labels appear at the top of each column of data.

import   A process by which Microsoft Access copies data from another source into your database.

join   An association between a field in one table and a field with the same data type in another table. *See also* relationship between tables.

join line   A line between fields displayed in field lists in the Relationships window or the Query window that indicates the matching fields in the underlying tables.

label   A control that displays text that you use as a title for a form or report or to identify fields on a form or report.

link   A connection between a source file and a destination file. A link inserts a copy of an object from the source file into the destination file while maintaining the connection between the two. When you make changes to a linked object, the changes are saved in the object's source file, not in your database file. *See also* embed.

list box   A control that displays a list of values from which you can select.

Mailing Label Report Wizard group   A tool that automatically creates mailing labels based on your answers to a set of questions.

Main/Subform Form Wizard   A tool that creates a form with a subform by asking you questions, and then creating the forms based on your answers.

many-to-many relationship   A relationship between two tables in which one record in either the primary table or the related table can have many matching records in the other table. *See also* one-to-many relationship *and* one-to-one relationship.

navigation buttons   The four arrows in the lower-left corner in Datasheet view, Form view, and Print Preview. Use these buttons to move to the first record (or page), the previous record (or page), the next record (or page), and the last record (or page).

null field   A field containing no characters or values.

object buttons   *See* database object buttons.

object frame   A control used to add, edit, or view OLE objects. There are two types of object frames: bound object frames and unbound object frames. *See also* bound object frame *and* unbound object frame.

object linking and embedding (OLE)   A protocol by which an object, such as a graph, in a source application or document can be linked to or embedded in a destination document, such as a form or report.

OLE object   Any piece of information created with an application for Windows that supports object linking and embedding (OLE). OLE objects include pictures, graphs, and sounds.

one-to-many relationship   A relationship between tables in which one record in the primary table can have many matching records in the related table. *See also* many-to-many relationship *and* one-to-one relationship."

one-to-one relationship   A relationship between tables in which one record in the primary table can have only one matching record in the related table. *See also* many-to-many relationship *and* one-to-many relationship.

operator   A symbol or word, such as > or And, that indicates an action to be performed on one or more elements of an expression. For example, the arithmetic operators +, -, *, and /, indicate addition, subtraction, multiplication, and division.

page footer   Text and/or graphics that appear at the bottom of every page of a report. A page footer typically displays the page number.

page header   Text and/or graphics that appear at the top of every page of a report. A page header typically displays a heading for each column of data.

Palette   A dialog box containing choices for color and other special effects that you use when designing a form or report.

parameter query   A query that asks you to enter one or more parameters—or criteria—when you run the query. For example, a parameter query might ask you to enter a beginning and ending date or a city name.

primary key   One or more fields whose value or values uniquely identify each record in a table.

Print Preview   A view that shows you how your form or report will look when it is printed.

property   An attribute of a control, field, table, query, form, or report that you can set to define one of the object's characteristics (such as size, color, or position) or an aspect of its behavior (such as whether it is hidden).

property sheet   A window in which you can view and modify the full set of properties for the selected object.

QBE (query by example)   A technique for designing queries. With graphical QBE, which Microsoft Access uses, you create queries visually by dragging the fields you want to include in the query from the upper portion of the Query window to the QBE grid in the lower portion of the window.

query   A Microsoft Access database object that represents the group of records you want to work with. You can think of a query as a request for a particular collection of data. *See also* Select query.

Query Wizards   Tools that ask you questions, and then create a query based on your answers.

record   A set of information that belongs together, such as all the information on one job application or one magazine subscription card.

record number box   A small box that displays the current record number in the lower-left corner in Datasheet view of a table, query, or form, and in Form view. To move to a specific record, type the record number in the box, and then press ENTER. There is a similar box in the lower-left corner of the Print Preview window that you use to move to a specific page in a form or report.

record selector   A small box or bar on the left side in Datasheet view of a table, query, or form, and in Form view that you can click to select an entire record.

row selector   A small box or bar that you can click to select an entire row in a table's Design view.

relational database   A database in which information is stored in tables, allowing efficient and nonredundant data storage and retrieval.

relationship between tables   The association between data in two tables that have fields with matching values. When tables are related, a new query or form can be created using data from both tables. *See also* join.

report   A Microsoft Access database object that presents data formatted and organized according to your specifications.

report footer   Text and/or graphics that appear once at the end of a report and typically contain summaries, such as grand totals.

report header   Text and/or graphics that appear once at the beginning of a report and typically contain the report title, date, and company logo.

Report Wizards   Tools that help you create a report by asking you questions and then creating different types of reports based on your answers.

select query   A query that asks a question about the data stored in your tables and returns a dynaset in the form of a datasheet, without changing the data.

shortcut key   A function key, such as F5, or a key combination, such as CTRL+A, that you can press to carry out a menu command.

Shortcut menu   A list of commands that is displayed when you click the right mouse button while your mouse pointer is on a toolbar, property sheet, control or other object. The list of commands depends on the object you click.

sort order   The order in which records are displayed — either ascending (A–Z and 1–100) or descending (Z–A and 100–1).

subform   A form contained within another form.

status bar   A horizontal bar at the bottom of the screen that displays information about commands, toolbar buttons, and other options.

table   A collection of data with the same subject or topic. A table stores data in records (rows) and fields (columns).

Table Wizard   A tool that helps you create a table. You can choose from a selection of more than 40 types of personal and business tables.

tab order   The order in which the insertion point moves through fields when you tab from field to field in Form view.

text box   A control that displays data from a field. A text box can display text, numbers, or dates, and you can use it to type in new data, or change existing data.

toolbar   A bar at the top of the Microsoft Access window containing a set of buttons that you can click to carry out common menu commands. The buttons displayed on the toolbar change depending on which window or view is currently selected.

toolbox   A box containing the set of tools you use in Design view to place controls on a form or a report.

unbound control   A control that is not connected to a field or expression. You can use an unbound control to display informational text, such as instructions about using your form, or graphics and pictures from other applications. *See also* bound control.

unbound object frame   A frame that displays an object that's part of the design of the form or report, such as a company logo. *See also* bound object frame.

underlying table or query   The table or query that contains the fields you want to display in a form, report, or query.

validation   The process of checking whether entered data meets certain conditions or limitations.

validation rule   A rule that sets limits or conditions on what can be entered in a particular field.

value   An individual piece of data, such as a last name, an address, or an ID number.

wildcard character   You can use wildcard characters, such as the asterisk (*) and the question mark (?) in searches using the Find and Replace commands. Wildcard characters can also be used in query criteria and other expressions to include all records or other items that begin with specific characters or match a certain pattern.

wizards   Microsoft Access tools that help you create a form, report, query, or table by asking you questions, and then creating the object based on your answers.

Zoom box   An expanded text box that you can use to enter expressions or text instead of using the small input area in a property sheet or in the QBE grid. You open the Zoom box by pressing SHIFT+F2.

Index

Special Characters

+ (addition operator), 271
* (asterisk as multiplication operator), 271
[] (brackets), 145, 212, 257, 272
, (comma), 272
& (concatenation operator), 212, 257, 271
/ (division operator), 271
$ (dollar sign), 272
= (equal sign), 212, 257, 274
= (equal-to operator), 271
! (exclamation point), 272
> (greater-than operator), 135, 271, 275
>= (greater-than-or-equal-to operator), 135, 271
< (less-than operator), 135, 271
<= (less-than-or-equal-to operator), 135, 271
<> (not-equal-to operator), 271
(number sign), 272
. (period), 272
" (quotation marks), 51, 212, 257, 272
– (subtraction operator), 271

A

Access. *See* Microsoft Access
Add-ins command, 247
addition operator (+), 271
addresses. *See* mailing labels
Add Table button, 112, 117, 118
Add Table dialog box, 110, 132, 137
aligning
    controls, 187–88
    data in text boxes, 189
Allow Editing command, 226
Allow Editing property, 226
ALMOND.BMP file, xvii
ALT key, xxvi
ampersand (&), 212, 257, 271
And operator, 271
angle brackets (<>), 271
Apply Filter/Sort button, 51, 52, 53, 55, 90
asterisk as multiplication operator (*), 271
Attach dialog box, 95
attached tables
    creating, 95–96

attached tables, *continued*
    defined, 94, 279
    deleting, 99
    field properties in, 96, 97–98
    vs. imported tables, 94, 98
    opening, 96
    using, 96–98
Attach Table command, 95
AutoForm Wizard, 148, 279
AutoReport Wizard, 156, 157–58, 246, 279
Avery mailing labels, 65–66
Avg function, 271

B

BACKSPACE key, 7
Bold button, 245, 257
Bonbons form. *See also* Presenting Bonbons form
    filtering records, 50–52
    opening, 19
    sorting records, 53–54
    viewing records, 19
Bonbons table
    linking with Boxes table, 117
    relationship with Boxes table, 115–16
Border Color property, 187
borders on forms, 187
Border Width property, 187
bound controls
    adding, 181–84
    creating check boxes, 184–85
    creating combo boxes, 219
    defined, 181, 279
bound object frames
    adding, 197–98
    defined, 193–94, 279
    fitting pictures to, 199–200
Bound Object Frame tool, 197
Box Details table, 117
Boxes form
    adding records, 35, 42
    adding subform data, 35–36, 42
    deleting subform records, 42–43
    opening, 35

R

RDBMS (relational database management systems), defined, xx
read-only forms, 225–26
record number box, defined, 284
records
    adding pictures to, 27–29
    adding subform data, 35–36, 42
    adding to forms, 35, 42, 102
    adding to tables, 81, 86–87
    adding with Ditto key, 29–30
    defined, 4, 284
    deleting, 40–41, 42–43
    displaying in tables, 11, 78
    in dynasets, 130
    editing, 9–10
    finding with Find button, 46–49
    hiding duplicate field values, 245–46
    moving among, 9–12, 19
    related, forms for, 205–13
    saving, 9, 81
    scrolling through, 23
    sorting, 53–54
    validating data, 37–38, 222–23
record selectors, 20, 41, 284
relational databases, defined, xx, 284
relationships
    creating, 109–12
    defined, xx, 285
    deleting, 111
    many-to-many, 115–17
    one-to-many, 107
    one-to-one, 107
    overview, 107–8
    querying related tables, 136–39
    restoring, 111–12
    saving layouts, 111, 113
Relationships button, 109, 112, 117, 118
Relationships dialog box, 113
Relationships window
    adding tables to, 110, 112–13
    Box Details table in, 117
    creating relationship, 110–11, 118
    overview, 109–10

renaming
    calculated fields, 146
    fields in queries, 144
    queries, 141
    tables, 99
replacing text, 25
report footers, 242, 252, 255, 285
report headers, 238, 241, 242, 255, 285
reports
    based on parameter queries, 156–58
    calculated control examples, 273–74
    customizing design, 244–45
    defined, xx, 59, 60, 285
    in Design view, 242–43
    detail, 237–47
    expressions in, 273–74
    grouped, 251–62
    parts of, 238, 241–42
    previewing, 61–62, 240, 241
    printing, 63, 241, 243
    printing groups together, 259
    quick, 237–47
    saving, 67
    single-column, creating, 157–58
    single-column vs. tabular, 239
    sort order, 257–59
    tabular, creating, 239–40
Report window, 243
Report Wizards
    defined, 63, 237, 285
    Groups/Totals, 253–55, 282
    Mailing Label, 64–68, 282
    overview, 243–44
    Single-Column, 239
    Single-Column vs. Tabular, 239
    Tabular, 239–40
Report Wizards dialog box, 64, 239
Required property, 224–25
resizing
    controls, 177
    labels, 179
    windows, xxv
Restore button, xxv
re-using queries, 151
rows, datasheet, changing height, 20
row selector, defined, 284
rulers, 187, 188

Running Microsoft® Software with Bestselling Books

Running Microsoft Access® 2 for Windows™

John L. Viescas

Packed with winning tips, notes, and strategies, this complete and thorough tutorial runs you through all the ins and outs of data access, the program's powerful tools, and its robust development environment. The bound-in disk includes a fully functional database that illustrates the examples in the book, as well as additional sample databases that show you efficient table designs for common applications. This book is perfect for users who want a full and solid understanding of this tool.

960 pages, softcover with one 3.5-inch disk
$39.95 ($53.95 Canada)   ISBN 1-55615-592-1

Running Word 6 for Windows™

Russell Borland

Master the power and features of Microsoft Word for Windows— version 6.0—with this newly updated edition of the bestselling guide for intermediate to advanced users. This example-rich guide contains scores of insights and power tips not found in the documentation and includes in-depth, accessible coverage on Word's powerful new features.

832 pages, softcover $29.95 ($39.95 Canada)   ISBN 1-55615-574-3

Running Microsoft® Excel 5 for Windows™

The Cobb Group with Mark Dodge, Chris Kinata, and Craig Stinson

Here's the most comprehensive and accessible book for all levels of spreadsheet users. It includes hundreds of tips and practical shortcuts for using the powerful new features of Microsoft Excel 5 for Windows. In addition to the step-by-step tutorials, straightforward examples, and expert advice, this updated edition features a new and improved format designed to help you find answers faster!

1184 pages, softcover $29.95 ($39.95 Canada)   ISBN 1-55615-585-9

Microsoft Press

Train Yourself

With *Step by Step* books from Microsoft Press

The *Step by Step* books are the perfect self-paced training solution for Microsoft Office users. Each book comes with a disk that contains every example in the book. By using the practice files and following instructions in the book, you can "learn by doing," which means you can start applying what you've learned to business situations right away. If you're too busy to attend a class or if classroom training doesn't make sense for you or your office, you can build the computer skills you need with the *Step by Step* books from Microsoft Press.

**Microsoft® Excel 5 for Windows™
Step by Step**

Catapult, Inc.

368 pages, softcover with one 3.5-inch disk
$29.95 ($39.95 Canada)   ISBN 1-55615-587-5

**Microsoft® PowerPoint® 4 for Windows™
Step by Step**

Perspection, Inc.

352 pages, softcover with one 3.5-inch disk
$29.95 ($39.95 Canada)   ISBN 1-55615-622-7

**Microsoft® Mail for Windows™
Step by Step**

Catapult, Inc.

Versions 3.0b and later.
224 pages, softcover with one 3.5-inch disk
$24.95 ($32.95 Canada)   ISBN 1-55615-571-9

**Microsoft® Word 6 for Windows™
Step by Step**

Catapult, Inc.

336 pages, softcover with one 3.5-inch disk
$29.95 ($39.95 Canada)   ISBN 1-55615-576-X

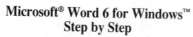

IMPORTANT — READ CAREFULLY BEFORE OPENING SOFTWARE PACKET(S).
By opening the sealed packet(s) containing the software, you indicate your acceptance
of the following Microsoft License Agreement.

Microsoft License Agreement

MICROSOFT LICENSE AGREEMENT
(Single User Products)

This is a legal agreement between you (either an individual or an entity) and Microsoft Corporation. By opening the sealed software packet(s) you are agreeing to be bound by the terms of this agreement. If you do not agree to the terms of this agreement, promptly return the book, including the unopened software packet(s), to the place you obtained it for a full refund.

MICROSOFT SOFTWARE LICENSE

1. GRANT OF LICENSE. Microsoft grants to you the right to use one copy of the Microsoft software program included with this book (the "SOFTWARE") on a single terminal connected to a single computer. The SOFTWARE is in "use" on a computer when it is loaded into temporary memory (i.e., RAM) or installed into permanent memory (e.g., hard disk, CD-ROM, or other storage device) of that computer. You may not network the SOFTWARE or otherwise use it on more than one computer or computer terminal at the same time.

2. COPYRIGHT. The SOFTWARE is owned by Microsoft or its suppliers and is protected by United States copyright laws and international treaty provisions. Therefore, you must treat the SOFTWARE like any other copyrighted material (e.g., a book or musical recording) except that you may either (a) make one copy of the SOFTWARE solely for backup or archival purposes, or (b) transfer the SOFTWARE to a single hard disk provided you keep the original solely for backup or archival purposes. You may not copy the written materials accompanying the SOFTWARE.

3. OTHER RESTRICTIONS. You may not rent or lease the SOFTWARE, but you may transfer the SOFTWARE and accompanying written materials on a permanent basis provided you retain no copies and the recipient agrees to the terms of this Agreement. You may not reverse engineer, decompile, or disassemble the SOFTWARE. If the SOFTWARE is an update or has been updated, any transfer must include the most recent update and all prior versions.

4. DUAL MEDIA SOFTWARE. If the SOFTWARE package contains both 3.5" and 5.25" disks, then you may use only the disks appropriate for your single-user computer. You may not use the other disks on another computer or loan, rent, lease, or transfer them to another user except as part of the permanent transfer (as provided above) of all SOFTWARE and written materials.

5. LANGUAGE SOFTWARE. If the SOFTWARE is a Microsoft language product, then you have a royalty-free right to reproduce and distribute executable files created using the SOFTWARE. If the language product is a Basic or COBOL product, then Microsoft grants you a royalty-free right to reproduce and distribute the run-time modules of the SOFTWARE provided that you: (a) distribute the run-time modules only in conjunction with and as a part of your software product; (b) do not use Microsoft's name, logo, or trademarks to market your software product; (c) include a valid copyright notice on your software product; and (d) agree to indemnify, hold harmless, and defend Microsoft and its suppliers from and against any claims or lawsuits, including attorneys' fees, that arise or result from the use or distribution of your software product. The "run-time modules" are those files in the SOFTWARE that are identified in the accompanying written materials as required during execution of your software program. The run-time modules are limited to run-time files, install files, and ISAM and REBUILD files. If required in the SOFTWARE documentation, you agree to display the designated patent notices on the packaging and in the README file of your software product.

LIMITED WARRANTY

LIMITED WARRANTY. Microsoft warrants that (a) the SOFTWARE will perform substantially in accordance with the accompanying written materials for a period of ninety (90) days from the date of receipt, and (b) any hardware accompanying the SOFTWARE will be free from defects in materials and workmanship under normal use and service for a period of one (1) year from the date of receipt. Any implied warranties on the SOFTWARE and hardware are limited to ninety (90) days and one (1) year, respectively. Some states/countries do not allow limitations on duration of an implied warranty, so the above limitation may not apply to you.

CUSTOMER REMEDIES. Microsoft's and its suppliers' entire liability and your exclusive remedy shall be, at Microsoft's option, either (a) return of the price paid, or (b) repair or replacement of the SOFTWARE or hardware that does not meet Microsoft's Limited Warranty and which is returned to Microsoft with a copy of your receipt. This Limited Warranty is void if failure of the SOFTWARE or hardware has resulted from accident, abuse, or misapplication. Any replacement SOFTWARE or hardware will be warranted for the remainder of the original warranty period or thirty (30) days, whichever is longer. Outside the United States, these remedies are not available without proof of purchase from an authorized non-U.S. source.

NO OTHER WARRANTIES. Microsoft and its suppliers disclaim all other warranties, either express or implied, including, but not limited to implied warranties of merchantability and fitness for a particular purpose, with regard to the SOFTWARE, the accompanying written materials, and any accompanying hardware. This limited warranty gives you specific legal rights. You may have others which vary from state/country to state/country.

NO LIABILITY FOR CONSEQUENTIAL DAMAGES. In no event shall Microsoft or its suppliers be liable for any damages whatsoever (including without limitation, damages for loss of business profits, business interruption, loss of business information, or any other pecuniary loss) arising out of the use of or inability to use this Microsoft product, even if Microsoft has been advised of the possibility of such damages. Because some states/countries do not allow the exclusion or limitation of liability for consequential or incidental damages, the above limitation may not apply to you.

U.S. GOVERNMENT RESTRICTED RIGHTS

The SOFTWARE and documentation are provided with RESTRICTED RIGHTS. Use, duplication, or disclosure by the Government is subject to restrictions as set forth in subparagraph (c)(1)(ii) of The Rights in Technical Data and Computer Software clause at DFARS 252.227-7013 or subparagraphs (c)(1) and (2) of the Commercial Computer Software — Restricted Rights 48 CFR 52.227-19, as applicable. Manufacturer is Microsoft Corporation, One Microsoft Way, Redmond, WA 98052-6399.

This Agreement is governed by the laws of the State of Washington.

Should you have any questions concerning this Agreement, or if you desire to contact Microsoft for any reason, please write: Microsoft Sales and Service, One Microsoft Way, Redmond, WA 98052-6399.

CORPORATE ORDERS

If you're placing a large-volume corporate
order for additional copies of this
Step by Step title, or for any other
Microsoft Press book, you may be eligible
for our corporate discount.

Call **1-800-888-3303, ext. 61659** for details.

The Step by Step Companion Disk

The enclosed 3.5-inch disk contains timesaving, ready-to-use practice files that complement the lessons in this book. To use the practice files, you'll need the Microsoft® Windows™ operating system version 3.0 or later, MS-DOS version 3.1 or later (MS-DOS 5.0 or later is recommended), and Microsoft Access® 2 for Windows.

Each *Step by Step* lesson is closely integrated with the practice files on the disk. Before you begin the *Step by Step* lessons, we highly recommend that you read the "Getting Ready" section of the book and install the practice files on your hard disk. As you work through each lesson, be sure to follow the instructions for renaming the practice files so that you can go through a lesson more than once if you need to.

Please take a few moments to browse the License Agreement on the previous page before using the enclosed disk.